INSIDE
THE
CRIMINAL
MIND

Co-Authored with Samuel Yochelson:

The Criminal Personality: A Profile for Change
The Criminal Personality: The Change Process

INSIDE THE CRIMINAL MIND

Stanton E. Samenow, Ph.D.

CROWN
BUSINESS
NEW YORK

The quotation from Anneliese Korner in Chapter Eleven comes from *Social Work,*
Vol. 10, No. 3, pp.41–50, copyright © 1965, National Association of Social Workers,
Inc. Reprinted with permission

Published by Crown Business, New York, New York.
Member of the Crown Publishing Group.

Random House, Inc. New York, Toronto, London, Sydney, Auckland
www.randomhouse.com

CROWN BUSINESS and colophon are trademarks of Random House, Inc.

Originally published by Times Books in 1984.

Printed in the United States of America

Design by Doris Borowsky

Library of Congress Cataloging-in-Publication Data
Samenow, Stanton E.
Inside the criminal mind / by Stanton E. Samenow.
Includes index.
1. Rehabilitation of criminals—United States. 2. Rehabilitation of juvenile
delinquents—United States. 3. Criminal psychology. 4. Juvenile delinquents—
Psychology. I. Title.
HV9304.S16   1983   364.3'01'9   83-45039

ISBN 0-8129-1082-6

20 19 18

In memory of

Dr. Samuel Yochelson,
teacher, friend,
source of inspiration,
and pioneer of a new
approach

ACKNOWLEDGMENTS

I am grateful to Dorothy K. Samenow, my wife, for her encouragement and sound advice throughout the course of my writing. I also thank my mother, Sylvia L. Samenow, for her many helpful suggestions and Marjorie Amidon for her fastidious typing of the manuscript and its revisions.

CONTENTS

Contents

Preface

It was 1968, and I had received my doctorate in clinical psychology. My internship had been spent in an adolescent psychiatric unit in Ann Arbor, Michigan. Eager and idealistic, I went to work at my first full-time professional job, serving as chief psychologist in a young adult unit at Northville State Hospital near Detroit. My clinical training had led me to become a dyed-in-the-wool Freudian.

In my new position at Northville, I was asked to diagnose and treat 18 to 20 year olds both from Detroit's inner city and from its suburbs. Many of these youths had been in trouble with the courts for antisocial behavior but had been regarded as sick rather than as delinquents. I plunged into treating them, applying the concepts and techniques that I had studied in graduate school and picked up by being a patient in psychoanalysis. I was repeatedly exposed to some rather raw slices of life, but I didn't see much improvement in my patients, who stubbornly clung to their disordered ways of thinking and acting. As I approached the termination of my work at Northville, it was time to decide what I wanted to do next.

Several years before, my father had introduced me to Dr. Samuel Yochelson, a friend of his from college days. At age 55, Dr. Yochelson had given up a large, successful private practice in Buffalo, New York, to begin what he regarded as a "second career" in psychiatry. From treating well-to-do corporate executives, he had moved to Washington, D.C., to direct a research project in which he would study and treat people who had committed serious crimes. His work was based at Saint Elizabeths Hospital, an immense federal psychiatric facility in Washington, D.C.

Knowing that I was pondering whether to remain in Michigan or go elsewhere, Dr. Yochelson invited me to become his associate in the Program for the Investigation of Criminal Behavior. Because I had no interest in criminals, I turned him down. Nevertheless, Yochelson asked me to visit Saint Elizabeths with an open mind to see what he was doing. I had come to know this man well during the past six years. I had heard him speak with great passion about his work and found him enormously likable, brilliant, and fascinating. I read some of his clinical notes and talked with a young man who, having been treated by Yochelson, had changed drastically since setting fires that had done millions of dollars' worth of damage. It seemed to me that I was being offered a singular opportunity. Yochelson told me that if I joined him I would come to understand why I had failed in my treatment efforts with so many adolescents in Michigan. While job hunting, I had visited a number of East and West Coast psychiatric centers that had adolescent units. At all of them, I saw corroboration for my observation that a shift was taking place in the type of adolescent being referred for treatment. No longer did psychotic or intensely neurotic youths populate the wards in large numbers. More and more, psychiatrists and psychologists were being asked to treat teenagers who were truants, thieves, and drug users. These kids were in conflict with society, not suffering from internal psychological conflicts.

Confidently, Dr. Yochelson predicted that by working with him I would become equipped with concepts and techniques that would be more effective with such people than anything else I had learned. Still, I wasn't too keen on the idea of committing myself to a project that entailed studying and eventually treating murderers, bank robbers, rapists, and drug traffickers. I think I regarded them as a pretty hopeless bunch. Why not devote myself to people who were desperately asking for help and who would change, I thought. Finally, though, admiration for Dr. Yochelson as a human being was the decisive factor. He clearly had embarked on a radically different path and was having some success with men whom others had given up on. In late January 1970, I moved to Washington and reported for work at Saint Elizabeths as a clinical research psychologist.

When I began this work, I believed that criminal behavior was a symptom of buried conflicts that had resulted from early traumas and deprivation of one sort or another. I thought that people who turned to crime were victims of a psychological disorder, an oppressive social environment, or both. From my work in Michigan with inner city youths, I saw crime as being almost a normal, if not excusable, reaction to the grinding poverty, instability, and despair that pervaded their lives. On the other hand, I thought that kids who were from more advantaged backgrounds had been scarred by bad parenting and led astray by peer pressure.

When it came to understanding Yochelson's "crooks," as he referred to them, I discovered that I had to unlearn nearly everything that I had learned in graduate school. Only reluctantly did I do so, debating many points along the way. But Dr. Yochelson told me that he had had to do exactly the same thing. His decades of psychiatric practice had left him unequipped to deal with these difficult patients. As he abandoned what he had long thought and practiced, he developed new methods to understand and treat people who had made crime a way of life.

During the six and a half years that I was Dr. Yochelson's associate, he and I worked on a three-volume technical work. We titled the first chapter of Volume 1 "The Reluctant Converts," disclosing our extreme reluctance to abandon our sacred theoretical cows and how he, and later I, gradually led those sacred cows to pasture and slaughtered them. We then presented in detail an entirely new approach to understanding and changing criminal behavior.

The essence of this approach is that criminals choose to commit crimes. Crime resides within the person and is "caused" by the way he thinks, not by his environment. Criminals think differently from responsible people. What must change is how the offender views himself and the world. Focusing on forces outside the criminal is futile. We found the conventional psychological and sociological formulations about crime and its causes to be erroneous and counterproductive because they provide excuses. In short, we did a 180-degree turn in our thinking about crime and its causes. From regarding criminals as victims we saw that instead they were victimizers who had freely chosen their way of life. Dr. Yochelson piloted a set of procedures that resulted in career criminals willingly changing their thinking so that they lived without injuring others and became responsible members of society.

Dr. Yochelson first had contact with these men at a time in their lives when things were going badly for them. They were about to be sentenced by the court, were already locked up, or had been faced with the loss of something valuable to them such as a family or career. In his initial interview, Yochelson asked few questions of the criminal but instead presented him with so accurate a picture of himself that the criminal could do nothing but agree. From then on, his objective was to teach these men to examine and change patterns of thinking that in the past had led to criminal behavior. Dr. Yochelson taught the criminals to become aware of and write down their day-to-day thinking without editing it in a self-serving manner. Daily, in small groups, the criminals reported that thinking, and Yochelson identified the "errors" and taught them corrections. He also instructed them in how to deter the massive amount of criminal thinking that occurred daily.

As the men saw themselves realistically, they became fed up with their old ways and made efforts to change. Their progress was not rapid or smooth, for even though they did not want to return to crime, they did not find living responsibly particularly appealing either—at least not for a while. The criminals had been accustomed to instant results in whatever they undertook, and these were not forthcoming. As they developed new patterns of thought and behavior, they slowly found that there were rewards, tangible and intangible. They did not have to look over their shoulders for the police, and they felt "clean." The criminals discovered that effort, competence, and reliability are usually rewarded and that they could accomplish worthwhile things without deception or intimidation. Responsible people, especially members of their families, began to trust them and react to them differently. The men were promoted in their jobs and began to acquire material possessions honestly. Gradually, criminal patterns were abandoned, and they acquired a new set of values by which they could live responsibly.

Dr. Yochelson did not live to see his work receive national recognition in the media and in professional circles. On his first out-of-town speaking trip, his heart failed and he died. After Dr. Yochelson's death, I stayed at Saint Elizabeths to complete the project. I then left the hospital to enter private practice but continued to evaluate and treat antisocial people. I worked with adult offenders while also pursuing my earlier interest in adolescents. But now, as Yochelson had predicted, I was in a position to see adolescent crime in a new light.

In the Saint Elizabeths study, our subjects were 255 adult men. Half of them were patients hospitalized as not guilty by reason of insanity or incompetent to stand trial, while the others came to us through agencies such as probation, the courts, mental health, and social service. In my clinical practice during the last five years, I have evaluated and treated several hundred offenders referred to me by courts, schools, lawyers, mental health centers, and word of mouth. Although I have treated and evaluated female offenders, they represent no more than 10 percent of my clients. In this book, I have chosen to speak in terms of male offenders, the group with whom I have had more experience. However, my clinical work with female offenders, limited as it is, leads me to conclude that the same thinking patterns underlie the criminal behavior of male and female offenders. I have also been told by people who work in correctional centers for females that the concepts of Dr. Yochelson's work are totally applicable.

Throughout the United States and Canada, interest in the Saint Elizabeths work increased. I was asked to talk about this work and consult with people in a variety of fields. Next to the economy, crime has been the number one social issue. I found inquiries pouring in not only from criminal justices and mental health professionals, but also from lawyers, judges, law enforcement agencies, educators, clergymen, and citizens' groups. Crime was escalating to new heights not only in the cities but also in the suburbs and rural areas. Fears that crime was engulfing our civilization had led to a crisis attitude of "do something now and fast."

Federal monies were pouring into law enforcement and correctional programs, with billions of dollars provided annually by the now defunct Law Enforcement Assistance Administration. Criminal justice programs proliferated at America's colleges, and professional training programs expanded. The 1960s had been an era of prison reform, and there was a surge of interest in rehabilitating offenders rather than just locking them up and "warehousing" them. Offenders were offered a smorgasbord of opportunities to develop skills and change their lives. In the 1970s, attempts were made to assess how effective rehabilitation was, and then the rehabilitative bubble burst. "Nothing works" was the grim conclusion of many evaluations, and the death knell of rehabilitation sounded. The courts were seen as having gone soft on criminals, and other parts of the criminal justice system were accused of coddling criminals. The cry came for stiff determinate sentencing, firmer parole guidelines, habitual offender laws that mandated long sentences, preventive detention, reinstitution of the death penalty, and trying in adult courts teenagers who committed violent crimes.

Sensing the mood of their constituents, politicians began to talk more of "law and order," less of rehabilitation. The political pendulum was swinging to the right on this issue as well as others. If the rehabilitation movement wasn't already terminal, a troubled economy and a new consciousness of limited resources dealt it a nearly lethal blow. But the desire to help criminals change never was totally snuffed out. And it is a good thing, because every man, woman, or child who is under court supervision for committing a crime will one day be released unless he has a sentence of death or life without parole. Studies show that most repeat offenders even after prison will continue to prey upon the community, and the costs, not measurable in dollars alone, will continue to be astronomical. Society cannot afford to give up looking for ways to help criminals become responsible, productive citizens.

While working with Dr. Yochelson, I saw impressive results as hard-core criminals changed 180 degrees to become responsible citizens. Dr. Yochelson's approach was a radical departure from anything I knew of that was being done in the United States.

In discussing this work in the United States, Canada, and

England, I have been perceived both as a dewy-eyed, liberal reformer and as a hard-line reactionary, although I am neither. Dr. Yochelson's work can be responded to in political terms, but it is apolitical. It is a new approach that warrants serious attention.

I look back and realize that, when I began this work, I had beliefs and preconceptions about crime and criminals. I discovered that years of study and training both at Yale University and the University of Michigan had been valuable to me in treating people who were neurotic and psychotic. But most of what I had learned had to be discarded to deal with a different type of person—the individual who makes crime a way of life. Only when I understood with whom I was dealing could I be effective in helping some criminals change. It is this knowledge that I want to share. I want you to consider what I have to say with an open mind. I ask you to bear in mind our nation's many failures to date to cope with criminals. In writing this book, I have as background 13 years of experience. I am drawing not just on the Saint Elizabeths study but most heavily on my observations during the last four years as I have evaluated and treated dozens of offenders. I am also drawing on the hundreds of conversations I have had with prison wardens, mental health professionals, correctional officers, law enforcement agents, court services workers, judges, educators, clergymen, social service workers, politicians, and adult and juvenile offenders and their families. In crossing this country many times to talk with and train people, I have found that most of them have not abandoned hope. They fervently desire to come to terms with this problem, which threatens to destroy the very fabric of our society. I hope this book will reinforce that hope and help them and others to see what can and must be done.

Stanton E. Samenow
Alexandria, Virginia
April, 1984

INSIDE
THE
CRIMINAL
MIND

Chapter One
A New Beginning

CRIME AFFECTS all of us. There is little we do without thinking, however briefly, that we might be victimized. Nearly every time we turn around it seems we risk being cheated, robbed, attacked, or preyed upon in some other insidious manner. Our cities turn into ghost towns at night because we fear to go out. We are afraid to keep jewelry, silver, and other precious possessions in our homes; so we must resort to safes, locks, deposit boxes, and security systems. We fear to leave our young children alone in the car for a few minutes while we dash into a store. Fearing sexual assault, women who live alone bar their windows, severely restrict where they go by themselves, and even fear to have their names on a mailbox or in a telephone book. Municipal parks and swimming pools are no longer oases in the asphalt for they have been taken over by muggers, robbers, and drug traffickers. People are threatened with weapons and even murdered just so their assailants can grab a few dollars. When we shop for clothes we are inconvenienced by security precautions that limit how many items we can try on, and we fear to leave our own clothes in the changing rooms. We fear for our children because the public schools are beset with disorder, vandalism, drugs, thefts, and violence. Fear that our medicine or food will poison us is no longer a paranoid's delusion. Such things have happened from coast to coast.

Americans, a once trusting people, now find themselves on guard, second-guessing the motives of the door-to-door salesperson, distrusting the mechanic to whom they entrust their automobile, worrying that a home repairman will cheat them and abscond with their money. Even when we intend to vacation, we are on guard: We fear that our car will be broken into, perhaps that belongings will disappear from our hotel room. Large public gatherings such as parades, fireworks, and concerts are marred by violence. Either we or someone close to us has been victimized. Indirectly, we all pay the enormous price of crime, whether it is our tax dollars subsidizing the criminal justice system or higher prices at the store not only because of inflation but because of losses suffered due to theft. It seems as though the very fabric of our civilization is being torn apart by rampant lawlessness. Certainly crime is destroying the quality of our life at a very frightening pace.

Perhaps as long as civilizations have existed, there has been speculation about what causes crime. During the last century, criminology, law, sociology, psychology, economics, and medicine have been looked to for an understanding of crimes and criminals. Theories about crime proliferate, and remedies based on those theories abound. The pendulum of public opinion has swung back and forth as some people have advocated rehabilitation and social programs while others have clamored for tougher enforcement laws, harsher penalties, and more prisons. The liberals have had their day and the conservatives theirs. Still we remain engulfed by a crime wave.

When newspapers are filled with details of a crime, people clamor to know not only who did it, but why. A shocked public speculates about a motive. Was it jealousy, desperation, greed, or lust? If the criminal is caught, a probing study of his personality may be ordered by the court. An initial assumption is that anyone who would commit such an act must be mentally ill, sick. If the killer grew up in a rat-infested slum without a father and with a drunken mother, people might conclude that the pressures of that environment drove him to commit a desperate act. If he has epilepsy, abnormal brain waves, or a brain tumor, it may be surmised that forces within his own body had something to do with his violence. We ask "why" to make sense out of a vicious, illegal, unprovoked act, hoping to learn something that will help us prevent similar crimes in the future.

My aim here is to show you why our current thinking about causes of crime is dead wrong and why our solutions have turned out to be no solutions at all. I shall expose the myths about why criminals commit crimes, and I shall draw a picture for you of the personality of the criminal just as the police artist draws a picture of his face from a description. I shall describe how criminals think, how they defend their crimes to others, and how they exploit programs that are developed to help them. I shall discuss what these people are like as children for, with systematic study, it is possible to identify at least some children who are predisposed to criminality.

To rethink this whole problem, we must return to basics and understand what criminals are really like. Let's throw out our labels and diagnoses and stop the fancy theorizing by which we convince ourselves that we are clever, even though we have been incorrect. We must understand how criminals think and realize that they have a fundamentally different view of the world from that of people who are basically responsible. I submit that this basic understanding, if it ever existed, has been lost in the fog of theoretical speculation and political rhetoric often espoused by people who have never even met a criminal.

Criminals cause crime—not bad neighborhoods, inadequate parents, television, schools, drugs, or unemployment. Crime resides within the minds of human beings and is not caused by social conditions. Once we as a society recognize this simple fact, we shall take measures radically different from current ones. To be sure, we shall continue to remedy intolerable social conditions for this is worthwhile in and of itself. But we shall not expect criminals to change because of such efforts.

Only if society knows who the criminal is can genuine progress be made in fighting crime. Here, I shall propose still another approach to the crime problem, a method of dealing with criminals that has had positive results and therefore offers a ray of hope. It begins with holding the criminal completely accountable for his offenses. This is to say that a person is responsible for having committed a crime, regardless of his social background or the adversities that have confronted him. However, the fact that a criminal commits crimes out of choice should not result *only* in locking him up for he will emerge from prison still a criminal. Just as he has chosen a life of crime, so a criminal can make choices in a new direction and learn to lead a responsible life. This is not an attempt to resuscitate rehabilitation under another name, for all the traditional rehabilitative programs in the world will be of no use unless the criminal *changes his thinking*.

Behavior is largely a product of thinking. Everything we do is preceded, accompanied, and followed by thinking. A train cannot fly for it is not so equipped. Similarly, as he is, a criminal is not equipped to be responsible. A drastic alteration must occur, and to accomplish this, a criminal requires help. The criminal must learn to identify and then abandon thinking patterns that have guided his behavior for years. He must be taught new thinking patterns that are self-evident and automatic for responsible people but are totally foreign to him. Short of this occurring, he will continue to commit crimes.

The perspective I shall present here may upset some people because it runs totally counter to their way of thinking. My criticism of current efforts to deal with criminals may also offend some people, especially if they are intractably wedded to a particular approach. The failure of our society to deal with crime is obvious. Without fresh thinking and the new approach I am recommending, criminals will continue to think and behave like criminals, whether incarcerated or not, and they will extract an ever higher toll from us in lives, physical injury, emotional scars, property loss, and damage, and our fear of victimization will overtake us even more as we go about our daily lives.

I know that readers will be wary of yet another solution—and rightly so. Many directions have been taken, and paths that have appeared promising have led to dead ends. I am not advocating a panacea for the crime problem. Rather, I am setting forth an alternative to what has been done. I am arguing that we cannot afford to ignore any alternative that has produced positive results.

Some will say that what I am proposing is too expensive, especially during this era of diminishing resources. I shall argue that it is far more expensive not to chart a new course. We must understand that criminals are different, that they do not think like responsible people and do not want the same things out of life. It is also time to realize that unless we help criminals learn to think differently, they will continue to prey on us all. We cannot afford to cling to our sacred theoretical cows and to familiar but ineffective procedures and programs. If we persist in traveling along well-trodden paths that are littered with failure, who knows how much worse things will get?

Chapter Two

The Basic Myths About Criminals

In the 1957 musical *West Side Story,* Stephen Sondheim parodied what then was the current thinking about juvenile delinquency in the song, "Gee, Officer Krupke." Delinquents were punks because their fathers were drunks. They were misunderstood rather than no good. They were suffering from a "social disease," and society "had played [them] a terrible trick." They needed an analyst, not a judge, because it was "just [their] neurosis" acting up. In short, their criminal behavior was regarded as symptomatic of a deep-seated psychological or sociological problem. Little has changed since then in terms of deeply ingrained beliefs about the causes of crime. In this chapter, I shall briefly discuss these beliefs. In subsequent chapters, I shall examine them in greater detail and show that the prevalent thinking about crime has been and still is loaded with fundamental misconceptions resulting in devastating consequences for society.

When a person commits a particularly sordid crime, his sanity may be questioned. Three men pick up two girls who are thumbing a lift. A joyride turns into a nightmare when the teenagers are driven to a desolate mountainous area where they are bound and repeatedly raped. Two of their tormentors dig a hole and tell them to say their prayers. However, the men decide to prolong the torture and spirit the girls off to an apartment and brutalize them again. The girls are saved by a suspicious neighbor who calls the police. Eventually, the court considers the rapists to be "mentally disordered sex offenders" and sends them to a psychiatric hospital, where they spend less than one-third of the time they would have served in prison.

Criminals learn to fool the psychiatrists and the courts in order to serve "easy time" in a hospital with the prospect of getting out more quickly than they would from a prison. From other criminals and from their attorneys, even unsophisticated street criminals learn the ploy of insanity. The game is for the criminal to convince others that he is sick so that he can beat the charge. After he is admitted to the hospital, he plays the psychiatric game of mouthing insights and behaving properly so that he can convince the staff that he is recovering and deserves to be released.

We, the public, may be so revolted by the gruesomeness of a crime that we conclude that only a sick person would be capable of such an act. But our personal reaction is totally irrelevant to understanding the criminal. True, what these men did to the teenagers is not a normal, everyday event. But the key question is, what are these men really like? A detailed and lengthy examination of the mind of a criminal (which is seldom made) will reveal that it is anything but sick. The criminal is rational, calculating, and deliberate in his actions.

Criminals know right from wrong. In fact, some know the laws better than their lawyers. But they believe that whatever they want to do at any given time is right for them. Their crimes require logic and self-control.

Some crimes happen so fast and with such frequency that they appear to be compulsive. A person may steal so often that others are certain that he is the victim of an irresistible impulse and therefore a "kleptomaniac." But a thorough mental examination would show that he is simply a habitual thief, good at what he does. He can size up a situation at a glance and then make off with whatever he wants. A habit is not a compulsion. On any occasion, the thief can refrain from stealing if he is in danger of getting caught. And if he decides to give up stealing for a while and lie low, he will succeed in doing so.

The sudden and violent crime of passion has been considered a case of temporary insanity because the perpetrator acts totally out of character. But again, appearance belies reality.

A man murders his wife in the heat of an argument. He has not murdered anyone before, and statistical trends would project that he will not murder again. It is true that the date, time, and place of the homicide were not planned. But an examination of this man would show that on several occasions he had shoved her and often wished her dead. In addition, he is a person who frequently had fantasies of evening the score violently whenever he believed that anyone had crossed him. He did not act totally out of character when he murdered his wife. He was not seized by an alien, uncontrollable impulse. In his thinking, there was precedent for such a crime. A person with even worse problems might well have resolved them differently.

If criminals are not mentally ill, aren't they nevertheless victims of poverty, broken homes, racism, and a society that denies them opportunities? Since the late nineteenth century, there has been a prevalent opinion that society is more to blame for crime than the criminal.

Sociologists assert that the inner city youngster responds

with rage to a society that has excluded him from the mainstream and made the American dream beyond his reach. Some even contend that crime is a normal and adaptive response to growing up in the soul-searing conditions of places like Watts and the South Bronx. They observe that in correctional institutions there is a disproportionately large number of inmates who are poor and from minority groups. These inmates are seen as casualties of a society that has robbed them of hope and virtually forced them into crime just so they can survive.

Crime knows no social boundaries, as the rising suburban crime rate demonstrates. Suburban delinquents are also regarded as victims—victims of intense pressures to compete, of materialism, of parents who neglect them, push them to grow up too fast, or are overly protective. These adolescents are perceived as rebelling not only against their parents but against middle-class values, seeking meaning instead through kicks and thrills.

Peer pressure is seen as a critical factor in the lives of youngsters from all social classes who turn to crime. Experts point out that among some subcultures the rewards are for being daring and tough, not for good grades and job promotions. Kids learn about crime from one another; they are schooled in the streets and go along with the crowd in order to acquire self-esteem and a sense of belonging. The belief that crime is contagious like a disease is more than a century old.

Every social institution has been blamed for contributing to crime. Schools have been singled out as forcing into crime youngsters who don't fit the academic mold. Churches have been accused of not providing leadership to wayward youth and to the community at large. Newspapers, television, and the movies have been charged with glamorizing crime. American business and advertising have been accused of contributing to distorted values and therefore to crime.

Economic hard times have been associated with an increase in crime. But then so have good times. Financial pressures are said to push despondent people over the edge. But then, when times are booming it has been thought that the gap between the "haves" and "have nots" widens and the latter, out of resentment, turn to crime. Economic troubles are also seen as contributing to crime by forcing mothers to go to work, further weakening the family. Their children have less supervision and guidance than before and are even more vulnerable to peer pressure.

Sociological explanations for crime, plausible as they may seem, are simplistic. If they were correct, we'd have far more criminals than we do. Criminals come from all kinds of families and neighborhoods. Most poor people are law-abiding, and most kids from broken homes are not delinquents. Children may bear the scars of neglect and deprivation for life, but most do not become criminals. The environment does have an effect, but people perceive and react to similar conditions of life very differently. A family may reside in a neighborhood where gangs roam the streets and where drugs are as easy to come by as cigarettes. The father may have deserted and the mother collect welfare. Yet not all the children in that family are in crime. In suburbia, a family may be close emotionally and well off financially, but that is not enough to keep one of the youngsters from using drugs, stealing, and destroying property.

Criminals claim that they were rejected by parents, neighbors, schools, and employers, but rarely does a criminal say why he was rejected. Even as a young child, he was sneaky and defiant, and the older he grew, the more he lied to his parents, stole and destroyed their property, and threatened them. He made life at home unbearable as he turned even innocuous requests into a battleground. He conned his parents to get whatever he wanted, or else he wore them down through endless argument. It was the criminal who rejected his parents rather than vice versa.

Not only did he reject his family, but he rejected the kids

in the neighborhood who acted responsibly. He considered them uninteresting, their lives boring. He gravitated to more adventurous youngsters, many of whom were older than he. Crime is not contagious like chicken pox. Even in crime-infested neighborhoods, there are youngsters who want no part of the action. Sure there is the desire to belong to the crowd, but the question is, which crowd? Criminals were not forced into crime by other people. They *chose* the companions they liked and admired.

The school does not reject the antisocial youngster until he is impossible to deal with. Many criminals have no use for school whatsoever. Still some remain in school, then use their education to gain entree into circles where they find new victims. More commonly, delinquent youngsters use the classroom as an arena for criminal activity by fighting, lying, stealing, and engaging in power plays against teachers and other pupils. Basically, for them, school is boring, its requirements stupid, the subjects meaningless. Just as the criminal rejects his parents, he does the same to his teachers. It is neither incompetent teachers nor an irrelevant curriculum that drives him out. In fact, the school may offer him an individually tailored program, but no matter what he is offered, it does not suit him. Finally, he is expelled for disruptive behavior or grows so bored that he quits.

The notion that people become criminals because they are shut out of the job market is an absurdity. In the first place, most unemployed people are not criminals. More to the point, perhaps, is that many criminals do not want to work. They may complain that without skills they can't find employment. (Of course, it was their choice not to remain in school to acquire those skills.) But as many a probation officer will observe, in most areas jobs of some sort are available but criminals find them too menial and beneath them.

Some criminals are highly educated and successful at their work. Their very success may serve as a cover for crime. If a person has a solid work record, he is generally regarded as responsible and stable. But money, recognition, and power are not enough to make a criminal law-abiding. The point is that what a person's environment offers is not decisive in his becoming a criminal.

The media have been criticized for making crime enticing by glorifying both specific crimes and criminals. There has been intense concern about the high incidence of violence in television programs that reach children. Neither scientific studies nor congressional hearings have shed much light on how much the media contribute to crime. Once again arises the erroneous premise that human character is easily shaped by external events. Television does not make a criminal out of a child; nor do movies, comics, magazines, or books. A person already thinking about committing crimes may pick up ideas from the media or become more certain about the feasibility of a particular crime. (Note the rash of skyjackings following extensive publicity about them during the 1970s.) But a responsible person will not be turned into a criminal by what he watches or reads.

Economic adversity affects us all. We may be pushed to work longer hours or to take a second job. Women who prefer to be at home may have little choice but to go to work. Families may have to make do with less and watch goals slip further out of reach, and people on fixed incomes bear a special burden. The responsible person responds to economic pressures by sacrifice and hard work. Even for him, temptation may be stronger to step outside the law as the economic squeeze grows tighter. Ultimately, however, it comes down to how each person chooses to deal with adversity.

What of the observation that a disproportionate number of people incarcerated for crimes are both poor and from minority groups? This is less a commentary on those groups than on the processes by which the criminal justice system arrests, adjudicates, and confines. If a white upper middle-class youngster is arrested for shoplifting, his parents may hire a lawyer and get the charges dropped by promising that the boy will visit a counselor. He never sees the inside of a courtroom and his record is clean. The black kid may become a criminal justice statistic. He goes to court, is convicted, then sentenced to a term of probation, and has a criminal record. For a more serious crime, the person with money and connections may get probation while the disadvantaged offender is imprisoned. Perhaps we need to examine the system by which people end up behind bars rather than focus on their color or economic status. It is unwarranted and racist to assume that because a person is poor and black (brown, red, yellow) he is inadequate to cope with his environment and therefore can hardly help but become a criminal.

So far, I have contended that criminals are not mentally ill or hapless victims of oppressive social conditions. But the psychiatrists, psychologists, counselors, and social workers still would say that a person is what he is largely because of his early experiences. They regard a man's crimes as "symptoms" of conflicts that are rooted in childhood and remain unresolved.

Too long have the social sciences promulgated the view that a human organism comes into the world like a lump of clay to be shaped by external forces. This view renders us all victims! What it does accomplish is to make explanation of behavior relatively easy. If any of us had taken a criminal path, something could be found in our past to explain why we turned out as we did. If your child has problems, you will be faulted for your child-rearing practices, whatever they were. If you were strict, you will be told that your child has been affected by your harshness. If you were permissive, you will be accused of being too indulgent. If you were relatively democratic, you might be considered wishy-washy or even indifferent. Worst of all, you might be tagged as inconsistent, something that we are all guilty of to an extent. Psychology always has a clever theory about any bit of behavior and offers an explanation, but only *after the fact*. There's the old line that if a patient arrives late for his psychiatric appointment, he's resistant. If he's early, he's anxious. If he's on time, he's compulsive. Although social scientists are sincere in trying to explain why we are the way we are, they are often incorrect.

In varying degrees, all human beings suffer trauma as they grow up. But if a domineering mother or an inadequate father produce delinquent children, why is it that most children who have such parents aren't criminals? Psychologists stress the importance of parents as role models, especially fathers for their sons and mothers for their daughters. Yet many children with weak or irresponsible role models become honest, productive adults. Conversely, some children with strong, positive role models become criminals.

When they are interviewed after being apprehended, criminals invariably relate a tale of horrors about their early lives. They seize upon any hardships in their lives, real or made up, to justify their acts against society. By portraying themselves as victims, they seek sympathy and hope to absolve themselves of culpability.

Some of society's chronic lawbreakers do come from volatile, conflict-ridden families where they have suffered abuse. But that is likely to be only part of the story. In their accounts, they relate only what others did to them, omitting what they did to make a bad situation even worse. A man may describe savage beatings by a maniacal father, but he never tells what he did to provoke such treatment. He conceals the fact that he taunted, deceived, and defied his parents to the point that his frustrated father finally lashed out at him physically. A complete account might reveal that the criminal was the only child in the family to have received severe corporal punishment, whereas his siblings were generally well-behaved. This is not to defend harshness in discipline. It is, however, to suggest that we ought not to limit our inquiries to what parents have done to children but strive to determine what children have done to their parents. A related point is that probably most children who are mistreated suffer long-range effects, but not all are criminals.

Criminals contend that their parents did not understand them and failed to communicate with them. They are often believed, and as usual, the deficiency is attributed almost entirely to parents. If we could be invisible observers in the homes of delinquent youngsters, we might reach a different conclusion. As a child, the criminal shuts his parents out of his life because he doesn't want them or anyone else to know what he is up to. When a teenager skips school, hangs out at a pool hall, joyrides, drinks, smokes pot, and steals from stores, it should be no surprise that he tells his parents little about his day. In fact, he will greet parental interest and concern with accusations that the parent is prying into his business. No matter how hard they try, mothers and fathers cannot penetrate the secrecy, and they discover that they do not know their own child. He is the kid who remains the family mystery.

In short, psychological theory, in its current state, is more misleading than illuminating in explaining why people become criminals. Far from being a formless lump of clay, the criminal shapes others more than they do him.

During the nineteenth century, there was a belief among many experts that people were born criminals. Attempts to identify criminals on the basis of facial or other physical features were discredited. However, the "bad seed" hypothesis never died. In the 1960s, for example, a controversy arose over whether criminals have special chromosome patterns. Evidence for an "XYY" syndrome or other chromosome anomaly remains inconclusive.

Another belief is that perhaps criminals suffer from a physiological dysfunction that may be hereditary or result from trauma. Brain lesions or tumors, temporal lobe epilepsy, blood chemistry changes, glandular abnormality, and hypoglycemia are among the organic factors that have been linked to criminality, but conclusive evidence of such a linkage is still lacking. Of the many people who are afflicted with these conditions, few become criminals.

There has also been a theory that criminals are *inherently* less intelligent than the general population, but this has been laid to rest. Empirical studies of criminals and noncriminals simply did not support such a proposition. Criminals may score low on IQ tests and lack basic information that most people acquire in the primary grades of school. However, their mental acumen and resourcefulness are striking to anyone who is privy to their complex, well-thought-out schemes. Criminals are remarkable in their capacity to size up their environment in order to pursue objectives important to them.

Still the belief lingers, especially among some educators, that criminals have an organically based learning disability. Experts point out that many delinquent youngsters seem *unable* to learn and fall far behind academically. They also observe that among prison inmates there is a sizable number who can neither read nor write. Another deficiency noted is that criminals do not seem to learn from past experiences the way most people do.

There are several problems with the learning disability theory. Many criminals who appear learning disabled are highly capable of learning but simply chose not to because school was incompatible with what they wanted to do. Furthermore, most children who are genuinely disabled in their capacity to learn, while experiencing blows to their self-esteem and severe frustration, don't react to their difficulties by becoming criminals. The observation that criminals have an incapacity to learn from experience is inaccurate. They may not learn what parents and teachers want them to learn, but they do utilize the past as a guide when it matters to them. They learn how to become more successful criminals.

No factor or set of factors—sociological, psychological, or biological—is sufficient to explain why a person becomes a criminal. So far, the search to pin down causation has been futile. Far more disturbing is that programs, laws, policies, and decisions about how to deal with criminals have been based upon these theories, and this has resulted in a tremendous waste of resources while crime continues in epidemic proportions.

What is clear is that criminals come from a wide variety of backgrounds—from the inner city, suburbia, rural areas, and small towns and from any religious, racial, or ethnic group. They may grow up in closely knit families, broken homes, or orphanages. They may be grade school dropouts or college graduates, unemployed drifters or corporate executives. In most cases, they have brothers, sisters, and next-door neighbors who grew up under similar circumstances but did not become criminals.

Despite a multitude of differences in their backgrounds and crime patterns, criminals are alike in one way: *how they think.* A gun-toting, uneducated criminal off the streets of southeast Washington, D.C., and a crooked Georgetown business executive are extremely similar in their view of themselves and the world. This is not to deny individual differences among criminals in their aesthetic tastes, sexual practices, religious observance, or favorite sports team. But all regard the world as a chessboard over which they have total control, and they perceive people as pawns to be pushed around at will. Trust, love, loyalty, and teamwork are incompatible with their way of life. They scorn and exploit most people who are kind, trusting, hardworking, and honest. Toward a few they are sentimental but rarely considerate. Some of their most altruistic acts have sinister motives.

More than a half-century ago, the noted psychologist Alfred Adler observed, ''With criminals, it is different: they have a private logic, a private intelligence. They are suffering from a wrong outlook upon the world, a wrong estimate of their own importance and the importance of other people.'' Adler went on to say that the criminal's crimes ''fit in with his general conception of life."[1] Implied throughout Adler's writing is the idea that people choose to be criminals, that they are a different breed. Even in 1930, Adler's was a lone voice.

Psychology and sociology long have advanced the view that the criminal is basically like everyone else but has turned antisocial because he has been blocked by others in fulfilling his aspirations. Thus the criminal is perceived as a victim of forces and circumstances beyond his control. Those who hold such a view go a step further, asserting that we are all, in a sense, criminals because we lie, lust, and yield to temptation. But it is absurd to equate the white lie of the responsible person with the gigantic network of lies of the criminal. It is equally absurd to equate a child's pilferage of a candy bar with a delinquent's stealing practically everything that isn't nailed down. At some point, we and the criminal are very different. He is far more extreme in that crime is a way of life, not an occasional aberration. It is misleading to claim that the criminal wants what the responsible person wants, that he values the same things that a responsible person values. Both may desire wealth, but only one will work steadily and earnestly to acquire it and then use it responsibly. The criminal believes that he is entitled to it and grabs it any way he can, not caring whom he injures, and then thirsts for more. Both may desire a family life, but the responsible person shows the give-and-take, the empathy, and the selflessness that family life requires. The criminal pays lip service to love while demanding that his spouse and children place his demands and wishes first.

By taking the position that the criminal is a victim, society has provided him with excuses for crime and thereby supported his contention that he is not to blame. Partly to atone for its alleged injustices to the criminal, society has offered him countless opportunities to "rehabilitate" himself and enter the mainstream. Surprise has given way to despair as the criminal rejects the very opportunities that he rejected before (work, school, counseling) or else shamelessly exploits them while continuing to commit crimes.

Attempts to improve the environment, no matter how worthwhile, have not altered the criminal's personality. Psychological methods have been equally unsuccessful because therapists have mistakenly utilized concepts and techniques suited to patients with a very different character structure. In the more distant past, castration, lobotomy, and drugs were employed in hopes of altering biological forces within the criminal, but to little avail.

The death knell of rehabilitation having sounded, the pendulum is swinging the other way—to "lock 'em up and throw away the key." Given the high recidivism rate of criminals who were considered rehabilitated, such a sentiment is understandable.

What about the function of punishment? Arrest alone or confinement undoubtedly deters some offenders, but contact with the criminal justice system has little lasting impact on habitual offenders. Warehousing a criminal in an institution gets him off the streets for a while, but one day he will be released to wreak havoc again in society. Because prison is expensive—costing the taxpayer more than a year's tuition at an Ivy League college—and because many prisons are dehumanizing, alternatives to incarceration are being developed. In this effort, rehabilitative proposals are once again being heard, but the term is not being used. Instead, it is "community-based corrections," which features a smorgasbord of offerings—vocational training, schooling, counseling, psychotherapy—as well as accountability to a probation officer. In addition, restitution and community service programs have proliferated as society considers finally not just criminals but people who are truly victims.

The more things change, the more they stay the same. The criminal's motivation is to avoid confinement. He sees his probation officer once every couple of weeks for a brief appointment. He may attend some programs if they are mandated by the court. And he may make restitution. But his personality does not change.

And so the criminal comes up against a world that either bleeds for him because he is a victim or else wants to remove him from the earth. Criminals have been imprisoned, educated, counseled, preached to, and even executed. But the policies and programs continue to be ineffective, largely because those conceiving and implementing them do not know with whom they are dealing. Decisions are made on the basis of misconceptions in an atmosphere of ''do something now and do it fast.''

A surprising number of people who deal with criminals do not know how criminals think. How a person behaves is determined largely by how he thinks. *Criminals think differently.* If we are thoroughly familiar with how they think, we are in a far better position to draft legislation, formulate policies, administer programs, render more informed decisions, and be more effective in direct contacts with criminals both in the institutions and in the community.

There is even a ray of hope that we can help some criminals change and become responsible citizens. But to undertake this task we must see the criminal as the problem, not society. Our approach to change must be to help the criminal radically alter his self-concept and his view of the world. Some criminals can be ''habilitated,'' that is, helped to acquire patterns of thinking that are totally foreign to them but essential if they are to live responsibly.

Chapter Three

Parents Don't Turn Children into Criminals

DELINQUENT YOUNGSTERS come from all social classes and from all kinds of homes. The variation in their upbringing is enormous. They differ from one another physically, in their talents and capabilities, and in many aspects of their personalities. Despite these differences, they are strikingly alike in that they all display the patterns that will be described in this chapter. This is true regardless of whether they come from the suburbs or the city, from well-to-do or poor parents, or from two-parent families or broken homes and regardless of whether their parents were strict or indulgent. Each of them thinks and acts differently from responsible members of his own family. At an early age, each begins making a series of choices to live a life that he considers exciting, a life in which he is determined to do whatever he wants, a life in which he ignores restraints and eventually turns against his family and

25

scoffs at those who live responsible lives. Each complains about unfair treatment and is perceived by others as a hapless victim of his parents' pathology or of a malfunctioning family unit. But this is not the case. The theories that purport to explain delinquency by blaming parents are misleading and potentially harmful. Such youngsters *choose* the life they want.

Many boys and girls defy their parents, tell lies, fight, succumb to temptation, and steal a candy bar or some other small item. However, this behavior does not become a way of life. The criminal child's departure from parental and societal expectations involves more than isolated acts. Beginning as early as during the preschool years, *patterns* evolve that become part of a criminal life style. As a child, the criminal is a dynamo of energy, a being with an iron will, insistent upon taking charge, expecting others to indulge his every whim. His appetite for adventure is voracious. He takes risks, becomes embroiled in difficulties, and then demands to be bailed out and forgiven. No matter how his parents try to understand and guide him, they are thwarted at every turn. This youngster is unlike most other children, including his own sisters and brothers. While the others are seeking recognition through schoolwork, sports, or social activities, this child thumbs his nose at it all. He establishes himself by doing what is forbidden. His mother and father do not perceive a pattern unfolding but assume that his waywardness is merely a stage of development. This "stage," however, never ends. The parents become the first in the criminal's string of victims. Only it is not a one-time victimization. The emotional turmoil of seeing their child injure others and jeopardize himself is like a persistent searing pain. The parents' interminable struggle to cope with this wayward youngster saps their energy, drains their finances, weakens their marriage, and harms their other children. But the criminal child remains unmoved and unaffected.

Case studies of criminal youngsters differ in their particulars, but they all reveal common patterns. The case of Bill, 15, is an example. He is the youngest of four children from a middle-class family. Both his parents are teachers. But there are youngsters just like him from inner city and upper-class families.

There is nothing unusual about Bill's appearance—scraggly, shoulder-length blond hair and intense blue eyes. Like his contemporaries, he dresses in snugly fitting jeans, a colored T-shirt bearing an insignia or design such as a motorcycle, and sneakers that are now gray from wear. You might find him bantering with a friend as he tinkers with parts of an old car, or he may be alone, slumped in an overstuffed chair, transfixed before a television screen. A stranger would find him easy to talk to, in fact quite charming. Usually he is stuffing candy bars or junk food into his mouth or else he is smoking a cigarette. Few people would suspect that this teenager is a liar, thief, vandal, fighter, and pot pusher.

Although Bill has spent all of his 15 years with his mother and father, he has never been interested in them as human beings. To him they are merely vehicles to gratify his rapidly shifting desires. As a young boy, he expected his mom and dad to buy him whatever he wanted. When he spotted a shiny red Schwinn bicycle, he not only took it for granted that he would own it but, in his mind's eye, he was already pedaling it down the block, receiving jealous stares from other kids. Bill's parents did not believe in overindulging their children, but it was tough to say no to Bill and hold their ground. When he didn't get his way, he'd erupt into a tantrum, then pout, and generally make life miserable. His mother recalled a time when her boy implored her to buy him a toy gun for $1.39. When she refused, he was heartbroken. Later, he returned to the store and snatched the gun off the counter. As he scurried toward the door, he was grabbed by a clerk who detained him and phoned his parents. His mother describes her reaction to Bill today as being what it was years ago: "He makes us feel so irrational, so guilty." At 7, it was a toy gun. At 14, Bill had his mind set on a room with thousands of dollars worth of furnishings—gold shag carpeting, an elaborate stereo system, water bed, and psychedelic lighting. His parents told him that if he started earning the money, they'd help him out. His idea of working was quite different from theirs—he became a vendor of marijuana.

Bill always tried to get his way through a process his parents termed negotiating. This was a one-sided ordeal, more like extortion, in which Bill tried to force his mother and father to make concessions by grinding them down through endless argument. Bill relished an argument the way he enjoyed chess. He was positive that if he persisted long enough he would vanquish his opposition. When the power of argument failed, Bill became belligerent and, as he got older, verbally abusive, calling his mother an "old bitch" and berating his father as a "bastard" and "stupid old fool." But perhaps his most effective ploy was to promise his parents good behavior in exchange for whatever he wanted. Implied or explicit was that if he did not get his way he would continue to do whatever he pleased. For example, his mother told him to remove nails that protruded from a pair of shoes. (Bill drove these nails in deliberately so that he could kick an adversary during a fight.) His response was, "I don't give a shit. I'll take the nails out if you'll take me where I want to go. I don't get any cooperation from you, so you don't get any from me. Here, I've also got my chain for fuckin' up people's faces." Bill's parents were in essence being blackmailed. Either they transported their son to whatever place he chose at any outrageous time or else he would persist in behavior they disapproved of. This was typical of Bill's attempts to manipulate them.

Constantly, Bill demanded things on his own terms because that was how he thought life should be. He pressed his mom and dad to justify even a simple request. When ordered to do something, he regarded it as an imposition. "I'm not going to be your little nigger," he'd snap. If he complied, he expected great fanfare. Not getting it, his attitude was, "Those slobs don't appreciate all that I do." He put off a chore until his parents tired of waiting and did it themselves. He developed an amazing knack for forgetting. A request made of him would slip from memory in 10 minutes, but recollection was sharp for something that he had asked for 10 weeks previously.

The older Bill got, the more blatant his defiance. When he spat out "fuck you," his parents had all they could do to control themselves, but as their anger subsided, they'd begin to wonder if they had been unreasonable after all. When they yelled, they felt guilty afterward. But if they ignored misbehavior, they also felt guilty. Reasoning always seemed to fail; nothing succeeded.

Bill regarded everything in his family's possession as belonging to him. He was well acquainted with the inside of his mother's pocketbook, having often rummaged for change without asking permission. Money was missing so often that his mother began taking her purse to bed with her. Bill became similarly familiar with his father's wallet. The amount he took depended on how much money was in the wallet. Once, when greed outweighed judgment, he swiped two 20-dollar bills. His father confronted him but backed down when his son looked at him with his large blue eyes and seemed totally devastated by the accusation. Bill then realized that he had a powerful psychological weapon. He said to a friend, "The next time he accuses me, I'll act heartbroken the way I did before, and he'll feel so fuckin' guilty." When money was hidden, Bill would find it, pawing through drawers and forcing open locks on file cabinets during his search. He was quite practiced in this for at nine he had begun sampling the family liquor supply and had introduced his friends to various beverages. A locked liquor cabinet posed no obstacle. He'd unscrew the hinges and remove the entire door.

Although Bill considered others' property to be his own, anything that legitimately belonged to him he deemed sacred. His parents had repeatedly asked him to clean up his messy room. One Saturday afternoon when Bill was out with his friends, his parents, unable to stand it any longer, entered his room with the intention of throwing out the trash and picking up some of the litter. While hanging up his son's Windbreaker, Bill's father heard something drop. He looked down and saw a pipe and a small plastic bag with a substance that he suspected might be marijuana. When he and his wife confronted Bill with their discovery, Bill vehemently denied knowing anything about it and refused to discuss the matter. His face contorted with rage, and he cursed his mother and father for daring to invade his privacy. Determined to prevent any further parental intrusion, he purchased a small, lightweight file box with a lock in which to stash and safeguard his drug paraphernalia.

All children are self-centered and shape their parents' behavior by acting in a particular manner to get what they want. In their egocentricity, they remember what matters immediately and drag their feet about doing anything disagreeable. Their parents frequently have to badger or even coerce them to do things, but not all of these children become criminals.

Bill's family was headed by two devoted parents, both of whom had placed their offspring's welfare highest in their priorities. They spent considerable time with their children and got along well with each other. There was no indication of maternal deprivation or paternal inadequacy that is so often cited as contributing to the character development of delinquents. Bill's mother was a warm, giving woman who displayed both idealism and common sense in bringing up her four children. She spent a lot of time at home, placing family ahead of her part-time teaching and other activities. Bill's father was gentle and even-tempered. Despite his career and many other interests such as singing, he treasured time with his children. Yet Bill belittled him, rejected him as a model of behavior, and spewed forth contempt for his entire way of life.

It has been claimed that children become delinquent because their parents overindulge them to the point that they continue to expect the world to cater to them. But like neglect, "spoiling" leads to different outcomes. Whereas some overindulged children remain self-centered and dependent on others, they do not function criminally. Other pampered youngsters are jolted into reality once they leave home, and they learn to become self-sufficient. Perhaps more to the point is that when a counselor attributes delinquent behavior to an overindulgent attitude of the parents, it is often based on appearance. The counselor sees that the youngster is behaving outrageously and seems to be getting away with it. But the counselor may not realize that for years the child has thwarted nearly all parental attempts at disciplining him. Rarely is he acting irresponsibly because the parents gave him free reign.

One counselor advised Bill's mother and father, "You just need to be strong parents." He saw that Bill was doing whatever he wanted and assumed that his parents had been weak. The counselor hypothesized that unconsciously Bill was begging for restraint. It made a good theory. But it was not true. Both mother and father had long believed in the importance of setting limits and in being consistent. With Bill, they found themselves being stricter than they had ever intended. When they tightened up, more of Bill's behavior went underground. Their determination to be "strong parents" with Bill had borne no fruit. They had even initiated a point system of rewarding responsible behavior by granting him privileges and restoring freedom that he had previously handled badly. But to no avail. It was Bill who modified his parents' behavior. So it is with any child of Bill's kind, regardless of social class or family structure. He dangles the incentive of good behavior in order to get what he wants. The promise of being good is effective bait, allowing him to extract trust, money, and material possessions. It is blackmail, a matter of the child promising peace but determining the price the parents will pay. As parental stamina and self-confidence wane, concessions mount.

It has been theorized that a child becomes delinquent despite parental discipline because he is acting out the parents' unconscious wishes. In a 1942 paper still cited today, S. A. Szurek wrote that parents "selfishly" attempt to gain satisfaction for urgent unconscious needs through their child's behavior.[1] The child is considered a victim, unwittingly propelled into delinquent activity in order to gratify his parents' unconscious needs. Regardless of how they consciously instruct the child, such mothers and fathers are said to take pleasure *unconsciously* at certain infractions by their child because they fulfill the parents' own repressed forbidden wishes.

Repeated contact in a clinical setting with Bill's parents revealed self-aware human beings, people with integrity who were struggling to rear their children responsibly. If they seemed to condone some of their son's irresponsibility by occasionally looking the other way, it was because over the years they had grown weary of being forced by Bill into the roles of policeman, prosecutor, and judge. This was a far cry from vicarious enjoyment of their son's deviance. If Szurek's theory were accurate, what are the implications? Must parents of delinquents undergo years of psychoanalysis to get in touch with their unconscious? Even if they did, would that ensure a change in the child? All such a theory results in is shifting responsibility from the child to the parents.

According to one theory of family functioning, a child may become delinquent because, to quote psychiatrist Norman Cameron, he is the one the whole family selects to "act out the forbidden impulses and fantasies of parents and siblings." When this occurs, the rest of the family can "enjoy vicariously what the scapegoat does without themselves experiencing responsibility or guilt for it."[2] It may well be that a disturbed family system can give rise to isolated cases of antisocial behavior, but there is as yet no convincing evidence from treating entire families that the disturbed system is the cause of a child's expanding and intensifying *patterns* of delinquent activity. In fact, what often happens in treatment is that the delinquent child scapegoats the family. While insisting that he is all right and does not require treatment, he blames the family for being "sick."

Bill's family entered family therapy, where it was assumed from the start that a disturbed child meant that mother and father had deep-seated problems. His parents felt as if they were on trial as Bill recited his list of grievances against them. Following the lead of the counselor, he was adept at shifting the spotlight to his mother and father in the quest to identify the cause of his behavior. With mom and dad becoming the focus, they had more problems because of the treatment than they ever before imagined and, consequently, even more guilt, bitterness, anger, and despair. The most outrageous part of it was the counselor's assumption that, because Bill was so clearly out of control, they were inadequate parents. Bill's mother still smarts from the sting of those sessions, which they endured while Bill quit. This left them with a counselor who offered no suggestions that were any different from what they had been doing for years. Bill's parents did not give up after this experience but consulted other mental health practitioners. The results were usually the same. Bill could be bribed to attend one or two sessions, where he'd hurl accusations at them, and then they became the patients.

One clinician who evaluated Bill arrived at the following psychodynamic formulation: "Bill's behavior may be understood not so much as the product of indulgence but rather of subtle demands for high performance in the presence of role models portraying and expecting excellence.'' This was a complicated way of saying that his parents, who were teachers, set unrealistically high standards and applied too much pressure on their son. At first glance, this seems a plausible theory. But it had nothing to do with the facts. Like most parents, Bill's mother and father wanted their children to do well at whatever they undertook. But doing well did not necessarily mean that Bill had to be a straight ''A'' student and later a teacher. His parents' aspirations were far more modest. They hoped that Bill would get along with other people and be competent at whatever life work he chose. As they discovered Bill's considerable mechanical aptitude and interest in electronics, they encouraged him and bought him equipment, to which he reacted first with a flash of enthusiasm and then with total disinterest.

A psychiatrist can always fish for some underlying problem and spot conflict in any family. But to conclude that criminal behavior stems from obvious family psychopathology is a mistake. In a middle-class family from the same county as Bill, seven youngsters grew up with erratic, volatile, and often cruel alcoholic parents. With the exception of the fourth-born, all the offspring are now leading responsible lives. That one child is in jail for the sixth time, in this case for violation of parole. How easy it would be to account for his criminality by viewing him as the unfortunate victim of his parents' pathology. But what of the other six who were exposed to the same unwholesome environment but are not in jail?

Many delinquent youngsters assert that their parents are too restrictive and untrusting. In reality, their mothers and fathers yearn to trust them but find it difficult after they have been lied to and exploited repeatedly. Every time such a child asks for something, his parents are in a quandary because he tries to push them into acceding to his every request while offering a bare minimum of information. When pressed for details, he is vague. If a parent continues to probe, he flares up. If they deny his request, he berates and threatens them.

Occasionally, the delinquent deliberately sets out to convince his parents that he is trustworthy. He puts on a show of shouldering responsibility at home by fixing something that is broken, cleaning up a room in the house, and helping with chores. This is a con job, a front designed to lull his family into thinking that he is changing his ways. At these times, he has no such intention. Later he hearkens back to his good deeds expecting them to blot out all misconduct.

Such a child puts his parents in a double bind. On the one hand, he perceives their kindness as weakness and exploits it. When they say yes, they are played for suckers. However, strictness sparks a new series of hostilities. Deprivation of privileges and restrictions breed only more argument and bitter resentment.

When brought to counselors and therapists, delinquent youngsters complain that their parents do not understand them. The picture is not simply of a communications gap but a yawning chasm that seems unbridgeable. Therapists conclude that the child's parents are aloof, uncaring, or perhaps irresponsible. But they are hearing only one side of the story and basing their assessments on that.

Most parents faced with such difficult children make extraordinary efforts to talk to and understand their offspring. However, the child is the one who constructs an increasingly impenetrable barrier to communication. He lives a life that he is determined to hide from his parents. After a day of skipping school, using drugs, and stealing from stores, he can hardly be expected to come home bubbling over about the day's activities. Regarding his parents' attempt to show interest as prying, he responds to their questions with the most minimal account, evasiveness, or belligerence. What he does he considers none of their business. Such youngsters blame their parents for poor communication, but they are the ones who choose not to communicate. "I communicate to the point it makes *me* happy," said one such teenager. "They need to communicate with *me*. I don't really want to hear anything they have to say. I don't have anything to say to them. We're just different kinds of people."

To the extent that it exists at all, dialogue between parent and criminal child is on the child's terms. Savvy enough to know that silence annoys others and makes them suspicious, the youngster may engage in polite conversation, tell his parents what is safe, and remain on neutral ground. When the parents of such a youngster speak to him, he hears but usually does not listen. He is highly practiced at screening out what is disagreeable. It is as though, with a flick of a button, he can control which parental messages reach his ear. There is indeed a communications gap but not, as many experts suggest, one created primarily by indifferent or neglectful parents.

The delinquent youngster spins an increasingly intricate and sometimes tangled web of secrecy. It begins as early as the preschool years. The child tells a lie to worm his way out of trouble. He relates to his parents only part of the truth, omitting that which would incriminate him.

All children may lie at one time or another, but lying does not become a way of life. As they grow up, youngsters respond positively to social rewards for truthfulness. They try to establish themselves as credible people. Occasionally they lie to cover up wrongdoing, to save face in an embarrassing situation, to avoid an uncomfortable situation, or to protect their image. But they don't experience the tremendous excitement and sense of power that the delinquent gains from lying. In fact, quite the opposite is true: Normally, children are reticent about lying, and when they do lie they suffer pangs of conscience afterward. In the child who becomes a criminal, lying becomes a reliable device for trying to get away with more that is forbidden.

Perhaps most distressing to the delinquent's parents is

that so many of his lies seem to have no purpose whatsoever. Their child revels in making fools of them by inventing things that never happened. Although his innumerable misrepresentations and embellishments appear senseless to his parents, they are purposeful to him. By deceiving his mother and father in even the most trivial matters, the youngster believes he has gained the upper hand. Never knowing when to believe him, his mother and father search for cues by scrutinizing his facial expressions and listening for a quaver in his voice. In contrast to a child who occasionally concocts a lie and whose guilty expression just about gives him away, the criminal child can look his parents straight in the eye and solemnly tell the most outrageous lies, his gaze never faltering, his voice never cracking. These children see nothing wrong with lying. Indeed, they view it as a necessity in order to get away with all that they do.

The delinquent lies so often and has done so for so long that his lying appears to be compulsive. Yet the lying is totally under his control. He can readily distinguish truth from falsehood and is prepared to tell either, depending on which best serves his purpose. From the time he is in grade school, he develops and practices at home the deceptive methods that he will use in dealing with the rest of the world. Neither his parents nor anybody else will penetrate the shield of secrecy long enough to really know him.

Brazen lying is hard for parents to tolerate, but equally distressing is their paralysis in dispelling the fog of such a youngster's vagueness. He is tentative and global, hard to pin down. Even in situations that clearly call for a "yes" or "no," he responds with "maybe," "perhaps," or "I guess." The delinquent youngster doesn't have to work at obfuscation. It is as automatic as his lying. Again, he is the one creating the bulk of the communication problem, not uncaring, indifferent, or hostile parents.

Although these children are exasperating to live with, they have a sensitivity and gentleness that is as genuine as their selfishness and destructiveness. They seem truly to have a Jekyll–Hyde personality. When their endearing qualities surface, they help with household chores and participate eagerly in family activities. At such times, they can be completely captivating. When the sunny side of these youngsters shines through their darker nature, parents find welcome relief from battle fatigue and once again have hope.

Such phases are not con jobs. Throughout his life, there are times when the delinquent is in earnest about reforming. He resolves to do well at school, and he cooperates at home. The desire to shape up may last hours, days, or weeks. Then it seems to vanish completely. A life of going to school, working, staying around the house, and generally living like the "straight" kids is intolerable to him. The praise that others lavish on him for the changes that he initiates pales in comparison with the excitement of the life he has been leading.

Although family members never know whether the child genuinely wants to change or whether it's all another hoax, they delight in every moment that he is thoughtful and considerate. His parents are reminded that he is troubled even during these relatively calm periods because they are witnesses to his restlessness, irritability, and explosive temper. It may take a shockingly dramatic event to convince them that things are far worse than they ever believed. This happened to the parents of a 15 year old named Tom.

Tom's mother and father regarded him as moody but good at heart. They thought that, like most boys his age, Tom was going through the typical ups and downs of adolescence. They tried to cheer him up when his spirits sagged and to accept him when he was angry and upset. They were demonstrative in their praise for things he did well—notably his high grades and clarinet playing. But Tom's mother was growing more and more disturbed by his increasing hostility at home. However, she did not suspect anything radically wrong until she came into the kitchen and saw Tom standing over the family's pet poodle, who was sprawled on the floor in a pool of blood. Only after his mother and father took their son to a psychiatrist did the truth emerge. Tom and his friends had gone on shoplifting binges and rampages of vandalism "just for kicks." While skipping classes, he had smoked marijuana and popped pills. Tom didn't tolerate disagreement. When he failed to get his way with his friends, he exploded with a string of obscenities and felt a pounding desire to beat them up, an urge to which he succumbed when he figured he'd come out on top. Finally, when the family pet destroyed the wiring on his stereo set, Tom decided he was not going to tolerate that either. He grabbed a kitchen knife and thrust it into the animal again and again. After the consultation with Tom's psychiatrist, any illusions that his mother and father had about his being a normal teenager were shattered.

As a child, the criminal has contempt not only for his parents' advice and authority but for the way they live, no matter what their social and economic circumstances. To him, their lives are plodding, dull, and barren. If his parents are poor, he scorns their lack of success. If they are affluent, he scoffs at their achievements. If they do not work at all, they are bums. He does not fathom how toiling at a job can consume the bulk of his parents' working hours, especially when they have to work on someone else's terms. He cannot comprehend their placing obligations ahead of convenience or pleasure. To him, having a good time is what life is all about. Work and other duties have nothing to do with having a good time. "What is life for? You live it and die," said one delinquent from a middle-class family. He had decided that he would live as he saw fit and not be a slave as his parents were. And that's what he did. *"They* decided to have *me, "* he said. "It's not a free ride. If they don't like the way I act, tough." He was totally impervious to the fact that it was his parents' sense of obligation, their patience, their sense of purpose—the very qualities that he derided—that had provided him with the comfortable home that he assumed was his birthright.

Many a teenager adopts a critical, if not despairing, view of his parents' life style. A developmental task of adolescence is to evaluate what one has been taught and subsequently internalized. The teenager may rebel during this period of intense questioning and doubt. Most of those who flirt with danger do not become outlaws. They discover that breaking away from legal and moral restraints to any great extent extracts too high a price. It jeopardizes their future and hurts people whom they value and who cherish them. Eventually, it dawns on them that being responsible offers a wealth of possibilities from which one can carve out a life and still be his own person.[3] Living outside the law drastically limits alternatives and thereby curtails one's freedom. For a criminal, it's just the opposite.

The child who becomes a criminal gradually slips beyond his parents' reach, becoming ever more secretive and defiant. The accumulation of minor irritants as well as major infractions is so debilitating to the parents that they frequently doubt they can stand another day under the same roof with him.

When there are other children in the family, they are victimized by their delinquent sibling, who bullies them, helps himself to their belongings, and pins the rap on them when any discipline is about to be meted out. This behavior is far more extreme than the rivalry that usually exists among siblings. Not only does the criminal youngster appropriate their toys, records, and clothes without permission, but he destroys or loses them. He also steals their money. Brothers and sisters, if younger or smaller, are cowed into submission. They are warned to keep their mouths shut about what they see and are told that if they squeal they will regret it.

As long as the delinquent is at home, his brothers and sisters know few peaceful moments and have virtually no privacy. The greatest tragedy is that, in a sense, their parents have been usurped. In a home simmering with dissension, mother and father have little time for them, their problems seem less urgent, and so they feel shortchanged. The family is not really a family. The moments they do have together are often anxiety-ridden because the parents are worn out and on edge and so have less of themselves to share. It is amazing to see how some extremely disturbed families are instantly at peace once the criminal member leaves home.

Even though the delinquent makes life miserable for his brothers and sisters, he sometimes acts as their keeper. No matter how shabbily he treats them, he will not permit anyone else to inflict harm on them and is quick to rally to their defense—with violence if he deems it necessary to protect them. On the one hand, he belittles them for being "goody-goodies," yet he rebuffs them for wrongdoing and threatens to tell on them. If a sibling who has been a good kid grows curious and wants to accompany him on some of his clandestine missions, he discourages it. He doesn't want anyone tagging along, being a nuisance. In addition, he wants to keep his brother or sister out of harm's way. On the other hand, if there is a sibling who shares his lust for adventure, he welcomes him as a companion and accomplice.

When an older brother precedes a younger sibling in taking a delinquent path, it is often assumed that the younger has identified with and been corrupted by the older. A psychological report on one 14-year-old pot smoker and thief cited his older brother's unwholesome example as having had a critically detrimental influence on him. This interpretation is based on psychiatric theories of role modeling and identification. Deviance is often attributed to identification with a deviant sibling or parent. In this situation, extensive clinical interviewing revealed that the younger boy considered himself a guy with his own mind. He *chose* to emulate his brother rather than emulate the other male in the family—his father—who was responsible. He was suggestible only to things that appealed to him as offering excitement, but he was not receptive to the predominant influences in his environment—parents, neighbors, teachers—that urged him to follow a more constructive path.

Identification theory fails to explain the process of choice in the lives of the delinquent youngster. A teenager wrote to Dr. Robert Wallace, an advice-giving columnist, recounting his horror when he discovered his father smoking marijuana.[4] When he confronted him, the father told the youth to live his life his way and he and the boy's mother would live theirs their way. The columnist advised the adolescent, "Do as your father said. Lead your life as an example for your parents to follow. It's sad that you must learn right from wrong by not doing what your parents do." Had the teenager been smoking pot, a psychiatrist likely would have asserted that it was because he had such poor role models. Many psychiatrists, psychologists, and social workers seem not to allow for the reign of free choice. Children do not inevitably pattern themselves after the qualities of their parents. Responsible role models may have an irresponsible child and vice versa. Children decide who they want to be like and in what ways.

As the personality of the criminally inclined child unfolds, his parents are gripped by a gnawing fear that something terrible is going to happen. Their nerves are constantly on edge. Every time the phone rings, their hearts sink. What is it this time—a distraught neighbor, a teacher reporting a fight, the police, or, worst of all, a hospital informing them that their child is injured or dead?

As their concerns mount, parents try new ways to cope with the youngster's misbehavior. They more closely restrict his movement and privileges but end up suffering more than the child, who sneakily circumvents the restrictions or blatantly flouts them. In fact, it is a relief to the parents when they can bring themselves to lift the restrictions. Then there are fewer battles.

In many of these families, corporal punishment is an unpalatable solution, the parents preferring reason. They find that resorting to violence is no solution at all. Whacking their offspring has virtually no long-range effect except to convey the message that violence is acceptable. The child absorbs the physical punishment and shows he can take it. He still does as he chooses.

Sometimes even the parent who believes he will never strike his child finds his patience depleted and lashes out in frustration, only to feel intense guilt later. These are not instances of child abuse, although the youngster may find an ear sympathetic to trumping up such a case. One 14 year old was totally incorrigible. He did exactly what he wanted, listening to no authority and screaming ''fuck off'' at his parents when they tried to control him. On one occasion, he met with his school counselor, who wanted to discuss the boy's repeated unexcused absences. The youth shifted the subject and complained about his home life, asserting that his father was violent and that he was subjected to repeated beatings. The shocked counselor referred the matter to protective services, and a caseworker contacted the parents. The boy's mother and father were mortified. The only particle of truth to their son's allegation was that several times, after repeated provocation, his father had slapped him. That was the extent of the child abuse. The family underwent a humiliating investigation that eventually resulted in the case being closed with no charges brought. Meanwhile, the youth was delighted at what he construed as his parents being called on the carpet. He now had a new weapon: ''If you touch me, I'll report you.''

Family profiles of some delinquents indicate that they truly were victims of child abuse. One psychiatric theory posits that they identified with the parent who was the aggressor and became violent themselves, which in turn led to their becoming delinquents. Another conclusion is that severe early punishment resulted in their becoming so submissive that they were rendered vulnerable to the influences of crime. One boy was punished as a child by being locked in the bathroom, tied up in the basement, and beaten with a strap. He was the only one of six children who enraged his parents to the point that they meted out such brutal punishment. This is not to condone his parents' methods of dealing with him. The point is that children like him, by their unrelenting provocation, may elicit a violent reaction even from a parent with a normally placid disposition. Rarely does that part of the story come out. A psychiatric school consultant, evaluating a 13-year-old delinquent boy, understood how a parent could be driven to extreme measures. He wrote in the youngster's clinical record, "This is a child who relates to adults in a manner that could easily move the adult to be physically abusive." There are no clinical studies that reveal why many, perhaps most, children who truly are victims of child abuse do not become criminals.

There is yet another type of response to the delinquent child. After years of assault upon their own values, some parents gradually embrace what earlier seemed to them to be radical ideas. For example, a mother who had regarded any illegal drug use with abhorrence became an advocate of legalizing marijuana after realizing that she was helpless to prevent her child from using it and after being convinced by him that everyone else was using it. Such shifts in attitude are a consequence of a parent's desperation to draw closer to a child who appears completely alienated. In a calculating manner, the youngster callously exploits his parent's desire to strengthen their bond. He believes that rather than risk a setback in the relationship, this parent will cave in on other issues. If the less susceptible parent continues to withstand such attempts at psychological blackmail, a major rift in the marital relationship may develop. In the long run, the parent being exploited realizes that he has been played for a sucker, that he has compromised himself before his family, and that he has been won over by the child into a destructive alliance against his spouse.

Parents Don't Turn Children into Criminals

No matter how much upheaval in the family there is and no matter how serious the wayward child's offenses, his parents believe for a long time that he is basically good. They have witnessed incidents of their offspring's totally unacceptable behavior from the time he was little. But looking at each occurrence, they hadn't seen anything particularly abnormal. As the child entered adolescence, they became perturbed because the frequency of serious incidents was increasing. Even so, they were aware of only a fraction of his delinquent activities as he was very adroit at covering his tracks. But to cling to a benign view of him in the face of his mounting difficulties becomes increasingly difficult and then impossible. One mother in this quandary said, "At first, we felt that he would just naturally grow out of this disruptive behavior pattern, but as time went on and things began to escalate, it became obvious that there was something else wrong." She had seen his traits as a young child—his daring, his sense of adventure, his cunning and persistent way of pursuing what he wanted, his occasional tantrums—give way to incessant lying, belligerence, defiance, and destructiveness. "The cute," she said, "gave way to the unbelievable." It is conceivable that parents might regard their own child as emotionally disturbed. It is unlikely that they'd consider him simply an antisocial person or a criminal. Even parents of adult criminals who are behind bars generally don't think in such terms.

Few parents remain indifferent or give up. They do what they can—spend more time with the child, enroll him in a different school, support his joining organized sports and clubs, send him to a counselor, seek counseling themselves. In grasping at possible solutions, the soul-searching goes on. Mothers and fathers blame themselves, each other, and people and events outside the family. The psychologically oriented devour books and then identify themselves as the causes of their child's delinquency. Some parents seek therapy.

There comes a time when parents of such a child have to face the fact that they are powerless to change the course of events. "I'm learning to let go," said one father. "I don't want to tie my life to this problem. It's like a very ill relative. You prepare yourself for the death of that person." Still the daily pain is great, and commonplace events become sources of humiliation. What can the parents tell grandma when she asks how her grandson is doing? What reassurances can parents offer to the neighbor whose little boy is in tears after being tormented by their son? It is mortifying to admit to a school counselor that they cannot control their child at home, much less what he does in school. Each incident serves as a powerful reminder to them that they have failed at what they consider perhaps the most important experience in life—raising a child. Through it all, the youngster has not a shred of comprehension or concern about his parents' agony. In his opinion, it is they who have inflicted the wounds on themselves by demanding that he be something he has no interest in being. Their worry is needless. He is fine the way he is. When asked how he felt about his parents' distress, one boy responded coldly, "It's like an operation. They have to live with the pain. It's their problem."

The criminal child knows that one way to be free of hassles is to strike out on his own. However, such children usually think things through enough to realize that, if they run away, their parents will summon the police and they will be caught and brought back, only to have more restrictions piled on. Besides, most have no place to go. They prefer that their parents leave. But no matter how unsatisfactory life is at home, it is still home, a familiar base of operation. One 15-year-old boy said, "All I want is three hots and a cot, nothin' more." And so these youngsters stick around, continuing to victimize those who care about them the most.

Parents often wish they could let their child leave and live the way he says he wants to.[5] But when he is under 17, the responsibility is theirs. Boarding school is usually an unten-

46

able alternative because of expense and the probability that the youngster won't stay. In families with a delinquent child, a major disagreement may arise when the youngster does become old enough to live independently. At issue is whether his mother and father have a right to their own lives after years of turmoil. When he is legally of age to be emancipated, some parents say good-bye. For most, it still is an agonizing experience. One mother wrote her friend, "Probably the most difficult step we *ever* had to take was finally to follow the advice of a respected judge, a doctor, and Art's psychiatrist. We were to let Art take off as he wished before finishing high school, and later we were told to stop bailing him out of trouble every time he called collect. Our sending money didn't help make him responsible for his many debts. We still run into people to whom he owes money."

A situation in which the youth refuses to leave is no easier to face. The parents are often terrified of forcing their son into doing something drastic if they try to push him out. One mother said, "We've been through a flaky suicide attempt. He slashed his arms close to the wrist. Believe me, I hope I never have to go through anything like that again. I can handle emergencies, but all that blood. The intense feelings of dislike after he was in the hospital scared me. Sometimes I think I need an analyst. These kids don't realize what they do to their parents."

A final break rarely occurs. Some sort of tie, no matter how tenuous, is maintained between parents and the very difficult child. One mother said, "While our boy was in prison, we sent food packages, art supplies, a radio, an electric fan, and some money, but he *demanded* more. We continued to write in spite of his stealing from us by ordering stereo equipment on our credit card. Again, he lied about doing it and then about being sorry. As usual, he promised to change. We did not feel we could afford to send him all the things he demanded. Therefore, he angrily told us off and said he never wanted to hear from us again."

Some parents finally conclude that confinement of their child is necessary both to bring him to grips with reality and to protect innocent people. One mother said, ''It's the most horrible thing in the world to say—I am afraid of my own son. I'm afraid I'll go to bed some night and never wake up in the morning.'' The parents of one 18 year old had done all in their power to help him, including shelling out thousands of dollars for his psychiatric treatment at a prestigious inpatient center. Not long after his release from the hospital, he was apprehended for the abduction of two girls and was sentenced to a long prison term. All that his father could say was, ''Justice has been served.''

Any parent who has read this chapter may be alarmed if he has a child who is showing any of the behavior just described. But before concluding that he has a budding criminal in the family, he should ask himself whether his youngster is showing isolated instances of the behavior or evidencing patterns over time that are expanding and intensifying. Every child who swipes a few coins from a cookie jar or steals a candy bar from a store does not become a criminal. In a classic textbook on child development, psychology professors L. Joseph Stone and Joseph Church cite ''normal or casual delinquent behavior'' that ''will usually be outgrown without any special measures'' because children who show such behavior ''develop their own inhibitions and controls without any action by authorities.''[6] This chapter documents patterns in a minority of children who eventually inflict enormous damage upon society no matter what their parents or others do to deter them.

The reader may conclude that I have let all parents off the hook, no matter what their inadequacies. This is not so. Parents who are abusive, neglectful, inconsistent, and psychologically disturbed are likely to have an adverse impact on their offspring. This is not to say, however, that they will invariably produce criminals. Fortunately for society, most youngsters who suffer neglect or abuse do not become criminals. Furthermore, it is striking to observe that some criminals are the sons and daughters of parents who are devoted, stable, and responsible. Unfortunately the best efforts of parents to help and correct this kind of child can and usually do fail. As it turns out, the parents are usually the victims, the child the victimizer, not the other way around.

Chapter Four

Peer Pressure: No Excuse for Crime

IF PARENTS of criminals were asked what went wrong in their children's lives, many would reply, "My child ran with the wrong crowd." They would maintain that their son was a good boy at heart but that he was corrupted by others. The belief is widespread that youngsters turn to crime, alcohol, and drugs because they succumb to the pressures of their peer group.

Peer pressure is a force that we all have to contend with from the time we are in nursery school until the time we die. But we choose which peer group or groups to belong to. As is the case with nearly all children, the criminal as a child chooses his friends. No criminal I have evaluated or counseled was forced into crime. He chose to associate with risk-taking youngsters who were doing what was forbidden. Once he worked his way into their confidence, he gained in-

creasing recognition, which meant more to him than acceptance anywhere else. His parents, teachers, and numerous
others tried to persuade or compel him to associate with
responsible youngsters, but they were rebuffed. The delinquent youngster scorns his contemporaries who are
"straight" and sticks with his own kind. Sometimes alone,
but more often with youngsters like himself, he commits
more and more crimes, bolstering his self-image in the process and finding that no one can do anything for very long to
bring a halt to his spiraling criminality. Certainly, there is no
incentive to break away from those who share his interests
and are very much like him.

It doesn't take a sociologist to point out that youngsters
are influenced by their peers, that they want to be in step and
belong to the crowd. But some sociologists and mental health
professionals regard the child as a hapless victim who is contaminated by pernicious influences. E. H. Sutherland, a sociologist who is still widely quoted after more than 40 years,
contended that people become criminals because of their
close contact with others who are in crime.[1] His "differential
association" theory posits that criminality is contagious,
much like a disease. People are thought to contract criminality through exposure, much as they pick up cases of mea-
sles. Yet one must ask why, if this is true, do so many
children in high-crime areas, including the criminal's own
brothers and sisters, not become criminals?

A somewhat different perspective on delinquency is set
forth by sociologist Martin Gold, who states that boys are
"driven" into deviant behavior because of repeated failure
to achieve status in society.[2] Gold contends that these youngsters discover that through delinquent behavior they can
"win status" among peers who "share these status problems."

The view that a youngster is *led* or *driven* into crime to gain
status ignores the role of personal choice. From the time he
was little, the delinquent has chosen the company he keeps

and has determined what kind of status he wants. Only when he was held accountable for his actions did he resort to blaming others, claiming, "Some kids got me into shoplifting," or "The kids I hung with led me astray."

Whether the delinquent is from a poor or wealthy family, whatever his neighborhood is like, he shares much in common with a boy like Tim, the fourth born in a lower middle-class Catholic family of six boys and one girl. His sister and brothers were, for the most part, obedient and conforming. Not Tim. His parents date the beginning of his criminal career to age four. The family next door had driven off for a picnic and left the front door of their home ajar. Tim walked in and cleaned out as many toys as he could stuff into his arms.

Stocky and strong for his age, he established a reputation as the neighborhood terror, a thief and a bully who would take on anyone in a fight. At six, he left the neighborhood and roamed across the boulevard, where he was forbidden to go because of the rough area and heavy traffic. There he was attracted to an older bunch of toughs who hung around street corners and who were far more fascinating to him than the "goody-goodies" on his block. A favorite activity of this group was to enter a store and, while one boy diverted the owner's attention, make off with as much as they could carry. Tim started drinking with these boys when he was 10, often supplying them with beer stolen from his parents' refrigerator. Tim's pilfering escalated during early adolescence to breaking and entering, lifting CB radios from cars, and stealing cars.

But Tim was not totally an outlaw. He surprised people by participating in some conventional activities, such as church functions, which he attended with his family. An excellent swimmer, Tim aspired to be an Olympic participant. In high school, he joined a local swim team, which at the time was having a losing season. Even in a legitimate enterprise, he was determined to do things his way. Because he was so highly valued, Tim got away with infractions for which his teammates would have been suspended. The only member with stringy, long hair, a moustache, and a headband, Tim sauntered in for practice whenever he felt like it, which was rarely. Tim recalls showing up for meets "reeking from pot" or "half-crocked on booze," but then executing a perfect dive. As long as he remained on the team, it compiled a winning record. He thrived on being a prima donna but spewed contempt for the suckers who showed up for practice regularly.

Everywhere he went, Tim gravitated to those who offered him opportunities for excitement. While in the army, he became friendly with an alcoholic priest whom he assisted in serving mass. The priest took a liking to Tim and invited him to imbibe wine after services. The priest used his influence to obtain extended passes for Tim, who would stagger back to his army post roaring drunk. One night, some of the men in Tim's unit who were fed up with his belligerence threw a "blanket party." After he fell asleep, they tossed a blanket over him and started pounding away. His reaction: "I went insane." He broke free and went after the sergeant, determined to kill him. It took several soldiers to restrain him. After one month, the army discharged him. Again, Tim had rejected living within a social unit.

When Tim tired of being home, he violated probation by taking off for his brother's home in St. Louis. His parents were hopeful that, away from his old associates, he might make a fresh start and find more respectable friends. Asking for the court's indulgence and consideration, Tim's father wrote the judge, "We believe that Tim's full recovery could be enhanced under the influence of his older brother, whose opinions he respects." Despite a change in environment, Tim chose to travel a familiar path. He found friends cut from the same cloth as he, returned to drugs and drink, and then began stealing from his brother, the very person who was providing a roof over his head. Today, at 22, Tim is serving a sentence for assault and battery.

In the preschool years, neither Tim nor others like him divides the world into good kids and bad kids. But such a child realizes that some children are adventurous while others are not. Like a magnet, he is drawn to those who are nervy and disobedient. It is often thought that this happens because the delinquent child has been exposed mainly to social misfits and hasn't had the chance to benefit from association with responsible children. But this is not the case.

In inner city and suburban areas throughout America, youngsters flock to organized activities practically from the time they are of age to toddle around in neighborhood play groups. As they meet new people and discover new interests, they become involved in team sports, church groups, scouting, community service, and school clubs. A process of socialization occurs as these children learn about cooperation, competition, sharing, and self-control. What peers think of them comes to matter a great deal, sometimes too much. Personal recognition and achievement in these endeavors nurture their self-esteem, while failure may leave lasting scars. For better or worse, their ego involvement is considerable.

What offers opportunity for fun and personal growth to the responsible child leaves the delinquent with little but a gnawing restlessness and mounting boredom. Some delinquents steadfastly refuse to participate in any organized activities. Some responsible youngsters do the same, but for different reasons. The delinquent refuses to subordinate himself to anyone else's authority. Invariably, he regards a coach or other leader as knowing less than he. Contemptuous of the activity, its organizer, and the other participants, he chooses instead to engage in something more exciting, often illicit. The responsible youngster, on the other hand, may reject organized activities because he feels inferior to others in a group or simply because he prefers to do other things that are constructive. The delinquent rejects the organized activity for an irresponsible alternative, while other youngsters usually do so for one that is responsible.

Some delinquents are attracted to competition, where they are determined to outshine everyone else. Then their entire self-image is on the line, and they resort to any tactic that they can think of in order to win. To achieve a personal victory, they strive to impose their will and either con or force others to operate by their rules. If they even begin to sense that they will not come out on top, they cheat, fight, or quit. They are impossibly arrogant winners or else revenge-seeking losers.

Eventually such a child grows contemptuous of the "knotheads" and "finks" who live an ordinary existence at home, in the neighborhood, and at school. To be part of that life is, as one 12 year old said, "like being put on a leash." Dissatisfied with his age, the delinquent seeks out the more daring, usually older youngsters, whom he regards as having all the fun. One young teenager told a counselor, "I've always wanted to grow up fast. I don't get along with anyone my age. I get mad because they act too immature." At 14, he was hanging around with a wild crowd of 18 to 25 year olds who were neither working nor in school.

Every secondary school has groups with different names— preppies, jocks, sweathogs, freaks, and so forth. Snarled one 14 year old, "Preppies, I hate 'em. They think they're so neat with their alligator shirts." He chose to associate with the "freaks," who skipped school, used drugs, and went on shoplifting binges. One father said of his son, "If Guy saw a group of neatly dressed students holding their books and talking about girls, cars, and sports and he saw a scraggly bunch of boys swaggering around, drinking, and cursing, he would always choose the second group."

Far from being enticed into crime, the criminal as a child admires and cultivates those who are in the action. In fact, to gain their acceptance, he must prove himself by demonstrating that he is tough and, even more important, that he can be trusted. He dresses as they do, apes their language, follows them wherever they go, and does whatever they ask. In time, he is no longer viewed as a tag-along, but as one of the crowd. He may feel used during his period of initiation, but he overlooks this because he values just being with them.

Some of these youths form a loosely knit alliance, while others belong to an organized group or gang. (Some don't mix much with anyone.) In the city, delinquent youngsters congregate on street corners and around pool halls, pinball arcades, and taverns. In the suburbs, they flock to shopping malls, fast-food outlets, game arcades, or wherever else kids gather just to see what's happening.

Responsible youngsters also "hang out" at some of the same places. But if one were to have a film of the conversation and activities of the two groups, striking differences would be observable. It is a matter not only of where teenagers congregate but of what they do once they get there. At the shopping mall, the more conventional kids might be spending their allowance or job earnings, engaging in window shopping, or standing around talking about the evening's date or basketball game. The delinquent youngsters would be wandering through stores thinking about how to abscond with merchandise or how to alter price tags without being detected. Or they might stir up excitement by picking fights, making unsolicited comments to shoppers, drinking, and becoming rowdy. For delinquent kids, a favorite hangout because of its safety is the home of someone whose parents are out all day. If his neighborhood is dead, the child travels to where the action is, even if it requires boarding a bus or hitchhiking across town.

The parents of these children rarely know where their offspring are. Contrary to what many counselors and court workers believe, usually this is due not to negligence but to the youngster's ingenuity at concealing his activities. He may check in with his parents to satisfy them that he is visiting a friend, but he fails to disclose where he will be heading later. He often says he is going one place but goes another. Not only do the parents not know where their child is, but often they are in the dark as to who his friends are.

If the family ends up in counseling sessions, the counselor is likely to be critical of the parents for not making their home a place where their child's friends feel welcome, thereby leaving the youngster more vulnerable to pressures of the streets. But the fact is that the youngster does not want his parents to know who his friends are. "My parents don't know half my friends," said one 15 year old. "If they got a look at most of them, they'd give me a rough time." He knew that his mother and father did not approve of his hanging around with a hard-drinking, school-skipping gang, some of whom had been in trouble with the police. Even suspecting the worst, many parents still prefer that the youngster bring his friends home instead of roaming the streets. "I've tried so hard to make our home a pleasant place for my son to bring his friends," said one such mother. "But he always goes out. They never come here." Her son knew that his buddies would be bored to tears at his house. What could they do, sit around and drink Cokes and watch television?

The delinquent youngster is intent on conveying an image of himself as unflappable and invincible. As each youth is attempting to prove himself to other kids, he is also struggling to overcome intense and carefully concealed fears. Fears of the dark, heights, water, and lightning persist into adolescence, sometimes into adulthood. These youngsters are also fear-ridden about their bodies. Although they exaggerate the significance of each ache, their physical distress does not propel them to the doctor's office because they fear that there even greater pain will be inflicted. Consequently, a minor ailment that is neglected may develop into a more serious infection or illness. These youngsters fret over their height, weight, strength, and physical attractiveness. Some worry so much about their penis being undersized that they refuse to attend physical education classes in order to avoid undressing. When one 15 year old shared a cabin with a group of boys on an overnight outing, he neither took a shower nor changed clothes. Despite the fact that he was well endowed, he did not want others to see his genitals. He was at ease in a group shower only when he was among much younger boys. In private, he tried to overcome his perceived inadequacy by tying a brick to his erect penis to stretch it.

Because the delinquent youngster is always striving to impress his peers, to have others sense that he is afraid is just about the most humiliating thing that can happen. To avoid embarrassment, he may stay away from whatever bothers him. Or he may try to push these fears out of mind and fly in the face of them. Some delinquents cope with apprehensions about physical weakness by lifting weights, taking up boxing, and learning karate and judo. Obsessed with a desire to display bulging muscles, one 13 year old lifted weights for two hours a day until he was able to lift 250 pounds. He was determined to be able to stand up to any threat. In addition, he thought that rippling biceps would impress the girls.

Responsible youngsters have some of the same fears. They too may be afraid of the dark, experience vertigo in high places, and be preoccupied with their bodies. Many a teenage boy has dreaded undressing in front of others with more pubic hair and larger genitals than his. But the responsible person handles both his neurotic and reality-based fears differently from the delinquent. He accepts fear as part of life and tries to overcome it. Fearing failure at school, he studies harder. Fearing disapproval from the coach, he gives his all at each practice. Neurotic fears may be embarrassing, and if intense enough they may disrupt his life to the point that he becomes phobic, in which case he lives disabled or is driven to seek help. The delinquent fears fear because it demolishes his superman stance, leaving him feeling weak, exposed, and vulnerable. He copes with fear by denying it or lashing out at what he thinks is the source of the fear or at any other convenient target.

Reputation is all-important. These youths build and maintain a "rep" for themselves through the way they talk, the style in which they dress, and the activities in which they engage. The profanity and street slang lacing the language of the middle-class delinquent is indistinguishable from that of his inner city counterpart. Even as a small child, the delinquent accepts dares from others to show that he is not "chicken." These youngsters prove their mettle by jumping from high places, careening down steep hills on skateboards, diving off the high board, riding the scariest roller coaster, racing a bike through someone's flowerbed, competing to see who can swipe the most candy from a store. They play rough and take unfair advantage both in organized sports and in their own sandlot games. They prove to one another that they are physically tough by deliberately inflicting pain—holding their breath, sticking pins in their arms, burning themselves with cigarettes. No tears at any time; they show that they can take it, whatever the source of the pain. One boy cracked several ribs during a playground accident. He did not shed a tear or even wince as the ribs were taped. Later that day, to prove that he was invincible, he carried several packages out of a store without so much as a grimace. As teenagers, these youths demonstrate their daring by drag racing, guzzling liquor, experimenting with drugs, and engaging in high-risk crimes.

"People aren't to fuck with me" is the youth's stance toward his parents, teachers, other kids, the police, and the world in general. The smallest slight to his self-image, the least hint of interference with his plans may trigger a violent reaction. One 16 year old said tersely, "If anyone aggravates me, I'm ready to kill him." He then added, "I just like to fight, to feel skin against my knuckles, to feel noses break. I always win, except when it's four against one." This same youth thought of lashing to a tree a boy against whom he had a grudge and turning dogs loose to tear him to shreds. In such a boy's view, anyone who backs away from a fight is a punk or sissy.

Many children get into scraps, and some go through a phase of fighting. But they respond to socializing influences and learn that compromise, tact, and persuasion are more effective than fists. The delinquent's attitude of "no one is to mess with me" persists into adulthood. A 38-year-old criminal expressed it as, "If you do me wrong, then you got to whup me."

Not all delinquents are tough guys. Some are terrified of physical injury and, transforming this fear into a virtue, they look down on those who are violent as crude, lacking class. Said one teenager with disdain, "I never hung around with rednecks. I wasn't violent." Such youngsters build their reputation by outfoxing others or verbally intimidating them. A 16 year old confessed, "I've got a fearless image on the outside, but inside I'm a scared guy. Fighting wasn't my thing. I don't have the weight." But he bragged that he didn't have to use his fists because "I can talk a good fight." What he meant was that intimidation worked.

Whether or not he is a fighter, the delinquent takes but rarely gives. He does not know what friendship is because trust, loyalty, and sharing are incompatible with his way of life. The delinquent does not know how to hold a discussion. He says his piece and ignores or shouts down those who disagree. Continually, he engages in a fiercely competitive one-upmanship, building himself up by bragging about his exploits, usually with plenty of exaggeration. He diminishes others at every chance through unrelenting goading, teasing, and deception. Even his best buddy is not immune to being conned or made to look the fool. If a youth can get a good chuckle at this fellow's expense, it's another victory notched in his belt. The youngster's humor is at the expense of others. He delights in mocking, mimicking, and other ways of making fun of people, his close associates included. He

61

guffaws whenever someone is taken by surprise or humiliated. Even an accident, such as someone toppling down a flight of stairs, produces a laugh. What is predictable is that nearly all his friends will be the same way.

Part of the delinquent youngster's social scene is alcohol use, which begins even before adolescence. Some experts attribute drinking to peer pressure. However, the delinquent rarely is pressured into drinking. It is just another forbidden activity in which he engages with his buddies. Hanging out and drinking are virtually synonymous for many of these youths. "All we ever thought about was partying," reflected one 20-year-old man. This was a direct reference to drinking, which for a time occupied a central place in his life.

Alcohol can only bring out what is already part of the person's thinking and emotional makeup. Youngsters who are not delinquent also drink under age and act irresponsibly. But for some delinquents alcohol knocks out fear so that they then have the "nerve" to engage in riskier crimes that in the past they might only have thought about.

The delinquent is in control of what he does, even though he may rationalize a crime by telling others, "I was blasted. I couldn't see beyond my nose." Adults who have to deal with him often fall for this and believe he was not in control of himself. They blame the alcohol and their child's drinking buddies, but not the youngster himself.

Alan's mother declared that alcohol was the villain. Not knowing of her son's crimes before he ever began drinking, she asserted, "When he didn't drink, he was a different person." Alan began drinking at 10, when he and other kids heisted beer and Boone's Farm wine from local stores. At 16, he could pass for 18 and altered his driver's license so he could buy his own liquor. Throughout his adolescence, every adult who knew Alan was positive he would be all right if he left alcohol alone and associated with a different crowd. But Alan admitted to his psychologist that he used liquor to fulfill desires that he had when he was totally sober. "I'd go

out and get drunk so I could commit the crimes I was thinking of," he said. "I controlled how much I wanted to drink
and when I wanted to drink." In other words, neither alcohol nor his friends put ideas into his head. They were already
there, waiting to be acted on. Even when he was plastered,
he could use remarkable restraint if it were in his interest.
When Alan was arrested for a break and entry, he was remanded to an alcohol treatment program, not confined in
jail. While in treatment, Alan continued drinking but sought
more kicks. "I wanted one continuous high all the time," he
recalls. "I couldn't drink enough or do enough drugs. Anything or everything I could get my hands on would go in my
mouth."

Drug use is seen by some experts as a norm of adolescence. A federal government publication refers to drug experimentation as a "rite of passage" for a large segment of
teenagers.[3] The drug-using teenager fosters such thinking in
adults when he asserts that everyone uses drugs, while at the
same time the media bombard the public with news reports,
films, and television productions that dramatize an explo-
sion in youthful drug abuse. But the statistics on this phe-
nomenon are often misleading. Who is considered a drug
user? Lumped together are the person who has experi-
mented once or twice and stopped using drugs and the person who has been getting high several times every day for
years. A decade ago, psychologist Francis King reported that
17 percent of Dartmouth College students responding to a
poll were marijuana users. But a breakdown of this figure revealed that, of the 96 users, 74 had tried the substance less
than a half-dozen times.[4] Unquestionably, the incidence of
experimentation with drugs has skyrocketed. However, many
teenagers, after a brief trial, discontinue drug use because
drugs do little for them. A University of Michigan Institute
for Social Research study showed that 70 percent of high
school seniors surveyed disapproved of regular marijuana

use and 34 percent disapproved of trying the drug once or twice.[5]

Against such considerations, the drug use patterns of the delinquent youngster should be seen in perspective. The first time a youngster experiments with a new substance, he may be apprehensive about the results of getting caught. But outweighing his fears is the excitement of the unknown and the forbidden. Such youngsters first receive drugs from their friends. Pushers rarely foist drugs on the innocent but instead protect themselves by selling almost exclusively to known users. As a youth becomes a regular in the drug scene, he learns where to make his buys. The drug supply areas of the city are notorious. According to one news report, dozens of Washington, D.C., suburbanites head to the inner city every day to purchase drugs. As one regular customer observed, when dealers "see a white boy in a car with Virginia tags, they will flag you down. They know what you're there for . . . drugs."[6] This is a far cry from being a victim of peer pressure. The delinquent knows how to find what he wants. He is open to anything new and exciting and has chosen to associate with others who are willing to accommodate him.

Whether or not the teenage delinquent resorts to drugs, his crimes become more frequent, more daring, and more serious. He is neither corrupted by others nor dependent on them for ideas. A torrent of schemes rushes through his mind, and he enacts those which are most exciting and feasible. The youth has his own tastes and preferences in crime and looks down on kids who take what he considers foolhardy risks. One 15 year old sneered, "I don't break into houses. It's too easy to get caught. These people don't think about the chances they take." Some youths operate as loners, others in groups, and some both ways. They detect frailty and vulnerability in people and proceed to stalk their prey. Some operate by stealth and run a string of con games. Others operate by force and rob newsboys, snatch ladies' purses, roll drunks, and mug the weak and unsuspecting. Some youngsters have had a longstanding fascination with weapons and in their fantasies have shot, bludgeoned, clubbed, and blown to bits any number of people. Eventually the fantasies are transformed into reality. A 13 year old boasted, "I have a nice arsenal." With a sadistic smile, he went on to enumerate his switchblades, chains, knives, and clubs. Virtually any convenient object can be used as a weapon. A stick becomes a club, a letter opener a knife. A stone can hit a windshield with the impact of a bullet when it is dropped from a bridge high overhead.

The automobile broadens opportunities for all youngsters, and there may be a new set of pressures from peers. Responsible teenagers see driving as lessened dependence on their parents to take them places. They may drive in a manner to impress their friends, and some take advantage of their new freedom and misuse the automobile. A preoccupation with cars is typical of many adolescents, but what delinquents do with a car far exceeds the norm and has nothing to do with pressure from peers. Impatient to drive, many a delinquent is behind the wheel before he is licensed. The car is unleashed as a weapon, and the youth drives as though he owns the road. Roaring about at raceway speeds, these teenagers terrify and aggravate motorists by cutting in, tailgating, screaming obscenities, and hurling objects out windows. In a car, more territory is accessible for criminal activity. The city kid can hit the more affluent areas, and the suburban kid can make contacts in the inner city.

Psychologists Elizabeth Douvan and Joseph Adelson write that the "actual power of peer influence" has been overestimated.[7] In the main, they appear to be speaking of adolescents who are in school and basically responsible. If this is true of the 3,500 teenagers whom Douvan and Adelson surveyed, it is even more accurate with respect to delinquents who look for, find, and prefer others like themselves. These youths are not forced into a deviant subculture. One teen-ager summed up her voluntary separation from her responsible peers when she said, "What straight people do for fun, I'll never know. What do they do? If they started partying, they'd freak out." She remarked that she had nothing to talk about with straight people and said that she had found that the kids whom she wanted to be with were people like herself—those who lived in what she called "life's fast lane."

Chapter Five

"The Hell with School"

SCHOOLS HAVE shortcomings, and valid criticisms can be made of them. Incompetent teachers, overcrowded classrooms, an antiquated physical plant, an unimaginative or rigid curriculum, and lack of discipline all have an adverse impact on learning. But only a minority of students exposed to any or all such adverse conditions are criminals.

For decades, schools have been accused of spawning criminals by failing to meet their needs when they are young and shutting them out of the social mainstream. In their book *Schools and Delinquency,* Kenneth Polk and Walter Schafter state that schools restrict opportunities for some students, and they contend that delinquency is "a result of blocked goal attainment."[1] Educator Edgar Z. Friedenberg asserts that schools disparage lower-class youngsters, who then react by becoming delinquents.[2] Such charges ignore the fact that criminals reject school long before it rejects them. As a child, the criminal is bored by school, and his objectives have little to do with academic learning. Instead, he exploits the school, using it as an arena for crime or else as a cover for it. Like the parents, the school is unsuccessful in socializing and educating the criminal. Even special education programs and counseling often fail to diagnose accurately the criminal pupil, much less change him.

The criminal as a child increasingly sets himself apart from those who take school seriously. One 12 year old snorted, "Nobody wants to talk about atoms and things like that. Who likes those brainy guys?" Delinquents build themselves up by tearing others down, and so the brainy guys are referred to in an assortment of derogatory terms. The "puny, cross-eyed bookworms" bear the brunt of the delinquent's teasing and bullying, especially those whom he labels teacher's pet. The youngster unmercifully preys upon any inadequacy or insecurity in his classmates and loves to embarrass and terrorize them. A child who is visibly afraid of him becomes a repeated target of harassment all year. He is called names, cursed, mocked, threatened, punched, and made a scapegoat.

Although the delinquent picks on the serious students, he makes trouble mostly with kids like himself. He provokes them with an obscene sign, a hurled object, or a menacing gesture so that the recipient rises to the bait and gets into trouble, while he, the instigator, goes scot-free. A child mutters an obscenity to another boy who responds by throwing a pencil. The teacher sees the flying pencil but then is confronted with each child blaming the other: "He called me a name," "He threw a pencil at me." A favorite occupation is the cutdown battle in which boys compete to see who can be the most vicious in verbally tearing one another apart. When such incidents erupt regularly, the teacher is like a fireman who is called to extinguish several blazes simultaneously.

All this troublemaking is an antidote to the boredom that

the delinquent experiences in the classroom while his fellow students are engaged in learning. What others find acceptable or even fascinating, he disdains. He stirs up excitement through a series of power plays designed not only to relieve tedium but to call attention to himself and establish a reputation. What others consider getting in trouble he perceives as a boost to his self-image.

If the youngster is doing little or no work, his teacher and school administrators wonder whether he is intellectually deficient, emotionally disturbed, inherently lazy, or a combination of these. Actually, the child is certain that he is smarter than the others. Typical is the statement of one boy who claimed, "I could get all A's if I wanted to, but school sucks." The youngster thinks it is not incumbent on him to exert effort except when he wants to. The idea is to get the work over with. He doesn't care about the product. He sets the standard for what is acceptable. So if he does homework, it is in an erratic, disorganized way. Some delinquents decide not even to go through the motions and do no work. One teenager said, "I didn't see the need for homework and told the teacher I wasn't going to do it."

The criminal child appears to have a short attention span for most classroom assignments. However, to his teacher's astonishment, his lethargy is transformed into a burst of concentrated activity once he finds an interest. One surprised teacher commented, "Timmy can be very interested in a project if it is something that attracts his attention." That is, in Timmy, the capability was present. The dilemma was that very little that the school offered captured Timmy's attention. One teenager recalled that whatever academic interests he had disappeared as soon as someone provided direction, tested his knowledge, or imposed a deadline. He said, "The interest would turn into a conflict when something had to be produced like a paper or test." His "conflict" was that he objected to others' telling him what to do, whether at school or anywhere else. Furthermore, he refused to tolerate others evaluating him. He reflected, "Grading systems always bothered me, because I just disagree with them totally. If there's anything I'm interested in, I can do it."

When they are allowed to plan their own schedules, such youngsters choose the easiest subjects. They detest courses demanding the drudgery of drill memorization and step-by-step reasoning. The parts of the curriculum that interest them are those appealing to their sense of adventure and thirst for excitement, such as a detailed account of a bloody battle or a dramatic science experiment. These youths often miss the main point of a story or of an episode in history because their focus is so narrow.

In any group project, such a youngster expects to take charge and receive credit for the final product. He has no sense of teamwork. He *is* the enterprise, whereas others are merely lackeys to carry out his wishes. If they prove not so amenable, he quits, dismissing the activity as silly and boring. If he is not permitted to withdraw, he demeans the efforts of others, insisting all the while that things should be done his way. If he is allowed to take over, he is certain that he has more expertise than anyone else and operates as a dictator. When problems arise and he is unsure as to how to proceed, he is like a captain of a ship who is aware that he has lost his bearings but doesn't want to admit it to himself or to others and instead stubbornly plows ahead, insisting he is on course. For such a youngster, to seek help is to acknowledge that he does not know all there is to know. Like the proud captain, he'd rather run his boat aground than admit ignorance.

Academically, most delinquent children function far below their potential. But because of strong social pressure and school attendance laws, they remain in school long enough to avoid hassles with parents, teachers, truant officers, and the courts. When they reach an age when the law says they don't have to be in school, many leave. A minority stay and do well in school. If they earn good grades, others are likely to think well of them. A's and B's provide a cover for crime.

Evan was an honor roll student and president of his high school's student council. People who regarded him as a model student and leader did not suspect that he was leading a double life. Outside school and away from his neighborhood, Evan was hanging around with a fast crowd that was drinking, using drugs, and stealing. He became increasingly involved in serious criminal activity but was not caught. Because of his accomplishments at school, he was beyond suspicion. For years, he had maintained a facade of the all-American boy, and so it was a shocked community that learned of his arrest for rape.

Some delinquents delight in raising hell in the classroom. If this starts in the primary grades, it is rarely regarded as a serious problem at the time. One teacher observed of a restless, pugnacious seven year old, "He has something cooking all the time." She sympathetically conceived of him as the class clown who was starved for attention. Parents and teachers strive to help such children through what is thought to be a period of adjustment.

Some delinquents go on a rampage of theft and destruction during school hours. If they want something that another pupil has, they snatch it when it is unguarded. Belongings vanish from desks, coats, and lockers, and items are missing from the teachers' lounge, from musical and athletic supplies, and from the cafeteria. Youths with stolen goods line up customers to take hot merchandise off their hands. The parking lot is a potential treasure trove for loot from unlocked cars. Drug sales to an eager clientele flourish. Vandalism takes an enormous toll as desks are carved, walls defaced, books marked up, windows shattered, and furniture broken.

Instead of being centers of learning, schools can become battlegrounds as delinquents stake out their territory and establish supremacy. It is extremely difficult for a child to concentrate on the morning's math lesson after he has just been approached by a tough kid who shakes him down for his lunch money and warns him that he better have more cash the next day. Study is next to impossible when a pupil has been told that, unless he regularly hands over money for "protection," he will be beaten to a pulp. According to one report, 22 percent (4.6 million) of secondary school students avoid certain bathrooms in their schools because of fear.[3] The school building may be a refuge, but once the child leaves he faces the prospect of being terrorized on the playground, on the school bus, and on the street. Fear stalks the corridors of some schools, where fistfights occur daily and youths brandish weapons. By displaying their toughness even in elementary school, these youths maintain a reputation as individuals who are not to be messed with. Commenting about a nine-year-old boy who attempted to strangle a classmate, a teacher said, "People are scared of Ricky. They don't know what will happen next and so they stay away from him." She went on to say that he lashed out seemingly without provocation. This teacher regarded him as a troubled, angry boy in need of help.

Schools and teachers are evaluated much in the same way as are parents, relatives, and friends. The delinquent praises virtually anyone who lets him do what he wants and reviles anyone who imposes limits. A group of adult inmates in a Minnesota prison brainstormed 77 ideas in response to being questioned about how schools could help eliminate crime. Their suggestions revealed a perspective unchanged from childhood, namely that school should cater to the student and make few demands of him. Among the inmates' suggestions were "more spontaneity," "dump dress codes," "more rap sessions," "supervise kids and not teach them," "let kids teach some classes," "let students choose teachers." Additional proposals were offered, but most were directed toward giving students free reign while requiring little personal responsibility.[4]

To the delinquent youngster, a "good teacher" takes the class on field trips, tolerates gum chewing and talking, assigns little work—generally is lenient. Teachers who make them toe the line are to be outwitted and made fools of, just like other strict adults. When a teacher reprimands them, they are likely to go on the offensive, first charging that the teacher was wrong in giving them a bum rap and then proceeding to curse, mock, and threaten the teacher. The incidence of assaults on teachers in American schools has skyrocketed. The National Institute of Education reports that nationwide 5,200 secondary school teachers are physically attacked each month.[5] In some troubled institutions, instruction is usurped by the necessity of devising survival strategies. In 1978, the administration of the Dayton, Ohio, public schools wrote into teacher contracts a provision for 45 days of "assault leave."[6]

Whenever possible, schools prefer to respond to pupil problems without involving parents. A handbook for students at the Winston Churchill High School, Montgomery County, Maryland, spells out a disciplinary code and lists five courses of "corrective action." In order of listing they are: student conference, parent notification, parent conference, police notification (required by law that the principal notify the local police department when a crime is committed on school property), suspension.[7]

A school must choose which among a staggering array of problems merits concentration of precious resources. A behavior pattern that is not terribly disruptive or longstanding may be temporarily overlooked. Nonattendance is one area in which many schools have refrained from imposing penalties, at least until it becomes a frequent pattern. When the school does take action, the child may deny having been absent, write his own excused absence notes and forge a parent's signature, or destroy notices the school sends home before his parents see them.

The school will summon the police when serious offenses

occur on school grounds. Because drugs have become so widely available at some schools, undercover police have been hired. The purpose is not so much to arrest the occasional marijuana user as it is to detect sources of supply and stem the flow of drug traffic. The delinquent who uses drugs regularly not only finds out about the hiring of police but seeks to penetrate their anonymity. One boy was certain that in his school with its staff of black janitors the new white janitor just had to be the "narc." He scoffed, "They have a secret cop, but that's so stupid. We all know he's a cop, but he doesn't know that we know. White janitors are a give-away." Knowledge that an undercover policeman is around may deter some delinquent youngsters from involvement with drugs on school grounds. But others are incited to out-wit police surveillance and conduct business as usual. A "drug bust" may drive the trafficking from the school grounds, but it returns as soon as things have cooled off.

As delinquents know, schools often fail to report crimes to the police. According to Dr. Robert J. Rubel, of the Center for Improved Learning Environments in San Marcos, Texas, there are two reasons for this. One is that because principals may mistakenly regard a crime merely as a disci-plinary violation instead of a criminal offense, they believe they should be able to handle the situation within the school. The other reason is that principals deliberately fail to report crimes because they do not want their schools (and thus themselves) to look bad. Rubel declares that "there are criminals" in schools and urges that their crimes be reported and that "criminal prosecution result."[8]

Each disciplinary step taken by the school poses a chal-lenge to the youngster, who wears his bad reputation like a Boy Scout merit badge.

Thirteen-year-old Joel was locked in combat with every-one. He constantly defied teachers and tussled with other pupils. Habitually he was truant or tardy and on numerous occasions was caught smoking in the lavatory. He was also a suspect in the setting of several mysterious fires. Counselors and the principal tried to reason with Joel, but he was impervious to a rational approach. His parents were at a loss. Keeping Joel after school, suspending him, and threatening him with expulsion had little effect. In fact, the more trouble he got into the more recalcitrant he became. Joel thrived on his "bad ass" reputation.

Pupils like Joel may be suspended, but in order to justify expelling them the school must have an airtight case. Furthermore, each time the school cracks down, it has not only the unruly students to cope with but also their parents and often the community.

When summoned by the school, some parents listen attentively and respond immediately by laying down the law to their child. But many parents are not so receptive. They find school conferences threatening because they hear the school asserting that if they were only better parents they would have better behaved children. Some mothers and fathers defend their child and do not recognize the seriousness of the problem. Then there are the parents who are virtually impossible to involve. They see their child's acting up as a school problem only and shrug off responsibility for taking any action, often because they are as powerless as the school.

Some parents believe that their offspring would be less troublesome if he were away from his friends and under closer supervision. A decision to enroll him in a different school is agonizingly reached because the parents know that he will be up in arms at the idea of leaving his friends and will recoil at the prospect of unknown authorities exercising greater power over him.

Many private schools will not accept a child who has a history of causing turmoil in the classroom. Those that agree to enroll him usually have many others just like him. If the change of school is made, from the first day the child sizes up the teachers and other pupils. What appears to his parents to be a new attitude is simply the child's early decision to lie low until he figures out the new situation. Eventually, he discovers that the school is not the prison that he imagined. After a few weeks, he has gravitated to other students like himself. A change of school has not resulted in a change in the child. His parents' flicker of hope again dies out. Only now they are spending a lot of money (in the case of a private school), and in some cases they have changed their daily schedule in order to drive their son to a school distant from their home. Some settings offer such close supervision that the child realizes he can't get away with much. If that is so, he is superficially compliant. Then his parents may preserve the illusion that he has changed, which lasts until the first phone call from an angry neighbor or the police.

These children are puzzling to the school because they are so changeable. Said one teacher, "When Ed is in my class, his behavior ranges from belligerent to spaced out." Even though these youngsters have been regarded as unmotivated, inattentive, passive, negative, sad, hostile, and withdrawn, teachers usually find something favorable to say. About one boy the teacher observed, "On a one-to-one nonacademic level, he is likable and eagerly responsive." About another, "He is a nice person, with a pleasing, friendly smile." Teachers comment positively on these youngsters' charm, perceptiveness, and generosity, which surface from time to time. However, school records starkly document the problems, which have existed in many instances since kindergarten. One boy's elementary school staff considered transferring him to a special facility when he was six years old and in the first grade. He was fighting, stealing, and prone to violent tantrums. Because he was bright and inquisitive, the school was loath to give up on him. In the hope that he would settle down the next year, a decision was made to postpone the transfer. Youngsters like this are often diagnosed as hyperactive and placed on medication. Rarely does this have a lasting beneficial effect, and so it is discontinued. By age 12, many of these children have been through the evaluation and diagnosis mill repeatedly. Still they remain an enigma, and their problems become increasingly grave.

When a delinquent is failing academically, his ability may be questioned. Results of intelligence testing may support a belief that he just is not very bright. Unfortunately, IQ tests are not always valid indicators of ability in such youngsters because the scores are partially dependent on knowledge gained in school. For example, one of the questions on a frequently used individual IQ test asks where a particular country is located.[9] Low scores result not only because of a lack of information but also because these youngsters have not acquired skills critical to success even on tests that do not rely on verbal skills. To do well on puzzles and mazes requires concentration, persistence, and thinking things through. A child may be bright, but this may not be evident because his restlessness, impatience, and distractability lower his scores.

Rarely is the problem a lack of intelligence. Rather, the child refuses to absorb academic offerings in the same way that he balks at learning what his parents try to teach him. He rejects that which is meaningless to him and consequently does not acquire basic information. A shocking example is that of a 14-year-old boy who could not write his complete address. An observer might conclude that he was mentally retarded. But as a con artist he could run circles around his teacher and was a genius at ferreting out weaknesses in people and exploiting them. His illiteracy was not a consequence of mental deficiency but of an attitude toward classroom learning described by one instructor as, "I dare you to teach me something."

Because some of these children do not learn to read, they are designated "learning disabled," a reference to an organically based condition. The presence of a learning disability is alleged to account for both their academic and behavioral difficulties in the following way. Because the child is learning disabled, he fails and grows frustrated and his self-esteem plummets. It is thought that because he cannot achieve recognition in school, he seeks it through antisocial behavior. However, an assumption of such a condition in antisocial children is unwarranted. Perhaps a tiny minority of delinquent children are truly learning disabled, but it has not been conclusively shown that there is a causal connection between learning disabilities and delinquency. A summary of current knowledge about the relationship between learning disabilities and juvenile delinquency published by the federal government states, "The evidence for a causal link . . . is feeble."[10] Many learning disabled children have psychological conflicts, but only a minority become delinquents. Many delinquent youths find too much drudgery in learning to read to make it worthwhile. One boy said about reading, "I can't stand reading a book. I have to really concentrate. It's like working. I'd rather see the movie. The last book I read was *Curious George* [a book for preschoolers]." That these youngsters are quite capable of learning to read is often borne out when they are confined in an institution. With time on their hands and little to do, they amaze teachers by how rapidly they catch on and begin to read.

The school may place the child in a special class for pupils who have learning disabilities or who for other reasons are slow learners. When this occurs, the delinquent discovers that, with less expected of him, it's easier to mollify the teacher and get away with more on the side. Many educators consider keeping such a youngster back a year but usually conclude that it will be of little value. The child will simply be one year older, one year bigger, and one year angrier. So he moves on to become another teacher's problem.

Although some teachers can't stand such children and treat them harshly, many are sympathetic. They firmly believe that these pupils are emotionally disturbed and victims of forces beyond their control. Their classroom strategy is to foster whatever strengths they can find in such pupils and to nurture in them a positive self-concept. They encourage the delinquent in what he can do well and downplay his academic weaknesses and deviant behavior. The child is lauded for his talent in art or music and for his prowess in athletics. Whatever good work he does is held up as an example to others. A teacher may go out of his way to establish a positive emotional relationship by finding an area of common interest no matter how unrelated it is to academic matters. Such an approach is calculated to provide the child with success experiences and to reduce his antagonism toward the teacher as an authority figure. The child laps up the praise and is inwardly triumphant when pressure to make him shape up is relaxed. With the teacher no longer on his back, he may settle down for a while. It appears that a constructive cycle is in motion. As his teacher accentuates the positive, he behaves even better, and the teacher has more to praise. Eventually, the youngster has the teacher where he wants him. Enthusiastically, the pupil expounds to his teacher on sports, cars, or hunting but assiduously avoids percentages, participles, and spelling. He figures that the instructor won't push him because he'll want to keep the peace. As soon as the teacher applies pressure for him to perform academically, the closely knit relationship unravels and the youngster acts as though an ally has betrayed him. Faulting the teacher, he once again presents himself as a victim of injustice.

The delinquent also perceives kindness as weakness in a sympathetic school counselor who regards him as emotionally disturbed. One 14-year-old boy regaled his counselor with a long, sad, and false story of how his parents didn't understand or trust him. The counselor urged his teachers to go easy on him because of the terrible problems he was having at home. The boy's mother, knowing her son very well, later reflected, "He used the counselor as a cushion. She was eating out of his hand after he convinced her that my husband and I were to blame for his problems." Some counselors are not so gullible. They designate such a child as emotionally disturbed not out of sympathy but because it is the most expedient way to remove a disruptive influence from the class-room and place him elsewhere.

In many school systems throughout America, there are no special services for such a child. As long as he is designated "socially maladjusted," he disrupts every classroom he enters and remains a thorn in the side of classroom teachers for years until he becomes so bored and fed up that he just quits. However, if educators fudge a bit, there is an out. Because the criteria for designating a youngster "seriously emotionally disturbed" are so broad, school evaluators can apply this terminology to the delinquent so that he then falls into the even broader category of "handicapped children." Under state and federal law, if the public schools cannot educate a handicapped youngster, then he becomes eligible for special services, which may include placement in a private residential school, the high cost of which is borne by the taxpayers. Thus a youngster who is antisocial and who deliberately rejects all that any school offers may be placed in a setting with children who are genuinely emotionally disturbed and who suffer from depression, severe anxiety, crippling neurosis, or even psychosis.

In some school systems, segregation into behavior modification programs is one means of managing these children. The objective is to equip them with skills so that they can return to their regular classrooms. Behavior modification entails systematically rewarding desired behavior and ignoring or penalizing undesirable behavior. Such an approach has proved effective in many skill development and training programs as well as in treating some problems in psychotherapy. When used with delinquents and criminals, it sometimes evokes short-term compliance. But there is no evidence that it promotes long-term changes in personality or that it produces sustained responsible behavior.

The delinquent eventually sees behavior modification as a game. He is presented with a system of earning points and fulfilling contracts to accomplish what some educators describe as getting the child to "buy into the system." At first, such a child opposes any program that removes him from his friends and imposes more stringent controls on his behavior. Consequently, during stormy confrontations, he may be sent to cool off in a "quiet room." The scenario is very much like that of prison, where the recalcitrant inmate is sent to the "hole" and the cooperative prisoner earns time off his sentence. The youngster wants the "good time" but despises earning it on others' terms. Eventually, he realizes that his stubbornness only prolongs his stay in the special program. Even though others have established the rules, behavior modification becomes a worthwhile game to play. If he goes along with the program or "buys into the system," he works his way back to his friends. His basic stance toward school is likely to remain as it was, but his conduct may become more civilized, at least temporarily. Some pupils steadfastly refuse to cooperate with any program and are not the least frightened by the prospect of expulsion or some other consequence.

Delinquents who find school intolerable just don't attend. If they are old enough, they find work or else they just roam the streets. A minority follow a different path. Educators are most baffled when a youngster has done well academically and then his grades take a nosedive. Thirteen-year-old Rob had been in a program for the gifted and talented, but he was failing eighth grade. Seeing that he was having problems, the school tried to accommodate the youth by allowing him to take less rigorous courses. A social worker wrote in her evaluation of the boy, "School personnel have been creative in attempting to modify their regular program to help his adjustment but have not yet been able to satisfy him." Rob's family was stable, and the social worker simply could not fathom the drastic change in his school performance. She finally concluded, "It is assumed that the stress of adolescence and the combination of hormonal changes with prescribed and illicit drug use is responsible for much of his difficulty."

When I evaluated Rob, I found a simpler explanation. Through the sixth grade, he had received high grades without ever working hard. However, in junior high school, he was no longer able to slide by when he had to meet stiffer requirements of many teachers. His refusal to apply himself was an old pattern, but the consequences of this were evident for the first time and seemingly overnight, once he entered junior high.

Delinquent youngsters who are bright enough to earn above-average grades, usually with little effort, can gain admission to college. There they continue to be dissatisfied with teachers, courses, requirements, and the routine. Their complaints about college are often echoed by other students who are not involved in crime. The serious students continue with their education despite their dissatisfaction because they have long-range goals in mind. Some who are not so persistent drop out but find other responsible areas of endeavor. The criminal, however, uses the college campus as an arena for his excitement seeking. He may get fed up and drop out. Or he may stick it out because he finds the life soft—"a four-year paid vacation," according to one sophomore who was knee-deep in crime. Those who remain in school emerge as criminals with degrees rather than as criminals without degrees. Their education serves them by helping them gain entree for their criminal operations into sophisticated, affluent circles.

If enough delinquent youngsters are concentrated in one place, the school is affected as though it is under siege. Students, teachers, and administrators are hostage to youths who create a climate of fear and paralyze the learning process. Recording her observations of the impact of one boy in her class, a teacher wrote, "The tension of the class is visible when he is in the class. Students are scared when he is around. Two students asked to switch classes because of his behavior. I personally would not be willing to have him in class since it causes *severe* problems, and the other students are being seriously held back. . . . He has exhausted all local school resources.''

School personnel perennially walk a tightrope in managing disruptive students. For example, they are berated, dragged into court, or assaulted if they restrain or isolate a violent child. But they can also be in deep trouble if they take no action and a child is injured. Suspension of an unruly youngster provides temporary relief. Expulsion is rarely a solution. An attempt to transfer such a child to a special program or facility is met with cries that he is being stigmatized, deprived of opportunities, and dumped.

The late psychiatrist Samuel Yochelson used to quip that the school could engage the delinquent and hold his interest if it offered courses in lock-picking, safecracking, and arson. However, even this seems dubious because if such subjects were *legitimate* offerings the delinquent probably would reject these also. Even the achievement of honor roll grades does not signify that he values an education. Reflecting a lifelong attitude, one 20-year-old criminal who maintained a B average in college commented, ''School was so meaningless for me that it's hard to imagine someone getting something out of it.''

Chapter Six

Work and the Criminal

THE CRIMINAL'S irresponsibility occurs as a *pattern* throughout his life. His deviousness and exploitation of people at work and his self-serving utilization of a job reflect how he treats the world. He scorns hard workers with modest aspirations. For him, it is far more gratifying to steal a television from the stockroom than to earn and save enough money to buy a set. Earning money is not a criminal's chief inducement to work because he may net far more from a single crime than from weeks of work. *The criminal's most pressing business is crime,* not his job. The criminal who holds a job may have the intelligence and skill to acquire substantial money and power through legitimate means, but even enormous wealth and supreme power, honestly earned, would count for little. If something is legitimate, to him it is hardly worthwhile.

Criminals are at heart antiwork. Some work rarely if at

all. Others intermittently hold jobs to appear respectable, meanwhile committing crimes under the nose of their employer. These individuals stick with a job until they become bored or until they suspect that the authorities are hot on their trail. Others hold a job for a long time and thereby secure a good reputation. This makes it easier for them to indulge in illicit activities without being suspected.

Unemployment and crime have long been linked. Almost any sociology textbook will assert that people turn to crime because they have been frustrated by a society that denies them opportunities to earn a living. A 1976 federal task force on juvenile delinquency said, "The high correlations between participation in delinquent and criminal behavior and unemployment and underemployment suggest that inability to obtain work may, indeed, be a major factor in producing this behavior."[1]

Unemployment can have a devastating effect on people. During the recession of the early 1980s, unemployment reached a post-Depression high as millions of Americans were laid off or lost their jobs when their employers went out of business. But people reacted differently to their plight. Some took any job, no matter how much of a step down it was. Others received unemployment benefits while continuing to search for work. Some became despondent and stopped looking for jobs. Although the unemployed and their families suffered terribly from stress, most of them did not become criminals. Economics writer Robert J. Samuelson stated that a 1982 drop in crime during a period of rising unemployment "constitutes one of those massive, unexpected assaults on conventional wisdom that prompts a reconsideration of how society functions."[2] The *causal connection* between unemployment and crime is weak. What one must look at is the personality of the individual and how he reacts to adversity, whether it is unemployment or anything else.

Dr. Frederick Spencer, a social worker, asserts, "Even when compared to other groups of hard-core unemployed individuals, the criminal offender is perhaps the most disadvantaged of the 'disadvantaged.' ''[3] Spencer points out that criminals released from prisons have low self-esteem, are subject to employment restrictions, and carry the "almost irreversible label of 'criminal.' '' The criminal is "disadvantaged" in the eyes of others because of his lack of skills. What frequently is not taken into account, however, is that many criminals were antiwork long before ever being incarcerated. If a criminal lacks vocational skills, it is not, in most cases, because he was denied a chance to acquire them.

For many criminals, work means to sell your soul, to be a slave. Small wonder that they refuse to equip themselves for that. Yet with few marketable skills, they refuse to assume the only positions for which they are qualified; these often involving routine and menial work. Rather than scrub floors, pick up trash, or carry luggage, they prefer to remain unemployed. Such labor is not at all in line with their inflated notion of their deserved station in life. Rejecting a janitorial job at a restaurant, one young man told his job counselor, "I ain't no peon." Another criminal, after being dismissed from his tenth job in one year, admitted, "If the job meant something, I would have been there."

When unemployed, the criminal's most frequent excuse is that no jobs are available. Probation officers and counselors constantly hear this refrain when the truth often is that the criminal neither made an inquiry nor submitted an application. He may report that a position was available but it did not suit him. One man had acquired the know-how to repair shoes, but when his employment counselor suggested that he look for work in this field, he retorted that shoe repair shops were going out of business. He argued that people do not get shoes fixed anymore but buy new ones.

Some criminals hold jobs intermittently, but when they work their perceptions of themselves and their jobs are unlike those of most of their co-workers. The criminal believes that because he is inherently more capable than others, previous experience and training requirements should be waived in his case. He is positive that his expertise and unique talents distinguish him from the common herd.

The criminal's fantasy has long been that, were he to deign to work, he would stride through the door, snow the interviewer, and land a high-paying job. He assumes that he will be a resounding success at anything if others will only recognize his talents and surrender the reigns of authority to him. He readily envisions himself the manager of a department store, but never would he conceive of himself sweeping the floor of that very store. With some education and experience, he may present himself so impressively that he convinces a company executive to offer him a position carrying considerable responsibility.

Having refused for months to look for work, 28-year-old Mike finally changed his tune after his wife threatened to take their two children and leave. Dressed in a chocolate brown pin-striped suit with tan vest, a subdued striped tie, and shined cordovan shoes, he strode into a bank and asked to see the manager. His immaculate appearance and air of confidence had impact. He was ushered into the manager's office and then seemed so knowledgeable about public relations and customer service that the manager hired him on the spot, even though there had been no vacant position. In addition, he offered Mike a choice of working hours. As part of a training program, Mike had to begin as a teller, but he was assured that he'd move up the ladder into the ranks of management. After three months of cashing checks, logging deposits, and updating passbooks, Mike became fed up. He saw no further need for training, resented not gaining a promotion, and decided he'd had enough. Again, he was unemployed by his own choice, but in talking to others he blamed his boss.

When doors do not open immediately to a criminal, he complains about lack of opportunity or discrimination. One criminal revealed the basic antiwork attitude usually underlying such gripes when he asserted to his rehabilitation counselor, "People like me don't like hard work, and we're not going to work. It's like trying to make a respectable butcher out of Jack the Ripper." One 25-year-old criminal hardly knew what work was, but conditions of his parole from prison mandated that he find out. Formally uneducated, but having a sharp intellect and persuasive tongue, he turned to sales. In two months, he became a top department store salesperson, for which management recognized him with a badge and salary raise. But still he had little zest for the work. By noon of each day, he felt sapped of energy, despite getting twice as much sleep at night as he did when he was unemployed and carousing until all hours. Selling shirts, slacks, coats, and sweaters day after day was insufferable. After quitting, he told others his boss was a tyrant and that no one appreciated his efforts.

Sometimes a criminal stays on the job for a while because he is placed in charge of something. For example, while sitting atop a gigantic crane and operating it in the construction of a 20-story building, one man felt extremely powerful. Had he been shifted to collating papers at a desk in the firm's office, he would have resigned. For such a criminal, even the acceptable becomes unacceptable, and within a short time period he demands a change or resigns. Eventually, the crane operator grew bored and quit even though he had no other job awaiting him.

Some criminals are relatively steady jobholders because they realize that employment is their badge of respectability. If the criminal works, others ask fewer questions about how he spends his time. (Often parents, spouses, and counselors think a criminal is mending his ways just because he holds a job.) When he chooses to put forth effort at a job, he learns quickly and is a fireball of energy. His employer values him, and he earns promotions. At least for a while, he basks in the recognition because it conveys publicly what inwardly he has been certain of all along—that he is a cut above the ordinary.

But that is about all it means for he still does not think of himself as a regular working man like his co-workers, and more than likely, he has contempt for the job and for the very people who promoted him. Nevertheless, he knows that just as good grades at school helped him or his buddies get away with things on the side, so can an impressive job history. In fact, people refuse to believe it when they hear that a crime was committed by a man reputed to be a loyal employee of a respected organization. Not only are they incredulous, but they are inclined to judge him less harshly than they might an unemployed ne'er-do-well.

Status and authority are far more important to the criminal than the quality of the work that he does. To rise meteorically to the summit is his due, just because he is who he is. On the job, he maintains that his way is the only way. He gives unsolicited advice and imposes his opinions. A ruthless critic of others, he bristles at anyone who offers even a minor suggestion to him. Co-workers resent his dogmatism, inflexibility, and closed mind. Frequently, he locks horns over trivial issues with fellow employees, subordinates, and supervisors. Authority that he holds legitimately is abused rather than exercised in ways beneficial to the company. As an executive, his decisions are reached in isolation rather than through consultation. Opinions and conclusions are stated as decrees. In the short term, the employee's self-confidence and certainty may be so highly valued by his supervisor that his shortcomings are overlooked. His executive style is a successful front until it becomes evident that not only is he antagonizing people but also he has no in-depth knowledge of the business.

Some criminals are smooth rather than contentious, ingratiating rather than surly, devious rather than intimidating. They pretend to be interested in what others say. Appearing to invite suggestions, they inwardly dismiss each idea without considering its merits. They seem to take criticism in stride but ignore it and spitefully make mental note of who the critic was. They misuse authority and betray trust but are not blatant about doing so. With the criminal at the helm, employee morale deteriorates. His method of operation sooner or later discourages others from proposing innovative ideas and developing creative solutions.

For the sake of perspective, it is important to acknowledge that people who are not criminals have some of the same personality flaws. It is a matter of degree. Some executives would be far more effective were they less dogmatic, more self-critical, and generally more sensitive to the needs of others. Still, they value their jobs, loyally give their best to the firm, and do not intentionally exploit their co-workers. A criminal values his job mainly as an arena for power seeking. He attains power at the expense of others, sometimes quite ruthlessly, and exercises it to further his own objectives.

It could be argued that to succeed in many fields requires scheming, slickness, manipulation, and unprincipled jockeying for power. A discussion of what is necessary to succeed at business or in any other occupation is beside the point here. Certainly, in any legitimate occupation there are people who rise to the top without compromising their integrity just as there are those who operate like the criminal.

It is the routine of a job that gets to many criminals, who seem allergic to routine anywhere in life. In order to overcome the tedium, some use drugs while at work. When the criminal is "high," his day is bearable for drugs help his mind soar from the mundane to the exciting. In addition, there is the intrigue of finding which fellow workers are users, locating new sources for buying drugs, or discovering markets in which to make sales. Because he performs satisfactorily at his job, the criminal's drug use is unlikely to be noticed by management. If he becomes lackadaisical or careless, his employer reprimands him and perhaps assumes that something is temporarily troubling him. If the poor performance persists, the criminal may be fired, but without his boss ever suspecting his involvement with drugs. In the unlikely event that the criminal is caught red-handed using drugs, his boss may advise him to seek treatment, perhaps at company expense. Some employers even shoulder part of the blame. Rather than penalize the user, they assume that unsatisfactory conditions at work drove him to drugs. The worst that is likely to happen is that the criminal loses his job, which to him may not be a particularly severe penalty.

Criminals utilize jobs directly for crime. Businesses suffer more from inside theft than from pilferage from customers. *The Wall Street Journal* reported that theft by employees accounts for three-quarters of what is euphemistically termed inventory shrinkage, or missing goods.[4] Employees abscond with millions of dollars' worth of merchandise and embezzle substantial amounts of cash. The stealing may be as brazen as an employee's backing up a truck to the loading dock and hauling away a stereo system, or it may occur on the sly from behind a desk as a company executive alters books, takes kickbacks, and sells confidential information.

Criminals set up their own businesses in which they purport to provide services or deliver products and then do neither. The home repair business is one of many that is plagued by fly-by-night operators. A contractor drives around a neighborhood, offers homeowners a good price for driveway resurfacing, pockets a deposit, and is never seen again. If a criminal has merchandise to sell, he misrepresents its quality. One man bought cheap foreign watches at $4.25 each. He slipped each one into a burgundy and gold velvet case and advertised it as a $70 timepiece marked down to $35. Customers snapped them up, certain that they had a bargain. The purveyor of this merchandise had a whole string of confidence games running by which he extracted money from trusting people. He was not beyond swindling widows on a fixed retirement income out of their meager savings.

Even if the criminal does not actually engage in crime at the work site, he may learn skills on the job that are eventually useful in crime, such as those of a locksmith. In the course of his duties, he gains entree to the homes and businesses of the affluent, who later become his victims.

Frank, an air-conditioning repairman, regularly cased out homes during customer service calls. During a casual conversation with the owner, he gathered information about the habits of the family, often succeeding in getting a customer to reveal specific times when no one was home. Frank gained the confidence of his customers because he appeared thorough in his service. By taking a long time to check out equipment, he had ample opportunity to scrutinize the premises closely. Examining air ducts throughout the house and tinkering with one mechanism and then another, he gained access to every room. When he inspected the outside condenser, he looked around for the best route to make a fast entrance and immediate getaway. He might notice that the condenser next door was running and, in the future, rely on its incessant drone on a sweltering day to conceal the sound of his footsteps.

Professionals working in the area of rehabilitation have believed that providing criminals with jobs will give them an alternative to crime. Opposed to this are findings such as those of the Rand Corporation, which surveyed 624 male felons incarcerated in California state prisons. During the three-year period in question, 27 percent said that they held jobs "most of the time," while 17 percent worked full time.[5] Clearly, being employed did not deter these individuals from committing crimes. This can be explained by the fact that most criminals do not have a strong investment in work. (As has been pointed out, even those who do hold steady jobs have an antiwork attitude.) They exploit the workplace as they do any other situation, using it for their own immediate gain or as a cover. Giving a criminal a job does not change what he wants out of life.

Chapter Seven

People as Pawns

THE CRIMINAL values people only insofar as they bend to his will or can be coerced or manipulated into doing what he wants. He has been this way since childhood, and by the time he is an adult he has a self-centered view of the world in which he believes that he is entitled to whatever he wants. Constantly he is sizing up his prospects for exploiting people and situations. To him the world is a chessboard, with other people serving as pawns to gratify his desires. This view of life is not only expressed in his actions but also pervades his fantasies.

The criminal conjures up visions of himself as a super-criminal, dramatically pulling off big scores that outdo the exploits of the most legendary figures. Typical of his fantasies are masterminding a worldwide diamond smuggling operation, working for a syndicate as a hit man, and living lavishly from the proceeds of multimillion-dollar holdups. By no means limiting his fantasies to crime, the criminal fancies himself at the top of the heap in any undertaking. He is the medal of honor combat hero, the secret agent, or the sleuth who cracks a murder case that has stymied an entire police department. He also envisions himself as the self-made millionaire luxuriating in a palatial seaside home, with his Rolls Royce, harem of women, retinue of servants, private jet, and yacht.

Many people might imagine themselves being heroes and multimillionaires. Such idle thoughts pass through their minds and either self-destruct automatically or are consciously pushed aside. Some fantasies recur and spur people to take creative initiatives and work hard to achieve what they want. And some individuals daydream. But the criminal believes that he is *entitled* to whatever he desires, and he will pursue it ruthlessly. Every day, illicit schemes cascade through his mind like a waterfall. Said one professional holdup man, "Every minute of my life I scheme." Many of the criminal's fantasies range beyond what is feasible, but once he comes up with an idea that seems plausible, he nourishes it until he is positive that he can enact it without a hitch.

Wherever the criminal is—sauntering down the street, buying groceries at the supermarket, driving in rush hour traffic, riding the elevator to his apartment—he visualizes people and property as opportunities for conquest. The sports car parked by the curb with the keys in the ignition could be his for the taking. The purse dangling from the supermarket cart is a tempting target. The bank he passes looks like an easy hit. And he is certain that the blonde on the elevator would find him irresistible. Put a criminal and a responsible person in the gift department of a department store and ask each as he comes out to recount his thoughts while there. The responsible person comments on the attractiveness, quality, and price of the merchandise, and perhaps on the efficiency of the service. In addition, he may describe a pretty salesperson or customer and recount a conversation overheard. The criminal notices little of this. He determines the best means to gain access to the merchandise as well as to customers' purses, wallets, and other personal belongings. He also notices the location of the cash register, the security arrangements, and the location of the nearest exit. In addition, he regards any attractive woman as his for the taking.

The criminal's attitude toward people is mercurial, dependent on whether they serve him. One day he may regard a person as his bosom pal and the next as his mortal enemy. Even his appraisal of his mother vacillates from saintly to satanic, depending on how readily she does his bidding. The transformation in his view of her is especially striking when he is confined. So what if he has caused her years of heartache; he still expects her unswerving loyalty and devotion. She is to visit, write, and mail or bring whatever he tells her he needs. However, if she fails to comply with his demands, she is reviled. An inmate affectionately closed one letter, "I love you, lady, and I hope you're taking good care of yourself." Not long afterward, this same young man cruelly berated his mother for unknowingly visiting him on the same day he expected his wife, thereby using up his quota of one visit per day. On the heels of that incident, he penned a letter riddled with sarcasm saying, "I am quite sorry that you were so greatly inconvenienced by my stupidities while I was out, and I am truly sorry that I have been such a poor son to you. I hope that you can find it in your heart to forgive me for my transgressions. At least I hurt you without malice. I try each day to convince myself that your hurting me here has no malice. Happy Birthday." A continuing expectation on the part of this inmate and others like him is that his mother will galvanize forces to turn the wheels of justice in his behalf. After this fellow wished his mother a happy birthday, he added a postscript instructing her to call the judge's clerk and maneuver to have another charge dropped that was still pending.

The criminal expects to prevail in every situation. He considers himself the hub of the wheel, never one of the spokes. Reflected one man, "I made myself a little god at every turn." Another recalled, "I always wanted to feel like a king." The pursuit of power per se is by no means exclusively a criminal characteristic. Power can be sought responsibly and utilized to benefit others as well as oneself. It is critical to achieving success in many walks of life and is wielded to some degree by everyone from a parent to the president. The issue is how a person pursues power and how he uses it once he acquires it. People rise to positions of power through besting the competition by being smarter, more skillful, more creative, or more interpersonally astute. They may also do it through intimidation and deception and by preying ruthlessly on others' weaknesses. When people are in a position of power, they may use it responsibly or irresponsibly. For example, a policeman may have to use force as a last resort in making an arrest, or he may get a kick out of brutally subduing someone when force is not necessary. Criminals crave power for its own sake, and they will do virtually anything to acquire it. Insatiable in their thirst for power and unprincipled in their exercise of it, they care very little whom they injure or destroy.

A criminal does not regard himself as obligated to anyone and rarely justifies his actions to himself. The justifications come later and only when he has to defend himself to others. Just the fact that *he* has decided on a course of action legitimizes it. One man who had committed scores of burglaries said, "I turn people on or off as I want. My idea in life is to satisfy myself to the extreme. I don't need to defend my behavior. My thing is my thing. I don't feel I am obligated to the world or to nobody." Other people and their property exist for his benefit. One criminal reflected that whatever his brother owned belonged to him also: "I just saw his money as being mine. I was just reveling in what I would do with 'my money.' " One man said of patrons at a neighborhood bar where he mixed drinks, "All the people there were pawns or checkers waiting for me to deal with them as I wished and to sacrifice any I wished." They were potential victims for his burglaries and rapes.

The criminal strives to gain the upper hand, but not through fair competition. Instead, he operates by stealth, loading things in his favor. His secrecy offers him great advantage and provides him with a sense of power. Others are unaware of the sinister intentions that lurk behind an often benign facade. Only he knows when and where he will strike. Assuming that everyone plots and conspires as he does, he enjoys "playing games with people's minds" and catching them off guard.

Intimidation is the criminal's other great weapon. His domineering manner may be so menacing that he need never utter a threat, raise his voice, or clench his fist. People cower in fear of the criminal's tearing into them, revealing their inadequacies, and making fools of them. There are times when a display of anger accomplishes his purpose. This may occur in a carefully orchestrated, dramatic manner to make a point, or he may simply fly off the handle. In either case, the result is the same. Snarled one man, "My girl friend has seen my anger. She is afraid of me and will do as I say." Getting one's way may be accomplished through raw violence. A 16 year old bluntly stated, "I like to bash faces in. Killing is on my mind." Those who tangled with him wound up with fractures, sprains, dislocations, concussions, and lacerations. This youth felt no remorse after hurling a brick at a person and leaving him sprawled unconscious in an alley.

Even after he has been apprehended for a crime, the criminal continues to show the world that "people don't fuck with me and get away with it." He harasses the victim and the victim's family as well as witnesses. He badgers his own lawyer and anyone else who might help his cause. Before the case is concluded, he may have successfully intimidated the plaintiff, who then drops charges, or he browbeats witnesses, who then bow out of testifying.

The criminal demonstrates his power even over other people toward whom he bears no malice. A high school student spotted his math teacher's green Plymouth with its black vinyl roof. When the school bell rang, he bounded out of the building to the parking lot. He delighted in the hissing sound as he released air from two tires and gleefully watched them go flat. When he saw the teacher gazing helplessly at the car, he strolled over and eagerly offered assistance. This boy was not rebelling against authority or retaliating for any alleged injustice. In fact, he rather liked the teacher. But he had scored a double triumph, first by deflating the tires without being detected and then by appearing innocently on the scene and posing as rescuer of a lady in distress. To him the teacher was just another person on his chessboard.

Contrary to popular image, the criminal is not anti-authority. He recognizes the need for someone to establish and enforce rules, maintain order, and impose consequences on violators. He not only expects a teacher to teach, a parent to restrain, and a policeman to arrest, but he supports such people in the exercise of their authority. Even the most hardened criminals who spout antipolice rhetoric to one another recognize society's need for police. Some have thought about being policemen themselves. The only time a criminal opposes authority is when that authority stands in his way. His parents, teachers, and the police are fine people until they interfere with his plans or later hold him accountable.

From early in the day until bedtime, everything must suit the criminal. His wife is to have his shirts pressed, clothes laid out, and breakfast on the table. His ride to work must be prompt. His boss must meet with him when he is ready. Service at the lunch counter must be impeccable. At whatever hour he walks in the door, dinner must be waiting and hot.

Although there is an urgency to his every demand, he is none too quick to comply with requests made by others. Despite their prodding, he puts things off, eventually defaults altogether, then offers excuses when in fact he had no intention of doing what they asked.

This description may appear to characterize many men who are domineering but not criminals. Tyrants that they sometimes are, most such individuals do not commit crimes, nor are they necessarily unprincipled. Because they attempt to control people close to them, their relationships are rocky. The criminal, on the other hand, tries to dominate in every situation and resorts to any tactic to get his way. Anyone who evades his control reduces him in stature and thus is seen as a danger. Whenever others fail to do his bidding, the criminal's entire self-image is at stake. Criticism or interference with his plans constitutes a monumental threat because it signifies to him that he is not the omnipotent person he thinks he is. Instead of modifying his expectations and changing his behavior, he insists that it is others who err, not he. His pride is such that he adamantly refuses to acknowledge his own fallibility. Unyielding, uncompromising, and unforgiving, his attitude is, "I'm going to hold my ground if it costs me everything," no matter how trivial the matter at hand.

Whether pride is a virtue or a flaw depends on its basis and on how it is manifested. Pride is an inner sense of satisfaction experienced when a person accomplishes something positive. A coach takes pride in his team's championship, or a student takes pride in completing his thesis. This is different from the criminal who is pretentious and whose pride is expressed in an attitude of superiority, in a refusal to yield to another's authority, in an unwillingness to compromise, and in a refusal even to listen to a different point of view. The criminal's gloating over triumphs and conquests is a far cry from the inner pride of quiet satisfaction that is experienced by others when they responsibly achieve a goal.

Because the criminal's inflated view of himself is imperiled so many times in a single day, those who live and work with him are afraid for they never know what might set him off. When he angrily explodes, he is in effect announcing that he is somebody to be reckoned with. His anger may be thinly disguised in sullenness, silence, or feigned indifference. It may spurt forth in ridicule and sarcasm or erupt into screaming and cursing. Its most devastating form is raw physical violence.

Frequently, the anger is invisible to the observer. However, the thinking behind the placid exterior may be shockingly sadistic. One man was enraged at a co-worker who criticized his printing layout. He pictured himself tying up this person, yanking his pants off him, then slicing off his testicles, tying them around his neck, and stabbing him to death. Figuring that the man was ''scum'' and that it wasn't worth risking his own neck, the would-be assailant did nothing. Deferring immediate action, the criminal may conceive of a scheme in which he will get even later. He retaliates at a time least expected and in a manner totally unanticipated.

Criminals are often portrayed as having unusually strong sex drives. However, it is the excitement of making a conquest, not a biological urge that provides the impetus for sexual achieving. Often, the criminal does not even conceive of his partner as a person, and so he has sex with a pair of breasts, buttocks, and a vagina. He brandishes his penis as a weapon before which others will succumb. Anyone may be vanquished, from the tramp in the bar to the wife of his best friend. A virgin is a special challenge.

Seeking a sexual experience is not in and of itself ''criminal.'' But criminals find little satisfying in a consenting sexual relationship. Sex is mainly an assertion of their own power, and as a result they usually give little thought to the feelings of their partners. Criminals often pursue their conquests through deception (sometimes by means of force) and with the intention of exploiting their partners.

Jake, a 31-year-old lifelong criminal, boasted that he would bed down on the first date "whoever I can get my hands on." This was true enough, given the sleazy women he knew. But Lisa proved to be a stubborn exception. That she would only kiss and hug made her all the more tantalizing and Jake all the more determined. As he dated her, he persuaded Lisa that he was in love. In fact, Jake half managed to convince himself that he might enjoy marrying and settling down. Once he proposed marriage, Lisa's resistance to intercourse melted. Having scored sexually, Jake began to feel restless, then trapped by the impending marriage. Several weeks before the wedding, Jake vanished, never to be heard from by Lisa again. He had achieved all that he had wanted.

No matter who the partner is, the process of winning her over is far more exciting than the sexual act. One criminal recalled that, as a young man, his penis led him to church. "I would go out looking for women to con. I felt that there were a lot of women in church, and I was right. They were dying to be loved." His approach was to offer to walk an unmarried congregant home from church, all the while conniving how to approach her sexually. Usually, he was invited to stay for refreshments. He described a scenario which occurred many times. The woman would excuse herself and go into the bedroom to change. He recounted his mode of operating.

"I sat there about two minutes, and I got up and went to her bedroom. I walked up behind her and kissed her on the neck. She turned around and said, 'I'm surprised at you.' The way she said that made me know she went in for more. So I sat down on her bed and pushed her back and kissed her. Then I ran my hand up her leg. At first, she was just lying there limp. She put both arms around me and she started kissing me back. Afterward, I made love to her. I don't have to tell you where I went to put the make on other women. I found other women who could give me money. Then I'd drop them and find others who could give me more.''

Another criminal recalled how he wooed a young widow by endearing himself to her little daughter. Charlie had totally charmed Vera's three-year-old daughter by buying her candy and ice cream and taking her to the zoo. He continued to shower her with attention. Charlie was genuinely fond of the child, but what he had in mind was marrying her mother, who was left financially well fixed when her husband was crushed to death in a head-on automobile collision. Charlie intended to help himself to Vera's money, significantly enhanced by the life insurance payment, then extract additional funds from her wealthy father. He figured that once the marriage got to be a drag, he'd take off.

The criminal believes that others find him singularly appealing as a potential sex partner. If a woman fails to confirm this assumption, she poses a challenge. He pursues his conquest through a soft sell of flattery and conning, or he employs force.

As he rode the bus, Carl eyed an ample-breasted, middle-aged woman wearing a sheer white blouse through which he could see her bra and bare skin. He observed that she wore no ring and concluded that she was single. Alighting at her stop, he walked behind at a safe distance and noted where she lived. That night, he returned, climbed up the fire escape, and jimmied open her apartment window. Removing his shoes, he slipped into her living room and tiptoed into the bedroom. After gingerly drawing back the bedclothes, he cupped his hands around her breasts and fondled them. The woman awakened, sat bolt upright, and was about to scream when Carl clamped his hand over her mouth and warned her to shut up. He unzipped his fly and jammed his erect penis into her mouth. Hearing her gurgle as though she were about to choke, Carl withdrew from her mouth, then commanded her to lie back and spread her legs. Yanking up her nightgown, he directed her to guide his penis into her vagina. When she meekly complied, he concluded that she was discovering that he was quite the stud and enjoying him.

As Dr. Ann Burgess, a pioneer in research on rape victimization, pointed out, rape is "an act of aggression and violence, motivated primarily by power or anger, rather than by sexuality."[1] It is an attempt to subjugate another human being and offers a challenge to get away with the forbidden. One criminal commented that if society legalized rape, he would have no interest in it. The rapist does not necessarily hate women, nor is he sexually deprived. In fact, he may regularly have sex with a girlfriend or spouse and still rape. An analysis published in a Washington, D.C., newspaper recounted some of the current theories about rape. One is that "these men are sadists and really seek to punish women." Another is that the rapist lacks self-esteem and believes that no decent woman would have intercourse with him. A third theory is that rape is "a symbolic attack on the aggressor's own parents—particularly the mother."[2]

People who rape are irresponsible in other ways and are likely to have committed other kinds of crimes even though they may not have been caught for them. Rape is just one expression of their attempt to dominate others, to seek excitement in the forbidden, and to build themselves up. There is no attempt to punish women, nor does the offender believe that a nice woman wouldn't have sex with him. In fact, he believes that he is irresistible to all women. At stake in a rape is the criminal's affirmation of his image of himself as powerful and desirable. The assailant believes that his victim already wants him or will want him once she gives him a chance. Her attempts to ward him off only heighten his excitement. Then he tries to reduce her to a quivering, pleading speck of humanity and helps himself to what he believes was rightfully his from the start. Brute force is rarely necessary because intimidation works.

Sex crimes may grow increasingly bizarre as the criminal searches for more and more excitement. Even rapes can grow routine to a man who has committed scores of them. Such a person may become bolder and more sadistic, as in the case of a young man who abducted a woman at knife point and dragged her off to an apartment where he tore off her clothes, lashed her to a bed, paraded around naked, leering and cursing, masturbated until he ejaculated all over her, terrorized her for another hour, and finally thrust himself upon her for intercourse. Does such a person hate his victim? Often he does not even know her. Is he acting out of an unconscious, long-smoldering hatred against some other woman in his life, perhaps his mother? One could always speculate this to be the case. But then what of the thousands of people who suffered rejecting and inconsistent mothers, crueler than his, but who resolved their resentments differently?

Some male criminals exploit men sexually. Those who engage in homosexual acts are likely to be bisexual and even prefer heterosexual activity. Homosexual prostitution can be highly remunerative, but neither money nor sex is the main motive. Rather it is the charge out of seducing, conning, or intimidating another human being into doing exactly what he wants. The criminal may indulge in a string of one-night stands, or he may latch on to one partner, quite possibly an older, lonely, well-to-do man. In such liaisons, the criminal may appear to be the passive, parasitic member. Actually, he is aggressively staking out his quarry and conspires to reap a host of benefits. In return for sex, he may be supported in high style and gain entree in the homosexual community to a new circle of potential victims. Blackmail is an extremely effective weapon for extracting just what he wants, especially if his partner has a respectable standing in the community. When the criminal tires of the relationship, he leaves, taking his benefactor's money and belongings, sometimes by force.

Rarely does the criminal speak of love. In fact, in the psychiatric literature, a hallmark of the "psychopath" (who in most ways is indistinguishable from the criminal) is that he "seems incapable of real love or real attachment."[3] One can debate whether there is truly an "incapacity," but certainly it is the case that the criminal chooses to view people only in terms of their use to him. They are like property. From adolescence, when the criminal refers to "my girl," he really is asserting that she belongs to him, but he considers her as disposable as an old tattered shirt. He does not develop a concept of what a love relationship entails. He may be charming, but rarely tender or considerate. He insists that a woman change to suit him, but he requires that she accept him just the way he is. He demands that *his* girl be totally faithful, while he has sex with whomever he pleases. Once a woman presses a criminal for a commitment, she risks being discarded. Snapped one criminal, "This is a man's world. I don't want a bitch telling me what to do. Because she has a pussy, that doesn't mean that she can control me."

The criminal may have his eye on a girl who is young and virtuous, but naive. During his early infatuation, he may treat her like a queen. This was true of Ted, 24, who courted Gwen, a 22-year-old teacher and minister's daughter. Romantic and affectionate, Ted was always full of surprises. On a beautiful spring day, he picked her up for a date and told her he was going to blindfold her and drive her to someplace fun. When they got out of the car, he led her into a lush evergreen forest in the mountains and removed the blindfold. Then he took out the picnic basket and jug of wine. Gwen was his in every way except that she still chose to remain a virgin. The luster of their relationship began to tarnish as her suitor seemed to turn into an egomaniac. An early sign was Ted's talk about outfitting himself to take her camping. This idea appealed to Gwen until she found out that Ted would be satisfied with only the best equipment on the market. No pup tent and sleeping bag on the ground for him. "He went on a spending spree like I never saw," she recalls. His purchase of three expensive tents and two backpacks was only the first sign of his extravagance. He also insisted on the best in clothes, restaurants, stereo equipment, and everything else. Believing that everyone has faults, Gwen was tolerant and patient. But it was hard to discuss much with Ted because he stated an opinion and that was it. His utterances were like decrees, not meant to be challenged. Eager to please, Gwen stifled her discontent. But gnawing at her were his lavish expenditures of sums of money that she knew he had not earned as a carpenter. Hesitantly, she wondered aloud several times whether he wasn't going overboard. Once when she summoned the courage to ask him directly where he was getting the money, he shot back, "Don't ask me any questions, and I won't tell any lies." Reluctantly, she acquiesced. One night Gwen got the shock of her life when the phone rang. It was Ted calling from the police station to inform her that he had been charged with a string of robberies. At first, she thought he was playing a practical joke, but she knew differently when his voice cracked. She was incredulous. How could her Ted have it within him to rob a store or a home? He made a decent living. She hadn't demanded much from him. But rather than condemn him, she concluded that she must be to blame. Somehow she had failed him and, in doing so, had driven him to desperation. With Ted in prison, she remained faithful, writing, visiting, and vowing to be more understanding when they were reunited permanently. It was harrowing for Gwen to live in a small town, where she was sure that everyone was gossiping about why she never went out. Gwen feared that if her narrow-minded supervisors discovered that she was planning to marry a convict they would find cause to fire her. This preacher's daughter found herself living a lie, trying to conceal all clues of her romantic association with a convict. Today, she awaits his release, still blaming herself but determined not to fail Ted again. As for Ted, he presently intends to marry Gwen, who has so loyally stood by him.

Some criminals do marry. In some cases, the wife is as irresponsible as her husband. (Said one criminal, "Us kinds are attracted to each other.") Such a woman would find life with a responsible man intolerably boring. Marriages of people who are both irresponsible are highly volatile, as each struggles to control the other. Often they terminate in divorce when husband and wife seek what each expects will be greener pastures. Other marriages resemble the relationship between Ted and Gwen, the spouse being responsible but naive. Then there is the woman who doubts that any man will find her suitable and so she latches on to any matrimonial prospect. Unaware of her future husband's criminality, she finds him bright, charming, and promising the security she craves. Hardly have the marriage vows been exchanged than serious problems arise. But much like Gwen, the responsible partner is inclined to fault herself long before she blames her husband. One young lady married to a criminal sought a psychologist's advice because she was sure that it was she who needed the help. Tearfully, she poured out her story and said, "If he doesn't get better, staying with him will destroy me." But then she continued, "I'm sitting here with a black eye from when he hit me. I wonder at times whether I am like I am because my father used to beat me when I was little and that I want to prove to myself that men who beat me still can love me. I need his love, but it's making me unhappy and him too. If you think I should see a therapist with my personal problems, please tell me. I am not unwilling."

When the criminal's wife discovers what he is really like, she is likely to minimize and deny the seriousness of his irresponsibility. Rather than seek a way out of the marriage, she becomes a reformer, confident that if she tries hard enough, she can have a steadying influence on her husband. As the magnitude of the problem strikes her, she may conclude that he has emotional difficulties and needs outside help. By no means does she regard him as malicious or any sort of criminal. Not wanting her marriage to fail and frightened to face life alone, she hangs on. Nurtured by any crumb of kindness thrown her way, she assures herself that he still cares. She attaches inordinate significance to any good deed, praying that it indicates he is mending his ways. After his wife's nervous breakdown, one criminal reflected, "She had been living on hope, just purely the hope that I would change."

The criminal expects family members to anticipate his desires and account to him for whatever they do. However, his conduct is not to be questioned. If he stays out until the wee hours of the morning, his wife has no right even to ask where he has been. If he spends money, she dares not request an accounting. In making purchases, only his preference counts. If his spouse argues with him, she risks being harangued, harassed, and assaulted. Repeated experiences with self-doubt, depression, and anger that follow in the wake of vicious arguments persuade her that few issues are worth pressing. In fact, even a seemingly minor disagreement may touch off a massive anger reaction. It is hardly surprising that, in their rages, many of these men batter their wives. The criminal is the ultimate male chauvinist. His wife is an object, not a partner.

When the criminal's wife has had enough and decides to leave, he is surprised, indignant, and angry. Since he regards her as the problem, he is at a loss to explain why she wants to separate. If she would only shape up, there would be no discord. Some of these men won't permit their wives to leave and hold them in bondage through intimidation and raw violence. If a woman lacks confidence, she may be afraid to leave for another reason, namely that she doesn't think she can make it on her own. She would rather stay with the known than be alone and have to start all over again.

Cynthia had been through a lot in her six years with Tony. He had thrown them into enormous debt, written bad checks, and forced her to sign checks that she feared lacked the backup funds. He went to the penitentiary, but she did not. When he was released, she watched her two young sons turn against her as Tony tried to court their favor by buying them gifts and subverting her authority. He allowed her to have no friends and flew off the handle if she talked to anyone too long on the phone. He was so demanding of her total attention that one night he upbraided her for sitting with their younger boy, who was suffering an allergy attack. Cynthia lived in terror of Tony's temper because in his rage he had broken down doors, smashed things, and beaten her. One time, she decided to flee to her mother's, but Tony came after her and rammed her car into a spot from which she could not escape. Sex was a major battleground because Tony demanded it daily and on his terms. He would post a rating score on a calendar and berate her when she didn't perform to his satisfaction. When Cynthia summoned the courage to say no, Tony told her he would pay her for each time. Cynthia declared that she wouldn't be a prostitute, but she didn't hold her ground because Tony informed her that unless she changed her tune he would never repay her parents the $2,000 he had borrowed. Even though Tony constantly belittled her, he didn't leave and certainly didn't want her to leave. While on probation, he told a counselor that Cynthia was like an old car; if he traded her in, he'd just get stuck with another ''model'' with a different set of defects. As for Cynthia, she finally sought counseling and began to realize that she was not the failure she had believed. She began to think that she could establish a life of her own, but having been browbeaten and terrorized, she believed Tony would literally kill her if she left.

Just as the criminal erupts into violence toward his wife, he may also brutalize his children. He may be physically violent, but the abuse often takes another form. Since the criminal is self-centered and willful, he places his desires and objectives ahead of everyone else's. Therefore, his attitude toward his own children fluctuates wildly, determined more by whim than by anything the child does. He may pamper and dote over a son or daughter who at times he adores. But then he is just as likely to ignore, neglect, or cruelly mistreat the very same youngster. The child is a burden not because of his misconduct but because his father's mind is on other things far removed from coping with the youngster's needs. The child never knows what to expect because dad acts so erratically. The same misbehavior may be overlooked one day but incur his wrath the next.

The criminal's appetite for conquests is temporarily appeased but never satisfied. There is virtually a never ending series of maneuvers to control others and build himself up at their expense. As the criminal achieves one triumph, he pursues the next. Rarely does the career criminal stick to one type of crime. The Rand Corporation found that 34 of 49 habitual felons had committed four or more types of offenses. Rand reported, "The picture is one of opportunism, and the offenders appear to have engaged in whatever types of crimes were available to them at the time and to have remained with them only as long as they were productive."[4]

A criminal becomes known to the police, the court, and the community for the immediate crime that resulted in his arrest. Even his family may not suspect the enormity of his involvement in crime. Little do others realize that a runaway youngster, classified simply as a "status offender," may also be a thief, vandal, and drug vendor. Nor can others know that a man arrested for the first time and charged with disorderly conduct may have committed scores of felonies.

Clearly, for our system of justice to work, there must be a presumption of innocence. However, people who conduct background investigations and make evaluations of offenders should be aware that an arrest may represent only a fraction of crimes committed, and there should be at least an attempt to determine how extensive the prior criminality has been. This would have some relevance to sentencing decisions. Indeed, judges are permitted to consider prior records in sentencing.

Arthur is a classic case of the successful career criminal.

He was a one-man walking crime wave. His stealing began at 5 when he swiped toy cars and soldiers, crayons, and books from neighborhood playmates. His thefts grew in variety and number as he became sneakier and more imaginative. At 9, he had gathered together a small gang of children who raided stores almost daily. At 12, he helped defraud customers at a carnival booth. As a teenager, he terrorized small boys until they emptied their pockets and surrendered every last penny. At school, teachers were forever pulling him away from fights. His specialty was breaking into neighbors' homes while they were away, often leaving the premises in shambles. As a young adult, Arthur still had a violent streak and was a party to several assaults, including one in which he vindictively mowed a person down with his sports car.

As he grew older, Arthur preferred conning to violence and fronted a host of fraudulent enterprises. One after the other folded, but only after he had raked off his "profits." When he worked for others, he arranged kickbacks and embezzled funds. While employed by a department store, a job he couldn't stand, he livened things up by stealing $4,000 worth of merchandise and embezzling $3,000 in cash in 18 days. Over a three-year period, Arthur illegally wrote and cashed checks ranging from $75 to $100 per day, this amounting to approximately $30,000 per year. Arthur swindled a bank out of $30,000 by borrowing against fraudulent securities. He stole close to $4,000 worth of securities and turned them into another bank as collateral for a loan. Impersonating a physician, he wrote prescriptions for drugs, which he sold or used himself. Subsequently, he became involved extensively in the marketing of illegal drugs.

Arthur had an infatuation with pubescent girls. When he was selling cosmetics and soap, he always hired teenage girls, to whom he would pay extra commissions for sex. Before his marriage, Arthur had established liaisons with women ostensibly for romantic purposes, whereas his real objectives were sex and money. He succeeded in obtaining both, the latter by conning women into giving him cash to invest. They never were quite sure what they were investing in, but Arthur seemed so honest and knowledgeable that they were certain he was looking out for their interest. Of course, he was looking out only for himself and absconded with their funds. His wife's money was no safer because, without her knowledge, he had written overdrafts on her checking account.

If one were to count every arrestable act during Arthur's 40 years of life—each theft, each assault, each bad check, each misrepresentation and embezzlement, each sex offense, each drug offense—the toll would climb into the tens of thousands of crimes. (Sometimes there were a dozen thefts or several bad checks in a single day, as well as other crimes.) Yet, this man served one brief prison term for drug offenses. He beat a few other charges through brief hospitalizations for mental illness, which was considered the underlying cause of his criminal behavior. The rest of the time, he was on the streets.

Arthur was a "player," ready for just about anything at any time. But some career criminals are more selective. They may reject crimes that they consider "chicken shit" or too petty. And if a criminal considers a crime too risky, he rules it out. Criminals who are terrified of physical injury shy away from situations where force may be necessary. Even the most daring and versatile refrain from specific acts that they find personally repugnant. Some are disgusted just at the thought of molesting a child sexually or of mugging an elderly woman.

Although criminals differ in the crimes they find acceptable, they are carbon copies of one another in their view of themselves and the world. All are liars and hide behind a mask of secrecy. They have an inflated self-image in which they regard themselves as special and superior and assume that people will do their bidding. Contemptuous of the world of law-abiding people, they share the view that the responsible world is a barren wasteland.

Some criminals thirst for violence. Believing that manliness is shown by forcefully overpowering a human being, they resolve differences with fists and weapons. When violence occurs, it is not necessarily according to plan. A burglar, surprised by a family's return home, gunned down a much admired Washington-area cardiologist.[5] The criminal came to the home to break in and steal, not to murder. But he was armed, ostensibly in order to do whatever he thought necessary if his plans went awry. Occasionally, when a victim offers opposition, the criminal flees. More often, such a challenge fans the flame of the criminal's determination to win out, and he resorts to more dire means than he planned. Victims are hurt when they do something that the criminal does not expect, such as physically resist or make a sudden move leading him to think that they have a gun. Said one holdup man, "When you go to rob a liquor store, you never know when the guy might pull a gun. So it's a calculated risk. You never know who is going to stop you or mess around with you. Of course," he added, "we don't go out with the intention of hurtin' somebody. We are always prepared to hurt somebody in self-defense."

If the criminal is later held accountable, he blames the victim for the violence because he interfered in the successful execution of the crime.[6] Exclaimed one man who shot his victim during a robbery, "That man must have been nuts! It wasn't my fault that he was crazy enough to risk his life over the fifty bucks in his wallet." Remorse for the victim, if existent, is short-lived. Said one 17 year old about a recent break-in, "If I started feeling bad, I'd say to myself 'tough rocks for him. He should have had his house locked better and the alarm on.' "

In nearly all his operations, the criminal has the advantage. He has an eye trained to spot vulnerable targets, and capitalizes on opportunities. Also working in his behalf is the fact that many of the crimes he commits are never reported to police. According to Department of Justice estimates, in 1979 personal victimizations went unreported in rape and attempted rape by 48 percent, in robbery by 42 percent, in aggravated assault by 54 percent, and in personal larceny with contact by 64 percent.[7]

Many reasons underlie the nonreporting of crime. Some citizens do not call police because they think the crime is not serious enough. There are people too embarrassed to admit that they were gullible, greedy, or careless. Some commercial establishments find that they save money by not reporting crimes. To report thefts embroils them in time-consuming procedures with the police and may ultimately result in higher insurance premiums. Furthermore, since a sizable proportion of theft is likely to be by a firm's own employees, it is better for the company's image to handle such matters internally.

Witnesses may not report a crime because they do not want to spend hours and perhaps days talking to police and appearing in court. They also fear becoming known to the offender and suffering reprisal. A victim may not report a crime even when he knows who did it because he fears retaliation. The role of terror at the prospect of being victimized again cannot be underestimated in accounting for either nonreporting or the dropping of charges. Unless the crime is serious and the evidence conclusive, the offender may get off scot-free or else be confined only briefly. As long as the criminal is on the streets, his victim lives in fear. Even if the criminal is confined, there is the apprehension that his family or friends will harass the victim. Finally, there is the haunting fear that the criminal might retaliate once he is released.

As a member of the President's Task Force on Victims of Crime, I witnessed firsthand a crisis of confidence in the criminal justice system.[8] Victims told of neglect or mistreatment from the time police arrived until after the case was finally disposed of in court. They reported missing days of work to come to court only to have trials or hearings postponed. Some described the harrowing experience of having to sit in the same waiting room with the defendant. Victims of sex crimes described the often humiliating investigative procedures that they endured followed by the trauma of the public trial. A crime victim may in fact be victimized twice, once by the criminal and then again by the system. All of this has some bearing on the reluctance of citizens to report crimes.

The criminal's skill in avoiding apprehension and the nonreporting of nearly half the crimes that are committed account for a high percentage of crimes that are never solved. The FBI Uniform Crime Reports for 1981 state that there was clearance of 19 percent of the "index crimes" of murder, forcible rape, robbery, aggravated assault, burglary, larceny-theft, and motor vehicle theft.[9] Clearing a crime means identifying the offender, charging him, and taking him into custody.

It is no wonder then that the criminal's sense of invincibility mounts. The simple fact is that he is unlikely to be confined. Some criminals grow so cocky that, although they execute a crime flawlessly, they betray themselves by carelessness, such as parking a getaway car in a loading zone, where police immediately spot it. On drugs, they may be especially brazen and reckless. But generally, the criminal is a pro at what he does. In crime after crime, he asserts who he is—a singularly special and powerful person with whom the world must reckon.

Chapter Eight

"Getting Over on the Shrinks"

WHEN A PERSON commits a crime that seems particularly bizarre or out of character, he may at some point prior to sentencing be referred to a psychiatrist or psychologist. The examining doctor is asked to explain *why* the defendant acted as he did. It is believed that an understanding of the motivation behind the crime will be useful to a judge, jury, or other authority who must make a decision about the criminal.

Usually, the criminal does not voluntarily seek the services of a psychiatrist or psychologist but is directed to see one by the court or perhaps by his lawyer. Since the criminal lies to his family and to others who know him well, it should come as no surprise that he will also deceive a person whose specific objective is to unmask him. As a result, erroneous conclusions are often drawn about his motivation for committing a crime.

In this chapter, the focus is on psychiatric misinterpretations of motives in four types of crimes: first, the so-called crime of passion (or crime that appears out of character); crimes that appear senseless and without discernible motives; then, crimes that appear to arise out of a "disorder of impulse control" (with special reference to repetitive stealing, fire setting, and substance abuse); and finally, crimes committed due to insanity.

Crimes of "Passion"

Sometimes a seemingly responsible person appears to lose control and commits an isolated, unplanned crime against someone he knows. Referred to as crimes of passion, these often occur within families as when, in the heat of an argument, a husband grabs a meat cleaver and murders his wife. Such an individual has not been a killer in the past and, according to statistics, is unlikely to kill again. The perpetrator may have had a reputation as a loyal family man, a reliable provider, and a pillar of the community. But only immediate members of his household who intimately know the man can look behind the public image to glean some understanding of the crime.

Both the crime of passion and the calculated, cold-blooded murder by a criminal are products of a mentality with similar features. A closeup of the enraged husband would reveal that he has much in common with the criminal in the way he views himself and deals with the world. Blustery, inflexible, and impatient, he demands that others do what he wants. He flares up whenever someone criticizes or disagrees with him. Instead of coping with unpleasant situations, he adds more problems by his manner of reacting. When frustrated or disappointed, he is quick to blame others and fly into a fury. While vowing to even the score, thoughts enter his mind of destroying the person who is thwarting him. The homicide that he commits may be preceded by a long series of threats or assaults that were hushed up within the family. Despite appearances, when the homicide is finally committed, it is by a man to whom violence was no stranger. The case of Stuart, who murdered his wife, illustrates this.

Stuart had been arrested for stabbing his wife, Angie, nine times in the parking lot of a government building. He had no prior criminal record and had been serving in the army for the previous four years. The court referred him to me for evaluation because it appeared to be a case of a stable man who had gone berserk and acted totally out of character. In fact, he had claimed that his mind snapped and that he didn't know what he was doing. My psychological study of Stuart revealed a different picture.

For 10 years, dissension had plagued this man's marriage. Shortly after he married Angie, she began making derogatory remarks about his family. Stuart described to me his characteristic reaction when he became upset with her: "When I get frustrated, I hit the ceiling. Anything in front of me has to move." Husband and wife separated on several occasions but got back together each time. The arguments continued, and Stuart grew increasingly violent, threatening Angie numerous times, striking her on several occasions, and one time attempting to drown her in the bathtub. Episodes of the preceding sort were not uncommon.

Stuart asserted that to the outside world he presented a "perfect attitude," and this probably was not far from the truth for he did not steal, cheat, or use drugs and he appeared polite, educated, articulate, poised, and confident. What finally happened was that after another of their separations, Stuart set a luncheon date with Angie. When she didn't arrive and he couldn't reach her by phone, he became despondent and angry. He went home and, to his great consternation, discovered that most of the furniture had been removed. Determined to track her down, he combed the area for six days until he spotted their van. During this period, thoughts flashed through his mind of "burning her up," squeezing her to death, and he conjured up other ways of getting rid of her. Although he had discovered the location of her new residence, he took no immediate action. Several days later, he drove to her neighborhood, followed her car to a subway stop, and parked where she did. Having no intention of harming her, he ran after her, pleading for an opportunity to talk and begging for reassurance that there was no other man in her life. Angie ignored him and got on a subway. In pursuit, Stuart jumped aboard and sat next to her. Still, she remained indifferent to his pleas and ignored his questions. When she got off he followed, now enraged. When they left the terminal and emerged into a parking lot, he continued to harangue her. Then from a brown bag he grabbed a pair of scissors and stabbed her repeatedly.

Because Stuart had been considered an upstanding citizen, his crime was widely regarded to be a result of a momentary lapse of control, a crime of passion. No one knew that Stuart had been violent before, and no one would have suspected that in his thoughts Stuart had many times murdered his wife.

This crime and others like it are not, in the strictest sense, premeditated. Stuart did not plan the date, time, place, or precise manner of the homicide. However, the act was neither the product of a deranged mind nor perpetrated by a man to whom violence was an alien impulse. The idea of ridding himself of his wife had occurred again and again. In that sense, he was programmed to murder his wife— programmed not by someone else but by his own *habitual* patterns of responding to conflict. He was determined to control his wife, to have total power over her, no matter what it took. In evaluating such crimes, it is essential that the examiner probe *antecedent* patterns of thought and action. Almost invariably, what will emerge is that the crime at issue is merely one example of other offenses actually committed or else contemplated.

"Senseless" Crimes

Sometimes a crime is committed that seems to have no iden-
tifiable motive. For example, a group of boys descend upon
an old man sitting in the sun on a park bench. They drag
him behind bushes, kick and beat him, then leave him to die.
Financial gain is not a motive, for this man is disheveled and
shabbily dressed; he is not even wearing a watch. Revenge
does not figure in the assault for he is a total stranger. What
the boys get out of the crime is kicks—just the thrill of doing
something daring and vicious and getting away with it in
broad daylight.

A pair of bank robbers are nabbed red-handed by police.
While checking the criminals' car, one of the officers discovers an attaché case containing $30,000 in cash garnered in an
earlier robbery. When the astonished officer demands an explanation for holding up the bank when they already had so
much money, one of the men replies blandly, "Well, ya' got
to do somethin'." What he means is that he and his companion are not satisfied with the earlier take and are after a
larger haul. They have given little thought to how they will
spend the proceeds. It isn't the money itself that is important
but rather the excitement of knowing that they can pull off a
really big score. Like these men, many a thief has given little
thought as to how to dispose of the loot. Criminals constantly
complain about being broke. This is because they spend or
give away the proceeds nearly as soon as they acquire them.

The common motive behind many crimes that appear
senseless is kicks—the thrill of doing the forbidden. There is
excitement in thinking about crime, bragging about crime,
executing the crime, making the getaway, and celebrating
the triumph. Even if the offender is caught, there is excitement in dealing with the police, in trying to beat the rap, in
receiving notoriety, and, if it gets that far, in the trial proceedings.

The "Impulse Disorder" Crime

To some observers, it appears that offenders repeatedly commit crimes because they are at the mercy of impulses over which they have no control. A child steals from home, from classmates, from neighbors, from stores, from construction sites. It seems that no matter where he goes, he returns with something that does not rightfully belong to him. He may be tagged a kleptomaniac, a psychiatric term for a person suffering from "an uncontrollable impulse to steal."[1] Behind the appearance of uncontrollable impulse lies the stark reality of the offender's *calculating* and proficient method of operating. Wherever he is, the thief habitually scans the environment to take advantage of opportunities. He does not have to develop an elaborate scheme for every single theft. He devotes about the same thought to some of his stealing as a person gives to driving. Both acts become matters of habit, and for each, vigilance is necessary.

But what is habitual is not necessarily compulsive and beyond one's control. To say that a person has a habit of doing something does not mean he lacks responsibility for his actions. Just as a person can adapt his driving to icy pavements, so a thief adapts his pilfering to current conditions—what kind of surveillance he thinks there is, the accessibility of the merchandise, the location of exits, the number of people between him and the closest exit. If the thief is apprehended, he may claim that he was compelled by an irresistible inner force to steal. By throwing the case into the bailiwick of the psychiatrist, he has hope of being evaluated as not responsible.

A person who frequently sets fires may be referred to as a pyromaniac, especially if readily understandable motives such as revenge or jealousy seem to be absent. Like kleptomania, pyromania refers to a condition in which there is a "recurrent failure to resist impulses" and an apparent "lack of motivation such as monetary gain.''[2] But I have found that the pyromaniac, too, is a calculating person who is very much in control of his actions. He chooses the time and place to set a fire and takes precautions to avoid detection. By setting fires, he wields a tremendous amount of power over human life and property. He can terrorize a community and inflict enormous devastation. Then he can enjoy his triumph as he smugly sits back, watches a building become engulfed in flames, observes the fire department struggle to contain the blaze, and all the while is reasonably certain that he will not be caught.

Some psychiatrists believe that kleptomania and pyromania are prompted by a search for excitement, but they assert that this behavior is really motivated by unconscious and compulsive attempts to relieve sexual tensions. In other words, mention excitement, and the Freudian psychiatrist thinks of orgasm. Special FBI agent Jim Reese has cited psychiatric literature that suggests: ''The desire for thrill or orgasm is the sole reason for the fire.''[3] Such reductionism leaves little room for free choice, despite the fact that the thief or fire setter makes decisions as to whether or not to commit offenses depending upon his calculation of the risks involved. If the offender is seen by the court as a victim of his own ungovernable impulses, he may be ordered to seek treatment. Then the therapist may institute a treatment plan based on misconceptions while his patient continues to steal or set more fires.

From my clinical observations, I have concluded that ''kleptomaniacs'' and ''pyromaniacs'' are simply people who enjoy stealing or setting fires. They are as much in control of their behavior as the bank robber or offender who commits arson for profit. The fact that the stealing or fire setting is repetitive only makes the issue appear more complex. Any criminal activity, repetitive or not, could be considered abnormal in that it is socially proscribed and most people do not engage in it. But this does not automatically make it a sign of illness or thereby exonerate the offender from responsibility. For behind such acts is a person who deliberates and acts with knowledge of possible consequences.

Criminals who have become dependent on drugs have been regarded as victims of their own impulses. Like kleptomania and pyromania, substance abuse is considered a "disorder of impulse control" by the American Psychiatric Association. The APA regards substance abuse as "pathological" under certain conditions, such as when there is an "inability to cut down or stop use" and when there is a "need for daily use of the substance for adequate functioning."[4]

For the sake of perspective, it is important to note that I am referring only to criminals, not to basically responsible people such as a housewife who abuses tranquilizers to cope with stress and then becomes dependent on them.

When held accountable, the criminal does his best to convince others that he is a victim of drugs. He asserts that the sole reason that he turned to crime was because his use of drugs got out of control. (In effect, he is alleging that he meets one of the APA's criteria of an impulse control disorder, namely, an "inability to cut down or stop use" of drugs.)

In every case that I have encountered, the criminal was immersed in crime *before* he ever smoked his first reefer, popped his first pill, or first shot heroin. Some criminals find that they need drugs in order to muster the courage to commit more daring and exciting crimes. Drugs knock out both fears of getting caught and considerations of conscience, and as a result, the criminal is prepared to *do* what previously he had only contemplated.

As a criminal seeks greater excitement, he may perpetuate a cycle of crime, more drugs, and then more crime, until he is supporting an expensive drug "habit." Taking advantage of his situation when he is eventually apprehended for a crime, he may then convince a doctor and ultimately the

court that he should be remanded to a drug treatment program instead of prison. The authorities do not realize that he
cannot imagine living without drugs *and* crime and that he
has long known of treatment programs but would not avail
himself of them. Nor do they know that several times he
withdrew from drugs without professional help. He did so
without any intention of giving up drugs permanently but
rather with the desire to reduce his habit so that he could get
a better high from less drug. The point is that others are not
aware that the criminal has made *choices* as to whether to use
or abstain from drugs. He leads others to believe that he had
no choice in the matter—that he has been a victim of drugs
and the authorities *owe* him the chance to be treated instead
of incarcerated.

Selection of a specific substance depends, to a great extent, on what is available. Any drug in proper dosage can
give the criminal a high. So when the supply of the drug of
choice dries up, he turns to another substance. The sophisticated user prefers specific drugs for specific purposes and is
well informed about the advantages and disadvantages of
each. Amphetamines provide a quick infusion of energy but
a severe letdown following the cessation of use. Opiates
knock out fear and thinking becomes sharp (given optimal
dosage), but there is the risk of dependency. Barbiturates
help him to assume an "I don't care" attitude, but dosage is
difficult to regulate and the risk of physical dependence is
high. Marijuana is a desirable party drug but not powerful
enough to be of much assistance by itself in high-risk crimes.
And so on.

With respect to marijuana, the pendulum has swung from
the "reefer madness" scares in the first half of this century to
a demand by reformers that marijuana use be legalized. Because marijuana is widely available, because penalties for its
use and possession have been reduced, and because there is
widespread experimentation with the substance, the drug is

receiving increasing acceptance. The public is being fooled into thinking it is relatively harmless.

Few parents who have watched a child become a regular marijuana user and few counselors or therapists who work with adolescent marijuana users will agree with this view. The long-range physical effects of the drug are unknown, although there is evidence of damage to the lungs and the reproductive systems of heavy users. But frightening to witness is the psychological damage—the so-called amotivational syndrome—as the frequent user turns off and drops out, rejecting his family, school, and responsible peers. If one probes carefully, he will discover that the youngster's dropping out and becoming irresponsible began *before* marijuana use but was accelerated by regular use of the drug. Once he is associating almost exclusively with other drug users, the teenage marijuana user is exposed to other drugs. It is in such situations that he may decide to try new substances just for kicks because marijuana has lost its excitement.

Some drug users reach a point where being without drugs is an unnatural state. One user commented, "I can't function unless I'm all wired up," by which he meant high on something. The great availability of illicit drugs contributes not only to more frequent crime but to more serious crime. The man who steals from stores and houses may have ideas about bank robberies flash through his mind, but without drugs he is too fearful to carry them out. Once he is on drugs, barriers to more daring ventures are overcome. The drugs do not *cause* a person to obtain a sawed-off shotgun and hold up a liquor store or, for that matter, commit any other crime. They simply make it more feasible for him to eliminate fears for the time being in order to act upon what he has previously considered. That is, drugs intensify and bring out tendencies already present within the individual user. They do not transform a responsible person into a criminal. The criminality comes first, the decision to use drugs later.

In short, criminals regulate their selection and dosage of

drugs with the intention of readying themselves for specific activities. Contrary to what they tell a psychiatrist or psychologist, they remain rational and in charge of their behavior. They control their drug use; it does not control them. Such individuals may appear "crazy" or not in control because, under drugs, they take greater risks and are more daring. But they have chosen to use the drugs, which then knock out fear and make these daring crimes more feasible.

Criminals usually exercise the greatest precautions to avoid being caught. Usually they are successful, but sometimes even a pro can get overconfident so that it appears that impulsiveness got in the way of judgment.

A young man strolled into a neighborhood grocery store late at night. All the nearby shops were closed, and the cashier was on duty alone. The customer looked around, picked up a six-pack of beer, and took it to the cashier. He dug into his pants pocket, took out his wallet, and reached into it as though he were about to pay. Some papers fell out, whereupon he quickly scooped them up and stuffed them with the wallet into his hip pocket. As the cash register drawer opened, his hand darted into his jacket pocket and whipped out a handgun. He ordered the startled cashier to remove the money and dropped it into a small insulated ice cream bag. Yanking the phone cord out of the socket, he ran out the door and took off in his car. The next day, he was apprehended by the police. In his haste to pick up the papers he dropped from his wallet, he left behind a dry cleaning ticket that bore his name.

When an offender makes such an obvious gaffe, a psychiatrist or psychologist may believe that the perpetrator of the crime really wanted to get caught. The basis for such a conclusion is in Freud's writings on unconscious guilt. In 1915, Freud stated that we all experience guilt, which is a remnant from the time in our lives when we had erotic feelings toward the parent of the opposite sex (the oedipal period).[5] He contended that children often misbehave in order to be punished, which then relieves that guilt. In "The Ego and the Id," Freud wrote, "It was a surprise to find that an increase in this unconscious sense of guilt can turn people into criminals."[6] Freud and his disciples extrapolated from findings on neurotics and applied them to criminals, even though they rarely treated criminals as patients. Present-day psychiatrists and psychologists do the same. Instead of seeing the offender as a person who is overconfident, they read into his motivation that he wanted to get caught or may even go a step further and claim that his behavior represented a cry for help.

Insanity

After being caught for murdering six young people and wounding seven others, "Son of Sam" David Berkowitz said that the devil had talked to him through his dog and commanded him to kill.[7] Later, a newspaper carried his acknowledgment that he had been feigning mental illness: "There were no real demons, no talking dogs, no satanic henchmen," Berkowitz said. "I made it all up via my wild imagination so as to find some form of justification for my criminal acts against society."[8]

During autumn of 1982, seven people in the Chicago area died after they had ingested Extra-Strength Tylenol ™ capsules laced with cyanide. Before there were even any strong leads, people were saying that the mind of the perpetrator must be deranged. In an editorial, Denver's *Rocky Mountain News* termed the act psychotic and went on to comment, "Almost every time a bizarre crime gets wide publicity, sick minds try the same thing, whether it be kidnapping or giving children apples with razor blades in them for Halloween."[9]

When a criminal commits a shocking crime, as did Berkowitz and the Tylenol killer, a gut reaction on the part of the average citizen is to say that he must be crazy. But this reveals only something about public perceptions, nothing about the mind of the criminal.

If a criminal commits a serious crime and believes that there is sufficient evidence to convict him, he may resort to the insanity defense to beat the rap. In the streets, local jails, and other detention facilities, he has heard that if a person can convince the authorities that he is crazy he will be sent to a hospital for treatment, not to a prison to serve a long sentence. In some jurisdictions, if a defendant is declared "not guilty by reason of insanity," he is free to walk the streets. In many instances, a hospital is far more comfortable and has a freer environment than a prison. More important, the local lore is that if the criminal plays the psychiatric game, he will be considered improved and will be released far sooner than he ever would from prison. (This applies only in cases where a long sentence is imminent.)

To convince the examining psychiatrists and the court that he is insane, a criminal must satisfy one of several legal definitions of insanity, depending on the legal test used in a particular jurisdiction. Does he know right from wrong (The McNaughton rule)? Is the crime a product of a mental disease or defect (Durham rule)? Does the defendant lack substantial capacity to appreciate the criminality of his conduct or to conform his conduct to the requirements of the law (American Law Institute Model Penal Code)?

Just as his crimes have been rational and deliberate acts, so is the criminal's scheming of his insanity defense. In the jails or wherever criminals are sent for observation, one learns from another, the psychologically sophisticated tutoring the unsophisticated. Some also get tips from their lawyers. Attempts to fake mental illness range from the subtle to the bizarre, depending on what the criminal thinks will be convincing. He may claim that he hears the voice of the devil commanding him to do evil. He may proclaim that he acted as a messenger of God. He may feign delusions of persecution, asserting that people are plotting to do him in or that

poison is being added to his food. He may pretend to be confused and disoriented and not know where he is. All this ma-
lingering is designed to demonstrate that he is irrational and
out of contact with reality and thus not responsible for the
crime. A suicidal gesture may accomplish what he wants. He
informs his cellmate that he will hang himself at 7 PM and
asks that a guard be summoned at that time to cut him down.
He figures that if he is considered a suicide risk, he will be
shipped immediately to a hospital.[10] There are many other
ways to make his case for a defense of insanity, including
feigning epileptic seizures, mumbling to himself, staring into
space, pretending to hallucinate, and self-mutilation. A case
for amnesia may be concocted even before his first interroga-
tion by police.

One man took precautions to lay the groundwork for a
psychiatric finding of amnesia. Upon learning that the police
were closing in on him for a crime, he abandoned his car,
tossed the keys into the river, buried all identification, and
wandered into a clinic looking dazed. He was hospitalized
for three months and then released on convalescent status.
There was no attempt to prosecute him.

The display of symptoms of mental illness may be dramatic in jail, during courtroom proceedings, or at a hospital
where the criminal is sent for observation. For example,
when a defendant smuggles a penknife into the courtroom
and lunges toward the judge, he anticipates that he will be
hauled off to a hospital. One defendant was derisive of the
flamboyance with which another was faking. He thought the
man was overdoing it and told him, "You try to save your
ass your way, and I will save mine my way." He had made a
study of psychological tests. In a quiet manner, he let signs of
psychopathology seep out during the testing. Appearing
withdrawn and anxious, he showed difficulty with memory
and concentration, often losing his train of thought. He gave
responses that were mutually contradictory. On the ink blot
tests, his reticence vanished, and he saw breasts, vaginas,

and lots of blood spilling over the cards. Later, he told a buddy, "What you have to do is see pussy in every picture." He was declared not guilty by reason of insanity and was sent to a hospital. By a successful insanity defense, he beat a potential sentence of 20 years for his crime of armed robbery and another 5 years for possession of the illegal weapon, a sawed-off shotgun.

How is it that highly trained professional psychiatrists and psychologists are sometimes fooled? Never for a minute does the criminal really believe that he is mentally ill. In fact, he is offended if anyone calls him crazy. However, he is willing to be called just about anything if he can beat a charge. He is a pro at examining people, having an uncanny knack for finding out what they want to hear and then feeding it to them. Either the strange behavior of the criminal at the time of the examination and/or the sordid nature of the offense may be sufficient to convince the examiner that he is dealing with a sick person. Thus the fact that the defendant has murdered his victim, hacked up the body, and then buried the pieces may by itself convince the examiner that he is dealing with an insane killer. A routine case of armed robbery is unlikely to be viewed the same way. But what may be extraordinary is not the crime but the defendant's apparent incoherence, mumbling, confusion, and general disorientation. If both the crime and the behavior during examination seem bizarre, the defendant has it made. He will be whisked from jail to hospital.

The experts may be misled in yet another way. If the defendant has an already established medical history of a disease, especially a disease of the brain such as epilepsy or narcolepsy ("sleeping sickness"), he may make the most of it and claim that it caused him to act without awareness. The examiner may then assume that the crime was a consequence of the disease and come up with a finding of diminished responsibility.

No sooner has the criminal been declared "not guilty by

reason of insanity'' and been admitted to the hospital than he starts trying to work his way out. He participates in programs for the purpose of convincing the staff that he is serious about change and is improving. In the hospital, the staff regards each activity as therapy. If the patient plays basketball, it is recreational therapy. If he makes a leather wallet, it is occupational therapy. If he has ground privileges and rakes leaves, it is industrial therapy. But the place to make a major impression is in therapy with the doctor, who will make the most influential recommendation about his release. In group psychotherapy, individual psychotherapy, and the therapeutic community, he feeds the doctor and the rest of the staff what he thinks they want to hear. He ventilates his feelings, talks about his past, and demonstrates insight into his mental condition. He also abides by hospital rules—at least to all appearances. The hospital's evaluation of him is based primarily on his cooperation and insight. Said one hospitalized patient, ''They don't care what you did on the outside as much as how you are doing inside.''

Playing the psychiatric game is exciting. Just like a crime, it offers a criminal opportunity to outsmart the system and make fools of everyone. About the only time that he is certain to fail is when the hospital staff is fearful of releasing him because he has committed a highly publicized atrocity. Then a decision is made to bury him in confinement. But he may have yet another alternative open to him. By becoming a troublemaker and administrative headache, he may succeed in pushing the staff to discharge him. One man kept filing grievances and writs against the hospital where he was confined. The administration became so weary of responding to his charges that it accelerated granting him privileges and eventually placed him on outpatient status. But if a patient is considered a truly dangerous case, or has attracted publicity in the past, he may instead spend many days locked in seclusion.

To the criminal, the hospital is a permissive prison. Because he is considered sick, his crimes of the past and violations of the present are treated therapeutically, not punitively. This means to him that he will be able to get away with a lot more than he ever could in prison. He figures, often correctly, that he can do as he pleases as long as he shows remorse and psychological insight later. If he assaults another patient, he can talk about his pent-up hostility. If he uses illicit drugs, he can explain it as his seeking relief from overwhelming anxiety. If he tries to escape, he can relate it to intense depression. Sometimes he gets away with such psychological rationalizations and may even be praised for them. Though he is ostensibly sick, at times the hospital will treat him as totally rational and responsible. Under the banner of the therapeutic use of authority, it may seclude, restrict, or deny him privileges. The criminal is never sure how the staff will react at any given time, but he worries about that *after* an infraction. He commits crime on the hospital wards and on hospital grounds as he preys on vulnerable noncriminal patients, many of whom are genuinely mentally ill. Robberies are frequent, drug rings flourish, sex with patients becomes a way of life, assaults, and, occasionally, homicides occur. Criminals misuse privileges and leave the grounds without authorization, wreaking havoc in the community and on their return importing contraband into the hospital.

There are some criminals, although relatively few, whose psychological defenses crumble after arrest and in confinement. Observers erroneously conclude that such a mental state must have prevailed at the time of the crime. Criminals showing signs of psychosis are often far too confused and disoriented to scheme and execute crimes that require an alert and precise mind. Freddie, a 28-year-old street criminal, is a case in point. Usually, Freddie was rational, but oddly enough, it was at those times he was the most dangerous. His stance toward the world was that nobody had better get in his way. When a man took a seat on a bus that Freddie had saved for a friend, Freddie fractured the intruder's nose. In addition to his readiness to fight, Freddie was a regular at break-ins, gambling, shoplifting, and virtually anything that seemed exciting. But at the hospital in a delusional state, he was fanatically opposed to crime. To the other patients and staff, he proclaimed that he was sent by God to rid this planet of evil.

Some criminals like Freddie cycle through alternating periods of crime and psychosis, the psychosis lasting as long as several months. But when the psychosis lifts, often with the help of medication, the patient who was irrational becomes totally lucid and in control of his behavior. There is no evidence to indicate that his transient psychotic phases *cause* his criminality.

The above suggests that all criminals are rational and that crime is never caused by a mental illness. I can speak only from my own clinical experience during the past 13 years and cite the work in this area by my late colleague, Dr. Yochelson, who had many opportunities to examine defendants adjudicated not guilty by reason of insanity. Neither Dr. Yochelson nor I found that any of the men we evaluated were insane unless one took tremendous liberties with the definition of insanity. And yet, there are mental health professionals who at this very moment claim they are treating people whose crimes were a product of their mental illness.[11] Clearly, the issue is open to debate and needs continuing study. There are several caveats to those who conduct these evaluations. One is that it takes many hours of probing to penetrate the defendant's self-serving statements and to study his thinking processes in depth. An hour's interview won't suffice. Second, it should not be assumed that because a person is psychotic at the time of the evaluation that he was psychotic at the time of the crime. Finally, even if it can be ascertained that the person was mentally ill when he committed the crime, it does not necessarily follow that he was powerless to act other than he did.

With respect to this last point, I am familiar with a case in which a young man murdered a former girlfriend. Sufficient evidence was collected by psychiatrists over many years to indicate that the defendant was in fact a "paranoid schizophrenic." However, despite his delusions of persecution, he schemed and carried out the homicide with deliberation and an awareness of consequences. He not only purchased a gun and stored it while thinking about the crime, but he took steps to locate the girl and cased out the place where she worked. In the meantime he had a discussion, ostensibly hypothetical, with a psychiatrist as to what would happen were a person in his condition to commit a serious crime. He concluded that he would be found mentally ill and avoid prison. Thus, even though this man was mentally ill, his condition did not diminish his capacity to understand fully what he was doing.

Psychiatric hospitalization gives the criminal an excuse for more crime. Each time he is treated at a psychiatric facility, there is more documentation of mental instability. Whenever he is arrested, he understandably will be regarded as an offender with psychiatric problems. Consequently, he may wind up again in a hospital rather than a prison. Thus to his considerable advantage he can continue indefinitely to outfox the shrinks.

Chapter Nine

Locked Up

IN MID-1982, there were 394,380 inmates in prison in the United States.[1] Over the last two decades, the prison reform movement has gathered strength, and much of the criticism leveled at correctional facilities has been constructive. However, one major thrust that is inaccurate and misleading is branding correctional institutions as schools for crime with the implication that people are turned into something that they weren't before.

Prison is a breeding ground for crime only insofar as a criminal expands his associations and finds support for anti-social patterns of thought and behavior. He hears new ideas for crime in prison, but *he* is the one who accepts or rejects those ideas. No one forces him to continue a life of crime either within the institution or when he returns to society. He is not a hapless victim who is corrupted by fellow inmates. He has made choices in the past and continues to make choices.

Criminals exhibit the same behavioral patterns inside prison as on the streets. Being locked up does not alter a criminal's perception that he is top dog. Once he adjusts to his surroundings, he becomes determined to establish himself, his stance being, "If you serve time, let time serve you." And so he continues his manipulations and power plays. Some inmates abide by the rules, but not because of any inner personality transformation. Rather, they are building themselves up as model inmates in order to gain special status or privileges. Then there are the inmates who find incarceration to be truly unsettling, if not a major crisis in their lives. They make genuine efforts to change, even seeking the help of institutional counselors, but the counseling that they receive usually turns out to be inadequate.

Wherever he is sent, the criminal believes that confinement is the final injustice in a string of injustices that began with his arrest. In the past, laws and others' rights meant little to him, but now that he is confined, he becomes highly legalistic about asserting his own rights. One inmate who was serving a sentence for a string of burglaries acknowledged, "You break a law to get what you want and treasure the law when it gets you what you want." The criminal looks for a way to beat a charge, and even long after he has begun serving his sentence, he seeks a means to overturn a verdict or reduce his sentence. Some spend hours poring over law books in the prison library and weeks laboring over writs. Among them are men who make a career in prison as jailhouse lawyers, conducting legal research and preparing documents for themselves and other inmates, collecting, in the latter case, money, property, and personal favors.

The assertion of rights continues throughout confinement and extends far beyond a preoccupation with legal statutes and procedures. As the criminal demands protection of his rights, he tries to intimidate members of the staff, who fear both lawsuits and violence. He insists on his right to join an activity if it appeals to him or insists on his right not to participate if he finds it distasteful. At different times, he may take opposite stands on the very same issue. He may demand treatment and threaten to sue to get it. But he may just as readily invoke his right to refuse treatment. An extreme to which inmates have pressed for their rights was cited by columnist Smith Hempstone. Several penitentiary inmates who were members of a newly founded, somewhat offbeat church initiated a lawsuit in which they contended that having steak and sherry at dinner was fundamental to observance of their religious faith.[2]

When the doors of prison first lock behind them, some criminals temporarily are frightened, remorseful, and depressed. These emotions are not strange because criminals experience them occasionally on the street when they weary of the daily grind, tire of looking over their shoulders, and regret disappointing people who care about them. Even on the outside, there were moments when life seemed no longer worth living. Behind bars, they have plenty of time to think. Old fears loom larger than ever and are more difficult to dispel. The present is grim, and the future seems bleak. Early in their confinement, some immerse themselves in prayer and Bible reading. Others ponder how to end it all. "I was just getting tired," said a 28-year-old armed robber, "getting to the point where I wasn't getting anywhere. I didn't see anything tangible I could call success. When my kids grew up, what kind of guy were they going to see? You never see anything accomplished. You're a nothing. You're scared." The turmoil and fear experienced by these criminals does not last. The man who trembles upon his entry to prison will, in time, be tough as nails.

Although even some of the most seasoned criminals begin their sentences in despair, others enter prison hardboiled. If a man has committed crimes but never before served time, going to prison gives him status. Now that he has made the "pen," he is in the big leagues. A distraught mother wrote to the judge in her son's trial, begging him for information about the 18 year old's adjustment to his first incarceration. He had been sentenced to two years for arson. In reply, the judge wrote, "He does not assume personal responsibility for his behavior and tends to negate it. So far, he does not even appear to be uncomfortable in prison. Rather, it appears that he is getting some status from it."

The behavior of an inmate may be geared initially to what he has heard about an institution before he enters it. Prisons gain reputations among their alumni and among other criminals who hear about them through the grapevine but have never been inside them. Some are maximum security institutions, notorious for being the end of the road for convicts who are unmanageable elsewhere.[3] These are often formidable fortresses with high barbed-wire fences, tall watchtowers monitored by guards armed with machine guns, electronically controlled gates, and interior surveillance by guards and closed-circuit televisions. Elaborate and costly security measures do not prevent highly volatile inmates from stabbing, raping, engaging in gang warfare, and rioting. The highest priority of an inmate is to survive. A new inmate knows that he will have to demonstrate from the beginning that he is as tough as the next guy. In institutions like this, the staff struggles to prevent inmates from taking over. Inmates occasionally win out and have the staff so intimidated that it depends on the prisoners to keep order. At the opposite extreme are minimum security facilities, which resemble college campuses. Inmates wearing their own clothing rather than regulation uniforms stroll to and from courses in education, art, music, and vocational training. They play tennis, engage in community-sponsored social activities, participate in work-release programs, and go on home visits. The atmosphere is casual, regimentation minimal. Such an environment is possible as the institution houses offenders considered less dangerous because they have not been convicted of violent crimes.

The toughness of the inmates and the tightness of the security are not the only factors determining an institution's reputation. Prisons are also known for their physical conditions. Some are antiquated nineteenth-century buildings that are crowded, dingy, ovenlike in summer, and freezing in winter. Others are modern but still stark with their gleaming metal and tiny windows. What also matters to inmates is whether it's a "joint" with a lot of programs expounding rehabilitative goals or a no-nonsense lockup where the staff goes strictly by the book. Given humane conditions, many prefer the latter because all they have to do is follow institutional rules and serve their time, not play what they call the "head games" of rehabilitation.

Despite being behind bars, the criminal still expects to do as he pleases. This is not surprising because it is a lifelong attitude. However, inmates have different methods of getting what they want in prison just as they did outside. Some wage open warfare with staff members, flouting authority and brazenly defying regulations. One teenager bragged about his defiance in a state institution: "I tore up my room. I loved hearing glass break." At another juvenile facility, several ringleaders assembled all the kids of one unit, barricaded the staff out of the lounge, and demolished the place. Some prisoners prefer to be locked in their cells or banished to "the hole" rather than capitulate to anyone. Even in their cells they can create a commotion by setting bedding afire or cause floods by stuffing up toilets. Said one inmate, "I am going to play my cards the way I want to and when I want to. Go straight—hell! I would rather remain a hoodlum than let anyone walk over me. No one is going to stop me unless they kill me."

In a struggle for status among fellow cons, the physically aggressive inmate is quick to lash out with a stream of profanity or throw a punch whenever he feels infringed upon. A prisoner who calls him a string of names may wind up with a fork jammed in his gut. A melee may erupt when someone switches the channel on the television. An unaware staff member may suffer a fractured skull from a flying chair after denying an inmate's request. One irascible inmate, displeased with the vegetable soup served at lunch, stared into his bowl, glowered at the man serving him, and complained that he had received the "dregs of the pot." He declared the "slop" unfit to eat and demanded another portion. When the worker ignored him, he threw the soup in his face.

An inmate may conclude that direct confrontations with staff or fellow prisoners is futile, that there is wisdom in restraint. The model inmate is the consummate actor. Contemptuous of everyone from the warden to the guards, he still plays up to them. By lining up allies, he expects to make life easier. Even the toughest con may decide that to score brownie points it is worthwhile to scrub his cell, buff the floors each morning until they gleam, and work diligently at his job. He is regarded as constructive, a good example for other inmates. In conversations with staff and while participating in counseling or therapy groups, he appears determined to reform. Good behavior may advance him toward an early parole. In some systems, an inmate can earn "good time" credits. Whenever he goes a specified number of days without an infraction, one day is lopped off his sentence.

Whether he locks horns with the staff or cons his way into their good graces, the criminal wages psychological warfare. With his customary finesse, he preys upon human insecurity, weakness, greed, and prejudice. Knowing how staff members feel about him and other inmates may be of considerable advantage. If he can touch a sensitive nerve, he may provoke a staff member into losing control. It is a triumph to divert attention from himself and put the other person or even the whole institution on the defensive.

Serving time for forgery, Carl, a tall, wiry man of 30, stayed to himself, determined to avoid a fight at all costs.

However, he had his own way of causing trouble. Without a trace of anger, Carl one day informed the social worker on the psychiatric service where he was housed that he planned to file no less than ten lawsuits, each alleging a specific form of malpractice as well as denial of psychiatric treatment. He declared, "I'll keep records on everything. I'll write down every irregularity. If the food isn't hot, I'll write it down." One of Carl's ploys had been to fake agonizing pain stemming from earlier surgery. His purpose was to persuade the physician to prescribe a narcotic drug. Denied the medication, Carl used the threat of a lawsuit to pressure doctors to transfer him to a different facility. He knew that all his legal maneuverings might amount to nothing, but he boasted to his friends that he would be long remembered for exposing staff incompetence and forcing the administration to defend itself.

The criminal is quick to detect dissension among staff members and exploit it. In many institutions, racial tensions run high. Fully aware of this, the inmate will invoke race where it is completely irrelevant to the issue but expedient for him. He cries discrimination to shift attention from what he has done wrong to a consideration of whether the staff is prejudiced. He injects race if he loses a privilege, if he is spoken to harshly, if he is ordered to do something he finds disagreeable, or if he has been blamed for an infraction and is about to be punished.

In prison, just as on the street, the dilemma of whom to trust hangs heavily in the air. Criminals don't know what trust is. If they use the word, it usually means that a person won't betray them. "Don't snitch" is a code among inmates. The price of squealing on another con may be a beating or even death. Even so, the inmate realizes that every man is out for himself and that even his best buddy may turn informant to save his own skin or to acquire privileges. Although convicts share an understanding of "no snitching," the dominant ethos in prison is, as it was outside, "Fuck everybody else but me.'' Writing in *Corrections Magazine,* Stephen Gettinger reports, ''Some prison observers say that the inmate code's prohibitions against informing are more honored in the breach than in the observance. The trading of information is as common, and as necessary, to the daily life of any prison as taking the count.''[4]

As he serves time, the criminal experiences psychological changes. There are periods of profound depression, similar to that which overwhelmed some upon arrival. As the days, weeks, and months drag by, prison life grates upon the inmate. The criminal never tolerated much in the way of a routine in the free world, but the regimen in prison is incomparably duller and more oppressive than anything he ever knew. Other people control his schedule, and there is little variation in what he will be doing each day during the months or years of his sentence. Outside, the criminal expected the world to suit him, and in prison he's no different. He seems to expect the institution to accommodate him as though he were a guest paying for a deluxe hotel room. His complaints resound with righteous indignation, as he ignores the fact that he is where he is as a consequence of the choices in life he has made.

Besides complaints there are genuine regrets. In contrast to the bleakness of prison existence, inmates glimpse life outside through radio, television, letters, periodicals, and occasional visitors. They are aging and life is passing them by. Their children are growing up, and their wives are finding new interests, sometimes other men. They have much to regret—not just their present incarceration but their previous indifference or opposition to the many opportunities to live a different kind of life. There is plenty of time to look in the mirror and reflect upon a life in the gutter, an immersion in what one man called ''a life of filth and slime.'' One 25-year-old vicious felon named Tony was serving a long sentence for a bank holdup but had never been caught for a string of armed robberies in which he had assaulted and maimed innocent people. In prison, he was doing a lot of thinking about his life and commented wryly, "I feel like a guy who was viewing the Virgin Mother and her child but who was so totally rotten that all he could think of was raping Mary and having sex with the child."

One outcome of such revulsion toward the self is to resolve to go straight. The inmate decides to avoid the incessant feuding and intrigues of the prison community and stays to himself. He cooperates with the staff, but this time he's not conning. Other inmates are highly suspicious of him, certain that he is putting on an act. If not that, they mark him as trouble because they think that he has sold out to the staff and become an informant. When their hunches turn out to be wrong, they may become convinced that he is sincere and really does want to change. But they remain skeptical because they know from their own experience that such determination never lasts. The basis for their skepticism is usually borne out. The man who aspires to straighten out finds that life without criminal excitement is intolerable. Gradually, his commitment to change erodes, usually in prison, but if not then, after he gets out.

An alternative to change is suicide. Some criminals had suicidal thoughts on the streets when things weren't working out. In confinement, an inmate's state of mind is such that he is despondent over the meaninglessness of his life and he is also raging at a world that he thinks never gave him a fair shake. Sighed one inmate who was considering suicide, "I wouldn't have to put up with shit anymore." There are no readily available statistics about the number of suicides in prison. Certainly, suicidal gestures dramatizing the inmate's plight are more common. A heavy but not lethal dose of drugs, a wrist slashing with a crude, handmade knife, or an inept job of hanging himself compels others to take notice and do something to help him. He may wind up in a prison hospital or psychiatric unit and receive treatment or, at the least, a less harsh environment in which to spend some time.

The despondent inmate may seek salvation in religion. Some criminals study the Bible, applying its passages to their own lives. They write for religious materials and ask their families or prison personnel to provide them with still more. They flock to the prison chaplain's discussion groups, sing in choir, share in readings of the liturgy in chapel services, and participate in other religious programs. Some experience a sudden flood of religious inspiration and overnight become converts to a particular faith. The "Biblebacks," as other inmates call them, quote the scriptures, zealously imparting their insights to others. These are not conversions of convenience calculated to impress the authorities. Rather, their whole existence becomes pervaded by religion. Their radios are tuned to church services and to gospel singing rather than to rock and soul. Their artwork is permeated by religious motifs. Their poetry, letters, and other writings resound with religious messages. Some inmates, less public about their absorption in religion, withdraw from others and quietly devote hours to reading and prayer.

Institutional staff members have no way of knowing whether the depression, spirituality, or attempts at reformation are genuine or whether the criminal is up to his old tricks. When genuine, these phases may last for months at a time. But phases they are. When they end, the criminal emerges with his basic outlook intact.

A criminal's absorption with crime does not necessarily diminish just because he is locked up. Despite the restrictive environment, he schemes, talks about, and continues to engage in illicit activities. Any external stimulus, such as a television cop show, a detective movie, or a lurid crime story in the paper feeds an already busy mind, as do his daily conversations with other inmates about crime. Through letters and visitors, the criminal hangs on to old ties in addition to establishing new ones in prison. To some, confinement means that the challenge to engage in illicit activities is greater than ever. Theft is rampant in prisons. Anything that a man wants to hold on to must be kept on his person or surrendered to a trustworthy staff member. An inmate may be robbed when he sleeps (if he shares a cell or dormitory), while he takes a shower, or at any other moment when he relaxes his guard. Inmates not only steal from one another but also pilfer personal belongings from the staff and food and other supplies from the institution.

Just as the criminal made sexual conquests outside confinement, he may attempt to do the same within. Homosexuality occurs not simply because the criminal is without a woman. Sex in prison is a powerful weapon to obligate and control others. A consenting sexual act may occur between two inmates in which sex is bartered for cigarettes, food, personal possessions, or money. Each criminal gets what he wants from the other and gives up little of importance. But sex in prison is often far less civilized. According to a *Washington Post* series on rape in prison, "Rape is common among heterosexual men because it is the best way for an inmate to command fear and respect among other inmates."[5] Many pairs of eyes rove up and down the body of each new young man who enters the institution, especially if he is of slight build and physically attractive. In his bed at night, a new inmate may be beset by a gang of inmates who threaten him with far worse than rape or sodomy if he resists or informs. It is a jungle in which the strong subjugate the weak. To obtain protection, an inmate may submit to becoming the lackey and sexual slave of one of the most feared inmates.

Criminals also attempt to solicit sex from staff members whom they think they can compromise. They test out personnel by telling dirty jokes and making suggestive remarks. Sexual rendezvous are most easily held in settings where criminals have their own rooms or have earned the privilege of leaving the unit accompanied by staff. If an inmate succeeds in having sex with a staff member, he owns him and can extract special favors in the future. For example, one inmate threatened to expose a female attendant with whom he had a sexual liaison unless she testified favorably in his behalf at a hearing. She did as instructed.

Gambling is a way of life in the institution. Like sex, it is a means by which criminals obligate others and build themselves up. Bets are placed in card games, pool, chess, sports events, and virtually every other activity in which the outcome is unknown. The gambling may be organized, as in daily numbers games linked to a downtown connection by a staff member. In many facilities, regulations prohibit criminals from having money on their person. Yet there are inmates who are flush with cash they have acquired by gambling, from visitors, or by doing favors for staff. In some gambling operations, inmates net more than a staff member earns in weeks. If cash is not available, anything that is valued can be currency in a wager. Some staff members are regulars in the gambling. When the inmate wins, he may acquire more than the sum bet. In lieu of demanding immediate total payment or charging losers usurious interest rates, he may cancel debts if the indebted staff member closes his eyes to certain violations and helps the inmate gain privileges.

Cigarettes are one of the most treasured commodities in prison. When an inmate smokes, he burns the cigarette down to the filter. Prisoners can be seen scrounging in ashtrays to redeem butts of cigarettes that appear still good for a puff or two. Cigarettes are the main currency for paying off debts, purchasing a sought-after possession of another inmate, buying sex, and bribing others for favors. When he runs out of cigarettes, a con may launch a full-scale criminal operation to restock his supply. Upon receiving his prescribed nightly sedative, a jail inmate secretly poured the liquid out of the cup into his own container, handed the empty cup to the guard through the bars of his cell, and then exchanged the medicine for cigarettes with an inmate who wanted to get high. Many a fight in prison has begun over an unpaid cigarette debt. This particular inmate was heard screaming at another man who owed him a pack, "You pay up, or I'll go through you like a hurricane."

Correctional facilities take precautions to prevent contraband from being brought in, but criminals are ingenious. A shakedown of virtually any correctional facility will yield a variety of contraband items, especially handmade weapons. Silverware may be smuggled from the dining rooms, although many institutions are meticulous in trying to account for every piece after each meal. In prison industries, metal or woodworking shops, and during other activities, inmates are in regular contact with sharp, heavy, and breakable objects that they can turn into weapons. Even a mop handle makes a good club. Inmates of one penitentiary collected all the glass containers left from Christmas gifts that they had received from family and friends. One night, angry at the early shutoff of the television, they urinated into the jars. The guards were startled when they were barraged with glass and showered with urine as jars without tops were hurled down from the upper tiers of a cellblock. From then on, glass jars were designated contraband.

Illicit drugs are nearly always floating around prisons and psychiatric hospitals housing criminal offenders. Friends ingeniously conceal drugs in packages which they send by mail. An innocent looking apple may have a drug injected into its core. A tempting chocolate cake may have drugs baked between layers. A sugary powder surrounding hard candy may really be heroin. Visiting at many institutions occurs without personal contact, inmate and visitor looking at each other through a pane of glass and talking through a telephone receiver. But institutions that allow contact visits experience an influx of drugs. A long kiss may not be an expression of love, but a means of transmitting capsules. Staff may bring in contraband from the outside or, knowing the sources for drugs inside the prison, may rifle the stock of unit medical supplies, the warehouse, or the pharmacy. The staff member knows that he has a permanent market and an easy way to make money. Instead of selling directly to inmates, the staff dealer finds one inmate whom he can trust to serve as distributor and conceal the source of the supply. For a job reliably done, the distributor is well compensated. He, too, stays behind the scenes, lining up other prisoners who will actually make the sales. Everyone gets a piece of the action, and the staff member remains insulated by others fronting for him. The total take from a prison drug ring may run into hundreds of dollars a week. Some criminals who leave on pass for home visits or work release engage in drug-related activities as well. The first stop en route home may be at a phone to arrange to meet his connection and stock up. If the risks are not too great, he conveys the drugs to the institution himself. However, if he is stripped and searched each time he returns, he buys the drugs but arranges with a visitor or staff member to bring them to the prison.

How widespread staff collusion with inmates and direct staff participation in illegal activities is in America's correctional institutions is impossible to say. Only rarely does a scandal hit the papers since usually such matters are handled internally. Whereas most employees in corrections are conscientious and responsible, some desire to work with or near criminals because they identify with them and find them exciting. These individuals relish listening to inmates' accounts of exploits, and they sometimes join in the endless bantering about crime, drugs, and sex. Such staff members would abhor working with the retarded, physically handicapped, or elderly. It would be far too tedious. Criminals intuitively sense which employees are very much like themselves and carefully test the waters to see who can be compromised. Some staff members will not risk their positions by direct involvement in criminal activity, but they get their kicks vicariously. Others are ready for action and collaborate with inmates in gambling, drug trafficking, theft, sex, and whatever else opportunity presents. The relationships are mutually exploitative. The staffer has his excitement, and his job becomes more than just work. The criminal expects to gain a potential ally who will not turn him in for infractions and who will help bail him out of trouble. If such expectations are not met, the inmate has the weapons for blackmail. The staff member, in turn, can threaten to report the criminal for any of a number of real or made-up offenses and thereby imperil his eligibility for privileges or release. If enough employees of criminal character work in any one part of an institution, their actions inevitably sabotage their conscientious colleagues, who then become disillusioned and demoralized.

All the above is intended to underscore the point that criminals are criminals, no matter where they are. In prison, their personality remains as it was. What may vary is the degree of risk they will take and therefore the method by which they operate. Those abstaining from crime still miss it, but they content themselves with fantasy and conversation about crime. Said a 22-year-old burglar, ''I'm still not afraid while I sit here in prison. The only thing I think about is stealing when I'm out of here in a few years and not the consequences. They don't mean anything.''

No criminal wants to return to prison, and no criminal expects to. Some offenders serve time, and that in itself is a powerful deterrent to further criminal activity. They do not repeat. But these are not the people who have made crime a way of life. There are no studies of these people and no figures as to how numerous they are.

Contrary to what some people believe, most criminals do learn from experience, but it is not what society wants to teach him. In prison, such a person has ample time and opportunity to learn how to be a better criminal. Some decide that upon release they will lie low, limit themselves to smaller crimes, and forgo the big-time ventures. Or perhaps they will mastermind a crime but stay behind the scenes rather than participate directly in the action. Such intentions are short-lived. Once they leave prison behind, their appetites become voracious for the high excitement of the old life. Some in fact do become more successful criminals, immersing themselves heavily in crime but being slick enough to avoid apprehension. Others avoid arrest for a long time but eventually land back in the slammer. Then there are the big losers. Hardly has the prison disgorged them into society than they slip up, get caught, and are charged with a new offense.

It is widely believed that criminals outgrow crime, but this is based on the fact that some never return to prison. Rand Corporation researchers observe that some criminologists have hypothesized that the criminal reaches a "burnout stage."[6] Dr. Richard Schwartz states, "By the time a man reaches age 40 his criminal career is essentially over."[7] The burnout theory may be based on the fact that some older criminals cease to get arrested for street crimes. It is true that as the street criminal ages, he is not as agile and literally cannot run as fast as he used to. He has mellowed only in that he takes fewer big risks and his offenses may be less serious. But his criminal personality remains unchanged, and people still suffer at his hands.

James grew up in the slums of a large Eastern seaboard city. He recalls his parents struggling to provide for him on what little his father earned working long hours for a moving company. Both parents were intent on his having advantages in life that they lacked. Though neither had more than a grade school education, they emphasized the value of learning and bought James books. His mother took him to the zoo, on picnics, and to parades. But none of this really interested James, who at eight years of age found hanging around street corners far more to his liking. As a teenager, he practically lived on the streets and in the alleys. After serving prison sentences for violent crimes and after treatment in a mental hospital, James was at 50 a free man. People who were acquainted with him thought that he was burnt out, mostly because he seemed less combative and had sworn off hard drugs.

A handsome black man with a neatly trimmed, graying beard, James wore suits wherever he went. He instantly appealed to many people because he had charm and charisma. He cornered people and spoke with great fervor as he interpreted social issues in terms of the Scriptures. (He was a self-educated man, having dropped out of school in the eighth grade.) Although some people regarded him as a religious fanatic, others admired him for his sincerity. Because he was required by the court to show evidence of employment, James waited on tables at a restaurant. Although he annoyed some customers by his inclination to preach, he kept his job. Management indulged his foibles because James seemed a trustworthy and loyal employee.

At 50, James indeed appeared to be a changed man, but he had a lot of people fooled. Never did anyone at his job suspect that he was stealing from tips that belonged to busboys as well as pilfering food and utensils from the pantry. As soon as he was no longer under court supervision, James quit his job and launched a criminal operation. He began working 10 hours a week as a phone solicitor for a company that sold household products such as light bulbs and brooms. Using his employer's phone list, he told potential customers that he was a minister raising funds for his church. This was the beginning of an enterprise in which James defrauded the public for years. All the while, he was collecting welfare and Social Security benefits, which began when he was declared mentally disabled in the hospital. Appealing especially to the black community, James posted signs on soft drink machines advertising counseling and pastoral services. Each week he rode a bus across town to upper-income white neighborhoods, where he hung around libraries and community centers strumming his guitar and soliciting passers-by for contributions to his church. He ingratiated himself with children, singing their favorite songs and offering free instruction on how to play the guitar. He'd find out where the youngsters lived and stop by their homes to ask their mothers and fathers for donations. It was awkward for parents to refuse this "reverend" who had been so kind to their children.

James had a talent for convincing people that he was personally interested in them, concerned about their welfare. If he heard that someone was sick, he promised to pray for that person and sent a card. His expressions of sympathy helped wring money out of ill patients and their families. James's enterprise flourished as he announced to potential donors that he was setting up a small store. If they would donate not only money but also furniture, clothing, and other belongings, they would help the poor purchase at cut-rate prices what they could never otherwise afford and at the same time support the church. The business never opened, but James did manage to add to his wardrobe and apartment furnishings.

From donations, Social Security, and welfare, James lived comfortably. He kept no accounting of his receipts and never filed an income tax return. By his own estimate, he had compiled a correspondence list of more than 400 names, whom he sporadically contacted by phone or letter. The most gratifying aspect of his activities was that James induced people to trust him with their hearts and respond generously with their pocketbooks. This was a triumph. It supported his belief that he could accomplish anything that he set his mind to.

James never severed his ties with other criminals. He once told a psychologist, "Some of my best friends are hardened criminals. What I admire is that they can make positive decisions. They are closer to being human than people who represent good, moral behavior." One day he was robbed of cash and some personal possessions. He turned this event to his advantage by proclaiming to potential donors that his ministry had been victimized and that it was imperative that the work of the Lord continue. Although he was not the lady's man that he had been in his youth, James still consorted with a 27-year-old prostitute and other irresponsible young women. He was off hard drugs but smoked marijuana and occasionally drank heavily.

This 50-year-old man was regarded as innocuous by those who had known him as a tough young street dude. Although he was no longer violent, James continued to live a criminal existence and in doing so inflicted more widespread, although less physical, injury than ever before. Neither years of confinement nor the process of aging had significantly altered his personality.

Chapter Ten

Criminals' Self-Image: "Decent People"

THE PLACE is the Oregon State Hospital, a meeting of a therapy group where dangerous sex offenders are receiving psychiatric treatment. Among them is a man who raped babies, a fellow who sodomized a 6-year-old boy, another who raped a 14-year-old girl at gunpoint, and 10 others who have committed almost every other imaginable sexual offense as well as other types of crimes. The therapist has just asked the men why society has rules. One man replies, "We have rules to protect society and so people won't hurt others." Another speaks up, "Society would fall apart without rules. There'd be mass confusion." A third says, "Rules are designed to teach people their responsibilities."

All these responses are rational and to the point. They come from the lips of men who, without question, know that rape, kidnapping, child molestation, and other forms of sexual abuse are wrong and why they are wrong. These men will acknowledge that, from society's point of view, they are criminals. But not one really regards *himself* that way. Every member of that group believes that he is basically a decent human being. How is it possible for a criminal to believe that he is a good guy when he has left behind him a trail of destruction?

The criminal knows right from wrong. He may be more knowledgeable about the laws than many responsible citizens. When it suits him, he is law-abiding and even takes pride in being meticulous about it. One ruthless teenage gang member, for example, would never spit on a sidewalk or break the speed limit when he motorcycled through a school zone. Despite his knowledge of what is legal and illegal, the criminal decides that he can make exceptions for himself just because it suits him at a particular time. The fact that *he* wants to do it makes it right. "I was born with the idea that I'd do what I wanted. I always felt that rules and regulations were not for me," asserted one 14 year old who then added, "Others may think I'll burn in hell, but at least I'll have a nice time doing what I want while I'm here."

If a criminal regards something as wrong for him personally, he will not do it. An act is wrong if it is too risky. An act is also considered wrong by a criminal if he thinks it is too petty. A big-time operator may consider shoplifting wrong only because it is not worth bothering with. If a criminal makes an error in judgment and is caught, he will say what he did wrong, but only because he was caught.

The semantics of this last point are interesting. One teenager said that lately he had been "messing up" and he needed to stop doing that. My probing into what he meant revealed a totally different message than his words conveyed. To the untrained ear, it might have sounded as if this youth wanted to reform, but that was not so. By "messing up" he meant getting caught. If he hadn't been caught for a crime, he would not have called it "messing up." What was wrong was getting caught, not his commission of the offense.

The criminal not only knows right from wrong, but he also believes that wrongdoers must be apprehended. Criminals are portrayed as hating the cops, but this is not so. As children, they admire policemen and imagine themselves in badge and uniform brandishing a nightstick and revolver and driving a speeding cruiser. Fascination with the police continues into the criminal's adult years, and he is an avid viewer of police shows and detective thrillers. He regards police as absolutely necessary to lock up lawbreakers, and, on occasion, he may help them out. After assisting officers in the arrest of a burglar, one criminal wrote to a law enforcement agent, "You have impressed me as a very efficient, no-nonsense guy who won't tolerate inefficient police work, and I really hope that you will match any criminal power thrust with an overwhelming display of power on the side of law and order." The criminal has contempt for law enforcement officials mainly when they pose an immediate threat to him.

Although the criminal may not accept what others consider moral standards, he claims to have his own set of morals. Other people are liars, perverts, scoundrels, and criminals, not he. Sociologist Joseph Rogers points out that even in prison an inmate "is not likely to see himself as a 'real' criminal." It is the other inmates, "whom he views as the 'real' ones."[1] He looks down on them as depraved because they do things that he would not. Specific crimes are wrong and thus off limits for him simply because he personally finds them offensive. Criminals differ as to what they find most revolting. One says that a child molester should be killed while another advocates that a rapist be castrated. But each considers whatever he does as beyond reproach. One tough guy of the streets said that sneaking up on an adult male and mugging him is all in a day's work, but if he were to see anyone do the same to a child or elderly lady, he would rip the attacker to shreds. To his way of thinking, the two situations are completely different.

If there is something that the criminal wants, he knocks down every barrier until he gets it. If this requires maiming or killing, so be it. There is no need to justify a crime to himself either before or at the time he commits it. In coldblooded fashion, he does whatever suits him; he is the only one who matters. A 25-year-old man who served a sentence for two counts of assault and battery commented, "A realistic person will have to admit that this is a dog-eat-dog world and basically every man is for himself first, others second. Only the fit will survive. Take what you want out of life, without any qualms or doubts, ruthlessly if necessary. But above all be true to yourself." He went on to say, "The question of being right or wrong is not a major one for when you are dead and gone some will say, 'He was a good son of a bitch' and some will say, 'He was a dirty son of a bitch.' Either way, you're a dead son of a bitch, and there won't be any dispute over that!"

The criminal does not think he has hurt anyone unless he draws blood. He does not see himself as harming his victims when he vandalizes their property, forges their checks, cons them out of savings, or breaks into their homes. Yet, if someone did any of these things to him or to his family, he would assist the police or personally seek revenge. One 15 year old had recurrent thoughts of sneaking up on old people and robbing them, but he said about the prospect of someone's doing this to his grandmother, "If I found the person, I'd kill him."

An exchange that took place in juvenile court reveals a characteristic attitude. Sixteen-year-old Stu was asked by the judge, "Why did you forge the checks?" Blandly, Stu replied, "It was an opportunity. I didn't need the money." Incredulously, the judge retorted, "It was an opportunity to be a thief!" Stu stared at the judge and said adamantly, "No, I'm not a thief." It might appear that Stu could not add two and two. Knowing that he had broken the law, he had admitted his guilt in court without excuses. Yet he declared that he was not a thief, a conclusion totally different from that of the judge or the victim. From his standpoint, Stu did what he wanted to; it was as simple as that. Thieves hurt people by causing them loss, anxiety, and inconvenience. Had Stu even imagined he was doing that, he would not have stolen the checks and forged them. When a criminal is confronted with tangible evidence that he has harmed someone, he blames the victim or minimizes the damage. At most, he passes it off perhaps as poor judgment on his part but certainly not as reflecting anything basic about his character.

Psychiatrist Willard Gaylin calls guilt "the guardian of our goodness." He says that feeling guilt is so painful because "it is like tearing apart our inner structure."[2] Most of us seek to avoid such pain and are usually deterred from serious wrongdoing. How does a criminal who experiences little guilt live with himself? He can maintain a view of himself as a decent person because psychologically he can do what most of us can't. Criminals isolate unpleasant emotions such as fear, guilt, and self-doubt so that they do not interfere with their objectives. Psychologist Hans Eysenck's explanation is a biological one. He maintains, "Criminality can be understood in terms of conditioning principles." He goes on to observe, "Criminals fail to condition adequately the socially adequate responses which society requires them to integrate into some form of 'conscience.' "[3] Freudians would explain lack of conscience in terms of a "superego deficit" due to disturbed "object relations" in the early years.

As I see it, criminals do experience guilt and remorse. They have a conscience, but it is not fully operational. When they commit a crime, they can shut off considerations of conscience as quickly and totally as they can shut off an electric light. Just the fact that the criminal can *feel* guilt, no matter how ineffective it is as a deterrent, helps him to maintain the belief that he is decent.

The criminal thinks so highly of himself because he has within him a deep reservoir of genuine sentiment. Amazingly, a violent street thug became impassioned about sparing the life of a bug, ordering his wife not to squash it. A criminal who indulged in fantasies of knife-point rape and homicide said to his wife when she proposed that they go to a tree farm where they'd be allowed to chop down their own Christmas tree, "No, I will not destroy living matter." Even while en route to a crime, a criminal may perform a good deed. One man dropped by a bar, treated a down-and-out alcoholic to a meal, and, feeling pretty good about himself, robbed a bank. Then there is the multiple murderer who wrote poetry about self-control:

> *So keep your mental balance*
> *When confronted by a foe*
> *Be it enemy in ambush*
> *Or some danger that you know.*
> *Be self-controlled and responsible*
> *When all around is strife*
> *And know, my friend, you've mastered*
> *The most vital thing in life.*

Idealism is by no means unique to the criminal. Perhaps all of us sustain a belief in our own goodness, partly because we espouse certain ideals. Even if we stray from them, we do not totally compartmentalize them from our daily living in order to inflict injury repeatedly on people. It takes a particular kind of mentality to break into an apartment, rape a woman, and then remain for 45 minutes to talk to her about religion. This in fact occurred in Washington, D.C.[4] The criminal's idealism and altruism are genuine and form part of a reservoir of good by which he sustains a belief in his own goodness. Still, he continues to commit crimes.

Sometimes the criminal persuades himself that in a different environment he will be a different person. He dreams of getting away from it all, retreating from the world and living a simple life in the country or mountains. Said one man incarcerated three years for felonious assault, "Damn, I don't ever want to own a bicycle or a car or any kind of transportation. I'd love to be on a farm or a ranch someplace alone for about five years and just sit there. No risks, no pressures, no nothing."

Many criminals are remarkably talented. Prison art shows display the work of gifted painters who have had little formal training. Some criminals are musically gifted, performing their own compositions on instruments that they learned to play totally by ear. Many who don't play an instrument may be music aficionados. An alumnus of a federal penitentiary with a passion for Bach declared, "To me, music is everything." Some criminals are excellent craftsmen, fashioning stylish leather goods and constructing handsome, sturdy furniture. Others have a knack for dismantling and repairing just about anything. Such talents and skills are often unknown to others, and when they are discovered, people are amazed and see vast potential in the criminal for becoming a constructive citizen. However, as with so much else, the criminal lacks the discipline to develop these talents. He has little interest in a training or apprenticeship program, which entails drudgery and perseverance. Instead, he expects to turn out a polished product or masterpiece overnight. If that is not possible, he loses interest.

People who are not criminals also fail to make use of natural aptitudes or to develop their talents. They may set such unrealistically high standards for themselves that they quickly become discouraged and quit shortly after embarking on a new undertaking. Some talented individuals have such a neurotic fear of failing that they give up before they put themselves to the test. Then there are the undisciplined, who grow bored, anxious, and impatient and don't see a project through. Some of these factors may be operative in the criminal. But the chief impediment to the criminal's actualizing his talents is that the *process* of doing so is devoid of meaning. The responsible person finds meaning in the process of achievement. He may be prouder of his determination in surmounting obstacles and sticking with an undertaking than of the final product. Not so with the criminal. When he is not an immediate success, then he asserts himself in criminal enterprises, which are far more satisfying.

A tattoo saying "mother" frequently seen on criminals reveals their deepest sentimentality. In most cases, mother has believed in the criminal, bailed him out of trouble, and never abandoned hope. On the one hand, he adores her, but on the other, he makes her life hell, cursing her when she opposes something he wants to do, stealing from her, threatening her, and causing her sleepless nights. Yet mother remains forgiving, always willing to help him pick up the pieces of his life. When the criminal is despondent, she is one person to whom he can turn. His awareness of what he has done to her is likely to be most intense when he is in prison. One inmate serving a sentence for bank robbery recognized that his distraught mother was completely bewildered by his life: "All this she cannot comprehend. She doesn't want to believe it, and yet she must, but still it's beyond her conception of her son whom she has loved so much and seen so little and wants so much to understand, to help, to protect, to ease and comfort through his tortured blind running." In a letter he entreated her, "Mom, please forgive me. I wish there were some way to spare you this. I've changed my name, went away, and tried to keep the truth from you, but you refuse to be happy unless I am happy."

Although the criminal violates everything for which his mother stands, he worries about her, especially about something horrible happening to her. One young man feared that, because his mom lived alone, she might become a victim of a criminal. He counseled her in a letter from prison, "You should devote several hours to a pure exercise in survival by just moving from one position in your room to another, imagining exactly what you would say and do if confronted by a robbery or assault.'' He went on to instruct his mother, ''Who's gonna train you? That's right! *You are.* What can you say that will calm an attacker? 'I won't hurt you' is the best opener. If he's worried about being hurt, he'll calm down. You can't reason with whoever it is while he's scared. I'm gonna change subjects because it depresses the hell out of me to keep thinking about you being in the position we're talking about, but please prepare yourself for the possibility by doing the things I have told you. You'll feel foolish standing in the living room yelling at yourself, but so what? If you can handle the playacting right, you may just spontaneously do the right thing someday and not get shot.'' Then he posed the question, ''Do you know why most people who get killed in robberies get killed?'' He rejoined, ''They do not know how to be robbed. That sounds absurd to you, I'm sure, and it is sickening that we live in a world where a person should be trained as a victim.'' The fellow writing this letter was an authority on the subject for he had committed numerous robberies.

Although sentimentality about mother may be deeply felt by most criminals, they differ greatly as to where their other sentiments lie. Some are so fond of animals that they will bring home a lost, injured animal and treat it more tenderly than their own children. Furthermore, these animal lovers will chew out and even assault anyone whom they find abusing an animal. Other criminals abuse animals or are completely indifferent to them. Similarly, some love babies, anybody's baby. It tears them up to hear an infant cry, and they rush to pick up a baby and soothe it in their arms. But there is also the criminal who doesn't care for babies at all, not even his own. A wailing infant may evoke murderous thoughts.

Usually the criminal conceals the soft side of his personality for fear that others will see him as a sissy. He is embarrassed if a buddy finds out that he went to an art gallery or that he listens to ''longhair'' music. To show compassion for someone is to be weak. The same with open expression of affection. The very qualities that he hides from his buddies are pluses in the eyes of the responsible world. To others the bad doesn't seem so bad when socially redeeming features are also evident. The "good points" work to the criminal's advantage especially in confinement because the staff thinks that there is hope for him when he returns to the outside world.

Responsible people frequently mistake fragments of sincerity and goodness for basic character. They conclude that the criminal at heart really is a pretty decent fellow whom they can help change by drawing upon his good qualities and reinforcing them. The sad truth is that the features that appear to be socially redeeming serve only to further the individual's criminality. The sentimentality, art, and music, the isolated acts of kindness all support the criminal's inherent view that he is a good person. He sincerely believes that any sin he might have committed is more than compensated for by the good that he has done. When others praise him for a good deed or for a talent or skill, he assumes that they are voicing their unqualified approval of him as a human being.

Some criminals are religious, and this figures prominently in their good opinion of themselves. Schooled in religion as youngsters, they took what they learned very much to heart. In the primary grades, they were not defiant or hell raisers. Rather, they were super good, regularly attending church and Sunday school, helping in the home, and looking out for kids who were the underdogs. Believing that God was watching them all the time, they tried to merit His approval. One criminal reported that as an eight year old he pictured God dwelling in a tower like a church steeple, looking down upon him, and judging everything he did to determine whether he'd rest in heaven or burn in hell. Another, at eight, was convinced that if he were bad the devil would snatch him and he'd die before his ninth birthday. One boy crossed himself each time the word "damn" slipped out of his mouth. As children, these criminals were ready to condemn adults and other children for the slightest impropriety. As for themselves, they believed that to remain in God's good graces, they had to be better than good, purer than pure. But their determination, though sincere, did not last. In a manner typical of criminals, they shifted from one extreme to another. As the youngster's world expanded beyond his family circle, there was both greater temptation and an ever more active mind that dwelled increasingly on the forbidden. The slow but steady erosion of his purity was almost impossible to observe. Those who thought they knew him were astounded when this model child suddenly exploded into antisocial activity. Yet religion was not abandoned forever. Criminals keep returning to it, some out of nostalgia for their childhood, others in a personal crisis when they long for the serenity of a church with its soothing music and familiar ritual. As with everything else, the criminal exploits religion to serve his own purposes. He not only presents God with his list of wants, but he also asks God to be an accessory to his crimes. He prays for success in his ventures and later, when he gets himself into a jam, implores God to bail him out. After the police apprehended one man for an assault with a deadly weapon, he silently beseeched the Lord from the patrol car, "God, if you'd only help me now, I won't do any more things." The criminal bargains with God for salvation after he is confined and resolves to mend his ways.

Fifteen-year-old Vic was shocked when a judge finally ordered him locked up after he had repeatedly violated probation. His first stint in confinement was sobering. There he began reading the Bible and a small book written by a minister. He devoted considerable thought to the nature of sin and resolved to sin no more. Vic found the smaller volume so absorbing that he considered swiping it to take it home. Then he was jolted by his parents' reminder that it was a sin to steal a book that he thought might keep him from sinning.

Leaving the book where it belonged, he reflected more on the nature of sin and told his parents with tears in his eyes that he wanted them to help him reform. Vic's sincerity was temporary. Nearly as soon as he was released from detention, he returned to crime.

Religion has little to do with how the criminal lives. As a child he may serve as an altar boy at a 10 o'clock service and two hours later go on a shoplifting spree. As an adult, he may pray in church in the morning and that very evening stick a gun to someone's head. (A *Time* feature on the Mafia reported, "A Mafioso cultivates the image of a solid, church-going, charity-supporting citizen."[5]) For criminals, religion and evil exist side by side, one compartmentalized from the other. A striking example of this is 30-year-old Bill, who had murdered his girlfriend. Bill had always considered himself a religious man. In his adult years, he still went to church, although not regularly. At the conclusion of one service, he went to the pulpit to talk with the minister and showed him a book on Christian ethics. Ethics book in hand, he lied to the minister by telling him that he had been released from confinement and was starting a new life. Actually, Bill was a fugitive from a federal institution, sought by the authorities.

The lament of most clergymen is that their congregants fail to live by the teachings of their religious faith. They emerge from church brimming with righteousness and feeling virtuous just because they managed to get out of bed and sit through a service. Then they curse their fellow congregants as they scramble to get out of the parking lot. But the fact remains that, despite their human frailties, unlike the criminal, they retain a sense of social boundaries, obey laws, and fulfill obligations. The criminal, on the other hand, has a remarkable capacity to shut off considerations of responsibility or morality from his thinking so totally that he can freely commit murder, rape, arson, extortion, and a myriad of other crimes. He perceives no contradiction between prayer and crime. Both are right for him, depending on what he wants at a particular time.

Ironically, the criminal's religiosity fosters crime for, when it is genuine, it bolsters his opinion of himself as an upstanding citizen. It is as though by having felt remorse, prayed, and confessed his sins to God, the criminal empties his cup of whatever evil it might have contained so that he has even more latitude to do as he pleases.

As the criminal sees it, he is a good person, making his way as he sees fit in a world that is his to conquer. But the world does not cater to him, and many times every day his unrealistic view of life is threatened. The slightest disappointment can trigger a total collapse of his inflated self-concept. Small daily frustrations that most people cope with routinely are calamities for him—having to wait in line when time is short, receiving criticism from his boss, having his wife disagree with him. These things are not supposed to happen. He assumes that he should give the orders, make the decisions, and not have to put up with the idiosyncrasies of others. His self-concept is easily shattered because he defines failure as being anything short of an immediate resounding success. If a kid wants to be known as a champion ballplayer, he shows up for regular practice. Not the criminal. If he isn't recognized right away as a top-flight athlete, that to him is the same as others regarding him as a spastic, and so he'll refuse to play at all. If he fails to be the most popular in a group, he'll believe that he is looked at as a social misfit. So he'll tell others to go to hell or will plot to get even. If a woman doesn't jump into bed with him, he'll consider it a threat to his manhood rather than recognize that she has a right to make her choice. The threat of being less than top dog, the possibility that he won't achieve unusual distinction, the chance that things will not go as he wants constitute a major threat to the criminal, almost as though his life were at stake. From his standpoint it is, because the puncturing of his inflated self-concept is psychological homicide. It is like pricking a balloon with a pin so that the entire thing blows apart. The result is a desperate and sometimes violent reaction to gain control of a situation and assert his worth.

Criminals, then, are almost always angry, even though they often conceal it. Only a slight jolt to the self-image sets them off, and anyone or any object in the vicinity may be a target. A derogatory name, a snide remark, a criticism may have an explosive effect similar to pouring lighter fluid onto a smoldering bed of coals.

Responsible people also get angry when things don't work out as they hope. But one frustration or disappointment does not threaten them with total psychological annihilation. They don't expect to be "number one" in everything or to be right on every occasion. Having learned to be self-critical, they realize that perhaps *they* did make a mistake, not the other guy. Consequently, instead of automatically thinking about retaliation, they are inclined to consider how to make amends or do better the next time. The criminal simply doesn't operate this way. He takes stock of himself only to try to ensure that he will come out on top the next time. What matters to him is not self-improvement but making a conquest.

Regarding himself as decent, the criminal approaches the responsible world with scorn. An ordinary life is a living death, clearly not for him. Said one youthful housebreaker and lock-picking expert, "I'd rather be dead than be a clerk." Yet, the criminal occasionally envies the responsible person. He eyes the trappings of success—a comfortable home, a car, a family, a high-paying job—and believes that the holder of these is on easy street. A 17-year-old delinquent said, "Sometimes I wish I was like regular kids." He saw his friends ready to graduate and driving cars which they bought with job earnings. He mused, "I could have had all that. Sometimes, I feel like a fool." But this youth quit school, would have no part of working, and turned his back on a devoted family.

Not only does the criminal think of himself as a good person, but he strives to convince the very people whom he holds in contempt of the same thing. He has help in this, because there is a tendency on the part of others to resist seeing the criminal as he is. People would like to find the source of the problem *outside* the individual. The criminal knows this and takes full advantage of it.

Adults dismiss much of the delinquent's early crime as inconsequential. Even when he is caught, he initially is dealt with compassionately. Society is predisposed to find explanations, which then serve as excuses. In fact, there are those who believe that his crime is a normal response to his environment.

Sometimes, of course, a youth who has no criminal pattern makes an error in judgment and gets in trouble. Such a youngster learns from the experience and does not become a repeat offender. Just the humiliation and pain of getting caught is enough of a deterrent. But it also happens that youngsters who engage repeatedly in criminal behavior are perceived as troubled but still basically good. It is not just parents and mental health professionals who hold such a view, but educators, clergymen, social service workers, and even policemen and probation officers.

Fifteen-year-old Al, who had been roaming the streets stealing, drinking, using drugs, disrupting classes, and assaulting students, was evaluated by a school social worker and a school psychologist. The social worker regarded Al as suffering from "undue environmental stress" and "inappropriate role expectations." The psychologist said that his behavior was "most probably the result of a relatively impoverished home life and some learning difficulties." During my evaluation, Al displayed blatantly antisocial attitudes, which had been longstanding. He asserted, "If people mess with me too much, I'll hit 'em." He guessed that if he had been arrested for all his crimes he'd be locked up for two years. It is significant to note that in the same "impoverished home'' lived two sisters and one brother, none of whom had been in trouble.

Because he is a minor and the full extent of his criminality is not known, people are inclined to want to help, not punish kids like Al. Unless he has been charged with a major crime and is considered dangerous, the delinquent may be let off with a warning or placed on probation. If he consents to receive psychological treatment, the charge may be dropped.

The adult criminal also is given breaks unless he has committed a violent crime or has a long police record. Those who deal with him, be it family, friends, or strangers, frequently fail to penetrate his thicket of lies, vagueness, and self-serving statements. And so, criminals go on committing more crimes, all the while continuing to regard themselves as decent people. Whereas they offer all sorts of justifications to others, they justify nothing to themselves.

Chapter Eleven

The Conventional Wisdom: How Wise?

SPECULATION ABOUT the causes of crime is as old as speculation about the nature of man. Human nature does not change, but theories and public opinion do, and it is these that guide a society in dealing with its criminals. The European "classical school" of criminology in the eighteenth and early nineteenth centuries saw man as responsible for his acts. It was thought that breaking the law was a willful act and that an offender should therefore pay the price by being punished. This applied not only to the adult criminal but also to the juvenile offender, for children were essentially regarded as miniature adults. The focus of investigations by the "classicists" was on law enforcement procedures, the judicial process, and technique of management of offenders after they were incarcerated.

During the late nineteenth and early twentieth centuries,

the "positivists" in Europe began to broaden the scope of investigations into criminal behavior. (Prominent figures associated with this trend were Hans Gross in Austria and Franz Von Liszt in Germany.) These investigators began considering the role of forces both external to the individual and within his psyche. Institutes were established, one of the most notable being that founded in 1934 at Utrecht, Holland, which was affiliated with a clinic where psychiatrists, psychologists, social workers, and nurses were involved in observational and diagnostic procedures. The impact of the positivist movement was that social responsibility for crime was emphasized and free will negated, for the positivists contended that it was up to society to make man responsible. If a man committed a crime, it was largely owing to a failure of society.

Sociological explanations of crime have long been dominant in the United States. Practically nothing is exempt from the sociologist's claim that the environment causes crime: urban blight and poverty, surburban materialism, broken homes, unemployment, racism, peer pressure, schools, television, comic books, pornography, advertising, moral bankruptcy in the society at large, alienation produced by technology. The following statements, which span a 34-year period, are illustrative of the direct cause–effect relationship that is alleged to exist between particular social conditions and crime. A 1939 U.S. Housing Authority report quoted by Clinard asserted, "Substandard housing is the direct cause of delinquency and crime, and its elimination would result in a crimeless world."[1] In 1953, Wertham called comic books, "primers for crime."[2] Loth said in 1967 that intense suburban pressures for status drive youngsters "to go outside the law to obtain money and other things."[3] In a global indictment of social institutions, Goldenberg stated in 1973, "Juvenile delinquency is basically the product of inappropriate, malfunctioning, and otherwise nonactualizing social institutions."[4]

In their environmental explanations of criminal behavior, sociologists have all but omitted consideration of the individual himself and the free choices he makes.

For example, it has been observed that a disproportionate number of inmates in penal institutions are poor and from minority groups. According to 1979 Department of Justice figures, 50.3 percent of the inmates in state correctional facilities were nonwhite.[5] (In the federal institutions, approximately 38 percent are nonwhite.[6]) Twenty-two percent reported having no prearrest annual income, and 49.4 percent had an income of less than $10,000. What do these figures tell us? Nothing about the characteristics of the poor or of minorities either as groups or as individuals. What the statistics reflect is that our system of justice falls short of being just. The well-heeled and influential with their access to competent counsel are more likely to avoid winding up behind bars, whereas, according to Barbara Babcock, a former Department of Justice aide, "legal representation for indigent persons—especially those charged with serious violent crimes—tends to be a macabre joke."[7]

Sociologists can help in analyzing the operations of the criminal justice system, but their formulations about the causes of crime continue to be flawed and often misleading.

Sociologists have argued that it is the laws themselves that make a person a criminal. Dismissing the idea that there is a "criminal mind," they point out that a person may engage in an act that is legal in one state but be hauled off to jail in another for engaging in the same act. They assert there would be fewer criminals if laws were changed and certain offenses, such as gambling and prostitution, decriminalized. The problem with this approach is that there are people who will break laws, whatever they are. One criminal said that if rape were legalized, he would not rape, but "I'd do something else." What he meant was that it is the kick of breaking the law that mattered, whatever the particular law happened to be. To understand crime, one must focus on personality, not laws and social mores. Crime resides within the person, not the environment. There are people who will be exploitative, larcenous, and violent no matter what the laws are.

The preceding chapters have shown that criminals have a similar manner of viewing themselves, no matter whether they are poor or rich, black or white, educated or illiterate. Their minds work the same way, regardless of their social environment. When policy makers and those making decisions about individual criminals regard them as victims of forces outside themselves, they only provide criminals with excuses for crime and grant them license to commit more crimes.

In the 1980s, an era of relative conservatism, there is still wide acceptance of sociological theories of criminal behavior. In the 1981 book, *Crime and Modernization,* criminologist Louise Shelley states that world crime patterns are "an understandable reaction to the rapid social changes."[8] Dr. Shelley discusses the change in crime patterns as different parts of the world modernize. Seeking an understanding of variation in type and amount of crime that results from changing social conditions may have merit. But there is little in contemporary sociology or criminology that will explain the origins of crime that are within the individual.

People continue to believe that, if social conditions improve, there will be less crime. The 1960s saw a host of programs enacted to remedy social ills. A 1967 presidential commission prepared a report that is quoted even today. The commission declared, "Warring on poverty, inadequate housing, and unemployment is warring on crime. A civil rights law is a law against crime. Money for schools is money against crime."[9] Partly because of movements for social change in the 1960s, opportunities were expanded for jobs and education, much substandard housing was torn down, and schools became more accommodating to different types of students. Progress was made in civil rights with equal opportunity and affirmative action programs. In the

1970s, many proponents of these programs became disillusioned, if not cynical, because a noticeable reduction in crime did not seem to result from improving conditions of life for thousands of citizens. Also puzzling to policy makers was soaring crime among those who had had abundant economic and social opportunities. Discussing crime in the "privileged precincts" of Los Angeles, author Larry Cole made the grim observation, "If you think violent kids are all on the east and south side of town, you'd better take a look at who's living in the same house with you." Cole went on to point out that the suburban crime rate was outstripping that of the inner city.[10]

Changes in the environment have improved the quality of life for millions of citizens, but the criminal remains a criminal, wherever he lives. The fact that crime is not significantly reduced by social programs does not invalidate those programs. Nor does it absolve policy makers of responsibility for improving living standards for people who need help to better themselves.

Psychiatrists and psychologists have approached criminality differently from sociologists in that they are interested more in a person's mind than his environment. But they too stress the effect of environmental factors impinging on the individual, especially during his formative years. For generations before psychology gained a foothold, people believed that if a youngster is bad there must be something wrong with his parents. Psychological research seemed to support such thinking. An early instance of this was a book published in 1936. In *New Light on Delinquency and its Treatment,* William Healy and Augusta Bronner reported that youngsters turned to crime largely because of "deeply emotionally felt discomfort" stemming from a lack of "satisfying emotional relationships in [the] family circle."[11] The "new light" in the work was the focus on the family's role in crime causation. Their findings led them to assert that "reconstruction of the parental attitude" is mandatory "for the solution of the delinquent's problems.'' Today the belief persists that young-sters turn to crime because of psychological trauma and con-flict experienced at the hands of the parents.

Some mental health professionals think that the criminal cannot help doing what he does because of unconscious mo-tives that propel him into crime. They further contend that he is destined to persist in antisocial behavior, no matter how severely he is punished. In fact, it is argued that the punish-ment itself may be gratifying and reinforce him in com-mitting crimes. Thus did psychiatrist Karl Menninger conclude that in addition to punishment being futile, it is it-self a crime.[12]

Such a view, like that of the sociologists, is deterministic. It is essentially the position that the child enters the world much like a formless lump of clay to be molded by parents and later by society. This perspective is not only clinically unsound but has proved damaging. Psychologist Anneliese Korner wrote that the ''one-way street'' view of child rearing that emphasizes what the parent does to the child has ''helped create a generation of guilt-ridden parents.''[13] Re-search during the last decade has documented what every parent of more than one child senses: that children are born with different temperaments. From the cradle, the infant's temperament has a considerable impact on how his parents treat him. A mother or father responds differently to a coo-ing, contented baby than to an infant who is colicky and cranky. In other words, the child raises the parents as well as vice versa. No one knows why the criminal opposes the social order from an early age. No one has yet been successful in identifying the critical factors causal to criminality. Efforts to help criminals change have met with even less success.

To understand antisocial conduct, professionals in the mental health field frequently are guided by the extensive lit-erature on the psychopath (more recently termed the sociopath or antisocial personality). This has been mislead-ing because the description of the psychopath reveals mainly the effect he has on others and very little accurate information as to how his mind works. The psychopath is characterized as lacking a sense of responsibility, lacking the capacity to profit from experience, and lacking a conscience; he is impulsive, emotionally immature, grandiose and self-centered, and unable to experience guilt or form meaningful human relationships. Although diagnosticians may make distinctions between the psychopath and criminal, for all ostensible purposes, one differs hardly at all from the other. Clinical descriptions of the psychopath are incomplete and in some important ways erroneous.[14] For example, to say that a psychopath or criminal is unable to profit from experience is misleading because there is no such *incapacity*. He does learn from the past, but he learns what interests him, not what society wants him to learn. To call him impulsive is to assert that he lacks self-control, whereas he actually has a rational, calculating mind that is very much in control. Conscience is present and the criminal has moral values, but he shuts off his conscience long enough to do what he wants.

To say that the psychopath or criminal is self-centered is to state the obvious. But this feature does not stem from some inherent incapacity to put himself in the place of another person and form friendships. He is a master at putting himself in others' shoes when he plans a crime. But true friendship imposes obligation and putting others first in ways that are incompatible with his sense of his own importance.

One could ask, "If criminals aren't made, are they born?" The question of whether there is a "bad seed" or born criminal is unanswered for we just don't know enough about genetics. Hans Eysenck, a British psychologist, has stated that studies of twins and of offspring of criminal mothers suggest that heredity does play a strong role in a person's predisposition to commit crimes.[15] University of California psychologist Sarnoff Mednick cited evidence from his research on twins in Denmark, which indicates that genetic factors do predispose some people to criminal behavior. He found that children who are adopted are more like their natural than adoptive parents with respect to criminality. However, Mednick acknowledged that other variables such as social conditions and parenting play a role in whether the genetic predisposition actually results in the individual's committing crimes.[16]

Social scientists react to such findings skeptically and, in many instances, ignore or dismiss them. The genetic issue is a hot potato because of its Orwellian implications. In a column on Mednick's findings, journalist Joan Beck writes, "At worst, a gene-for-crime theory could tempt an unscrupulous political leader to link it with the growing popular fear of crime and terrorism and jump into a Nazi-style horror of compulsory behavior modification, concentration camps, and extermination of 'born criminals.' "[17] Since Mednick's findings, Dr. C. Robert Cloninger, professor of psychiatry and genetics at Washington University in St. Louis, (with his colleagues) discovered that children of petty criminals can inherit a tendency toward antisocial behavior.[18]

Physiological psychologists and biologists believe that we stand on the threshold of a new era as more and more is understood about our genetic and physical makeup. Some scientists report discovering, for example, physiological components of anger reactions, but they still don't know what makes a person a criminal.[19] Robert Hare and Janice Frazelle hypothesize that criminal psychopaths may differ from normal people "in the way in which brain functions are organized."[20] We are still a long way from solving the puzzle of causation. Certainly, research into a possible genetic contribution should be conducted, notwithstanding fears of the implications of possible findings.

Dazed and slurring his speech, Andy awoke at about noon in the emergency room of a psychiatric hospital. The night before he had gulped down sleeping pills and other medication that he found in the family medicine chest. At 19 he was "tired of life."

Andy was the next to last of four children from a troubled marriage that ended in divorce when he was 10. His mother, warm, stable, and intelligent, had tried to do everything possible to meet the emotional and material needs of her family. She recalled that, as a toddler, Andy was a whirlwind of activity, far more boisterous than his brother and two sisters. Although 18 months is a difficult age for many children and their mothers, Andy's behavior was extreme. He was restless, irritable, and, young as he was, unresponsive to adult supervision.

By the time he entered kindergarten, he kept the class in a turmoil as he wandered away from the group, darted out the door, disrupted activities, and picked on other children. In the first grade, he was unruly and lagged so far behind academically that his teacher recommended that he repeat the grade. However, the principal insisted upon his transfer to a school that offered special programs. This was the first of a long series of special programs and schools. But the environment seemed not to make a difference because, wherever he was, Andy just didn't learn.

At one clinic, Andy was diagnosed mentally retarded, and his obstreperous behavior was believed to have been caused by his frustration at having to compete with children who were much more capable. Andy's mother realized that her son was not learning, but yet she knew he was inquisitive and had an almost uncanny knack for sizing up situations and anticipating people's reactions. Refusing to believe that he was mentally retarded, she continued her quest to determine what was wrong. A doctor evaluated him as suffering from a lack of myelination of the nervous system and therefore as susceptible to being driven into a frenzy by even a low level of stimulation. (Myelin is a white, soft material, somewhat fatty, that forms a sheath around the core of a nerve fiber.) Following this diagnosis, Andy was withdrawn from school, and his mother paid a tutor to come to the home so that he could learn at his own pace and without the distractions of other children. Andy did concentrate somewhat better in the tutorial arrangement, but his behavior with other people was still intolerable. By provoking and intimidating his brother and sisters, he kept the household in an uproar. He seemed not to recognize rules and limits and would strike out on his own to do whatever he wanted, leaving the house to join older boys who also were having considerable difficulty with the adult world.

When Andy turned 11, conditions at home had changed and were more to his liking. His parents were divorced, and his mother had custody of all the children. She felt guilty because she believed that the marital difficulties had been especially troubling to Andy. Yet none of the other children was as emotionally unbalanced, and only Andy was stealing, fighting, and setting fires. His mother hoped that Andy would settle down now that her husband was out of the picture. Andy's father had not been a criminal, a drunk, or social misfit. Nor was he cruel to his family. It was a marriage in which each partner went his own way because they came to share little in common. After the divorce, Andy still was unmanageable. At her wits' end, his mother concluded that a total change of scene would be good for him.

When he turned 14, Andy went abroad to live with his father, who welcomed his son, despite his knowledge of the boy's severe problems at home. Andy seemed to thrive in the new setting, but the calm did not last. Andy began exploring uncharted territory, roaming the streets, shoplifting, receiving stolen goods, and stealing bicycles and motorcycles. Andy was ready for any new kick, and so it took no enticement by others for him to turn to drugs. With his growing immersion in the drug world, there were larger and more daring thefts and growing homosexual and heterosexual promiscuity. Finally, Andy's luck ran out, and at age 16 he was apprehended for a break-in that had netted him several thou-

sand dollars' worth of jewels. He spent the next year in a reformatory for teenage boys. A baby-faced, slender teenager
with a soft voice and pleasant manner, Andy was solicited for
sex almost as soon as he walked in the door. He didn't have
to be forced into it; he was eager for any kind of action.

Released at 18, Andy returned to his father's home, but he
rarely spent a night there. He found that selling his body to
men could gain him a lot more than an orgasm and some
money in his wallet. Homosexual prostitution (although he
didn't consider it prostitution) introduced him to a whole
new world. With his lithe, youthful body, easygoing manner, and engaging sense of humor, he had his pick of clientele. He chose the richest and ended up sharing luxurious
penthouses, dining in fancy restaurants, gaining entrance to
the poshest clubs, and occupying front row seats in theaters
and concert halls. For a while, Andy lived with a rock star
who had him chauffeured around town in a Rolls Royce and
kept him well supplied with drugs and anything else he
wanted. It didn't take long for Andy to grow accustomed to
this way of life and expect nothing but the finest. However,
even these indulgences seemed like nothing special after a
year. Andy figured that there must be more to living.

Eager for a new scene, he decided to return to the United
States, where his mother offered to help him get a fresh start.
No sooner had he moved into her house than he plunged into
the drug world but refrained from returning to his other
criminal patterns. Instead, he became intrigued with a
group that was involved in Far Eastern religion. For several
months, he was absorbed by this novel experience and
stayed out of trouble with the police. However, something
was missing, and Andy grew increasingly anxious and despondent. He thought about going straight, even giving up
drugs, but he couldn't see himself putting up with the routine, the obligations, the demands. Yet he did not want to go
back to crime because he had broken his mother's heart too
often and had spent more than enough time in prison. Often

he thought about ending it all because no solution seemed acceptable. In desperation one night, he swallowed pills and landed in the hospital. Andy's mother saw no alternative but to have him committed for psychiatric treatment.

Andy was interviewed and tested by the hospital's clinical staff. His IQ was 99, placing him in the average range of intelligence. He was diagnosed as suffering from a longstanding schizophrenic disorder. His thinking was considered irrational because, in the words of the examiner, he "unrealistically linked up events and ideas." He was placed on medication often dispensed to psychotic patients.

Andy recovered quickly from his depression, thought treatment was a farce, and was determined to put as much distance between himself and the hospital as possible. He became a model patient so he could earn privileges to leave the ward without accompaniment. One day, he strolled down the hall to the snack bar but kept right on going out the front door. It was mid-winter and, liking his comforts, Andy found hitchhiking in the cold and being broke too rugged. In St. Louis, he was arrested for vagrancy and, not unwillingly, was escorted by a marshal back to the hospital. Again, he impressed the staff with his insight and good behavior, but this time he waited until spring before taking off for California. The hospital decided not to pursue him, entered a release on his chart, and thus did not notify the police of his escape. Having arrived in San Francisco, Andy wrote his therapist one night when he was "stoned" on speed, lamenting his return to his old ways: "It's the same old thing. I do real great. Then I fall in a hole." Several months after that, the therapist received an inquiry from the state of California asking if Andy was eligible for public support on the grounds that he was psychologically unfit for work. Although the therapist responded in the negative, somehow Andy succeeded in having his welfare application approved.

All his life, Andy had frustrated and puzzled parents, teachers, and others who came into contact with him. They differed greatly in their explanations of his enormous energy, incessant activity, apparent intellectual slowness, severe interpersonal conflicts, antisocial activities, and sporadic depressions. In fact, Andy had received almost as many different diagnoses as there were experts who had evaluated him: mental retardation, an adjustment reaction to the instability of a broken home, hyperactivity, a neurological deficiency, an impulse disorder, latent schizophrenia, and psychopathy. Andy's criminality was seen as a desperate attempt to strike back at a world that had shunned him and made him an outcast—a world that he, in turn, had come to distrust and hate.

None of these theories held water. Even though one clinician found him so lacking in basic information as to merit the diagnosis of mental retardation, those who knew how Andy outwitted others were astute enough not to believe it. The diagnosis of a neurological impairment resulted in no specific treatment and led others to expect little of him because they thought he was a victim of a permanent disability. Hyperactivity was a label pinned on him simply because he was restless and hard to manage. He was placed on medication for a while but showed no improvement. If Andy's wreaking havoc was an adjustment reaction to his parents' conflict, it was a reaction totally different from that of his siblings and cannot be explained by the home situation alone. Antisocial as he was, rather than being shunned by society, Andy was deluged with concern and assistance. But he turned his back on parents, schoolteachers, private tutors, social workers, and therapists.

Far from being at the mercy of uncontrollable impulses, Andy engaged in a series of calculated, complex schemes and became a slick operator. He was totally in contact with reality, knew the difference between right and wrong, and when the time came, was able to assist in his own legal defense. Yet he was termed schizophrenic.

* * *

There are many Andys with whom few people achieve the desired results. This is often because they fail to grasp how such a person's mind works. As in Andy's case, the professionals have a multitude of theories and explanations about *why* he is the way he is, but these do not lead to effective solutions, and many turn out to be misleading. So busy were the doctors and other professionals trying to *explain* Andy's behavior that they never understood his view of the world. No one even referred to Andy as a human being who made choices. Instead, he was regarded as a victim of the environment or of a physical abnormality.

Depth psychology, effective in its analysis of many troubled individuals, is not as successful in unraveling the complex personalities of criminals. A major reason for this was discussed earlier (Chapter Eight), namely, that psychiatrists and psychologists derive their clinical data from a highly unreliable source—the criminal. A master at feeding others what he wants them to know, the criminal carefully tailors his account to provide what he hopes will be a convincing account of *why* he did what he did. However, it is an after-the-fact explanation that is self-serving and has little to do with what was in his mind before, during, and after the crime.

Another reason that criminals like Andy are not understood is that those who evaluate them use interviewing techniques that are appropriate for many types of clients or patients but are counterproductive when utilized with criminals. While providing some information, conventional mental status examinations and psychological tests reveal little about the criminal's view of himself and the world. Questions that are aimed at constructing a psychodynamic understanding of underlying motives give the criminal an opportunity to offer any justification that he wants.

Perhaps the most formidable barrier in trying to understand a criminal is that people approach the task with a set of theories and concepts that simply do not apply to criminals, although they may apply to other types of individuals. In fact, in my days as a psychoanalytically oriented psychologist, I totally missed the boat in evaluating delinquent kids. In one instance, I wrote an article for a professional journal about Paul, a 15-year-old adolescent patient whom I treated on a university hospital psychiatric unit.[21] That case shows how easy it is to develop a misconception about a person even when one acts in good faith to apply the diagnostic tools he has been trained to use.

I assumed that Paul's truancy, shoplifting, drug abuse, and car theft were symptoms of a deep underlying personality conflict. I thought that a major source of anxiety and trauma had been that Paul's parents had defaulted on a promise years earlier to arrange for him to have an operation to bring down an undescended left testicle. I wrote in my case summary, "Paul had been unsuccessful in getting the help he wanted with his undescended testicle. In time, he lost faith in adults' ability to be gratifying or stand for anything. His attitude was to get away with things until he was forced to quit, and then to turn to something different." In other words, I regarded Paul's delinquent acts as symptomatic of his frustration about the undescended testicle. During Paul's psychiatric hospitalization, he requested and had an operation in which the undescended testicle, which had atrophied, was removed and a prosthesis was inserted into the scrotum. I wrote: "The 'ultimate deception' was no more. The operation had been promised to Paul by his therapist, and it had occurred." Thus the expectation that he would no longer act out his frustration and anger about this matter. For a while, Paul's behavior on the unit did improve, but this was only temporary. The last I heard was that after Paul had been discharged from the hospital, he became involved in more serious crimes, including possession and use of a firearm.

As I look back, I recognize that there was nothing in my entire report that shed light on the boy's antisocial behavior, nothing about his delight in deception, his search for kicks, his belief that the world was his chessboard. In fact, this evaluation could as well have described a neurotic adolescent with little inclination to commit crimes.

The appeal of psychodynamic psychology is that it seems to offer answers. After the fact, it can explain anything. The human mind desires closure and especially to make sense out of what appears senseless. Unfortunately, it is not so simple. As it has turned out, conventional theories from modern depth psychology are largely irrelevant or misleading in understanding the criminal. Ultimately, it is more important and beneficial to piece together the structure of his thinking, to understand his world, to grasp what makes life meaningful for him. Probing and then reporting on an offender's *thinking* about himself and the world can be of inestimable value to a judge, probation officer, or anyone else who will make decisions about him. Such an approach is of far greater value than the traditional expedition into the criminal's past to dredge up an explanation of what might have caused him to do what he did.

During most of the twentieth century, theories about crime and attempts at crime reduction have been deeply rooted in beliefs about causality. Those who have thought that the environment causes crime have recommended changes in the environment as remedial and preventive. Some searched for answers in psychology, believing that the individual rather than the environment must be the focus. Their thinking, however, was that criminality was a *symptom* of a deeper maladjustment and that it could be treated like other emotional disorders and problems of living. Psychological concepts and techniques that were effective in treating disturbed but responsible patients were utilized in clinical work with criminals. Hanging on to beliefs about root causes as an approach to reducing crime has resulted in an enormous waste of resources. The guiding conventional wisdom, based on concepts of causality, has not altered a situation in which the nation's prisons bulge and citizens are prisoners in their own homes.

Chapter Twelve

Coping with Criminals: Dusty Trails and Dead Ends

EFFORTS TO help criminals become responsible often have failed because they have been based on shopworn and inapplicable theories, ingrained preconceptions, myths, fads, and emotion. Because so many people in the criminal justice system and in the community at large do not understand how criminals think, they have slavishly followed dusty old trails or else all too rapidly dashed down unexplored paths that resulted in a dead end. Punishment and rehabilitation both have failed to reform criminals. Rehabilitative programs have been rooted in theories about crime causation instead of in an understanding of how criminals think. Based on erroneous premises and misconceptions, rehabilitation's failure was inevitable. However, this does not mean that criminals cannot change. There are times when they are open to making far-reaching changes. What has been miss-

191

ing is an accurate conception of the scope of the task of change and the tools to effect change.

In the wake of the failure to rehabilitate or successfully deter criminals through punishment, society has become polarized between the so-called bleeding hearts who want to help the criminal and the so-called law and order forces who want to lock him up for long time periods and forget him. Former U.S. Attorney General Ramsey Clark has said that society must rehabilitate criminals, not punish them. He declared, "Rehabilitation must be the goal of modern corrections. Every other consideration should be subordinated to it."[1] Representing the opposite point of view, syndicated columnist Max Rafferty stated that "retribution and restraint seem to be the only answers."[2]

What does the criminal think about this? He regards punishment as unjust because it interferes with the life he wants to lead. He is restricted, although not totally stopped, from pursuing the triumphs and conquests that nourish his self-image. While he is behind bars, society is protected. But some argue that he becomes hardened and more of a public enemy in the long run. As I pointed out earlier (Chapter Nine), imprisonment does not alter a criminal's basic personality. Whether he is on the streets or in prison, he develops contacts, learns new tricks of the trade, and passes on a few tips of his own to others. Both the streets and correctional facilities are schools for crime. Although one 30 year old said to me, "Incarceration has given me the credits to become a teacher of crime," he was already quite knowledgeable in that area before he was ever behind bars.

For some offenders who have not made crime a way of life, prison has a deterrent effect in that once they are released from custody they refrain from committing new crimes. But for the chronic offender, confinement is simply an interruption or a time-out from his customary activities.

The terms "corrections" and "reformatory" suggest that the criminal justice system intends to correct and reform.

But since the early 1970s, a deep pessimism has spread with respect to the feasibility of rehabilitating criminals. The person most often cited as the bearer of the tidings that "nothing works" is the late Robert Martinson. This researcher's conclusion was based on his extensive review of reports on programs that attempted to rehabilitate criminals. Martinson summarized his findings as follows: "With few and isolated exceptions, the rehabilitative efforts that have been reported so far have no appreciable effect on recidivism."[3] Five years later, a National Academy of Sciences panel asserted, "The promise of the rehabilitative ideal makes the debate about rehabilitation one of the most important of our time." But the panel sounded a somber note when it declared, "There is not now in the scientific literature any basis for any policy or recommendations regarding rehabilitation of criminal offenders."[4]

Attempts to discredit rehabilitation did not totally succeed. In 1973, a national commission stated that offenders had a "right" to rehabilitation programs,[5] a point of view widely held among people who deal with offenders on a daily basis in the courts, in institutions, in schools, and in the community. This is especially true in the area of juvenile justice. America is reluctant to give up on its youth, to write off any youngster as a hopeless delinquent or a criminal. Even citizens of the conservative state of Texas recently indicated that they believed that rehabilitation is a legitimate function of prison. Questioned in a survey as to what they think the main purpose of prison should be, Texans were equally divided between rehabilitation and punishment.[6] In the early 1980s, top policy makers had not abandoned rehabilitation. Edwin Meese, counselor to President Reagan, said in a 1981 newspaper interview, "Now, there are some who believe there is no hope of rehabilitation. I don't believe that. I believe there is some percentage—and no one knows for sure what it is—of those who've been convicted of a crime that, given the right kind of assistance and treatment, will never commit another crime.''[7]

The thousands of correctional counselors, case workers, educators, vocational teachers, and mental health professionals in both juvenile and adult institutions consider themselves to be more than custodians of a warehouse. Most prisons and psychiatric facilities for criminals offer inmates a variety of programs. Some are mere time fillers, but most claim to prepare the criminal to reenter society. What is being done today in the name of ''rehabilitation''?

Vocational training is given top priority by many in corrections, their rationale being that a person without job skills will continue to prey upon society because he is locked out of a legitimate way to earn a living.[8] In some institutions, work experience is limited to prison industries where inmates make items such as license plates, prison clothing, or institutional furniture. Other institutions hire special teachers and purchase elaborate equipment so inmates can learn a trade, such as carpentry or auto mechanics, or a skill such as typing. At the ''Wynne Unit'' in Huntsville, Texas, more than 500 inmates are being trained to operate thousands of dollars' worth of information processing equipment so that they can then process motor vehicle title transfers and other records for state agencies. Local correctional facilities, such as jails, permit inmates to hold jobs outside the institution. Generally, penal institutions keep a tight rein on the inmates, even making spot checks during the day as to their whereabouts. But work-release programs are criticized severely whenever inmates take liberties with the lack of supervision and are caught committing crimes while they are supposed to be on the job.

Cynics may contend that the criminal sees vocational training only as a way to impress others and earn his way out of confinement. Even though this is often so, it is no indictment of job training. If a criminal lacks job skills, there is every reason to help him acquire them. But the result of doing *only* that is a criminal with job skills rather than a criminal without them. He remains a criminal with the same patterns of thinking and behavior that he had before.

Proponents of prison education assert that without remedial instruction, inmates who can't read and write will remain barred from opportunities to achieve any legitimate success and, consequently, out of frustration, will continue their criminal careers. Institutions offer a range of services, from individual tutoring in basic reading skills to permitting inmates to attend college classes on a nearby campus. With time on their hands, some inmates are eager to further their education. Teachers find them rewarding to work with because they are bright and, when motivated, learn rapidly, mastering in months what they failed to grasp in years.[9] Some inmates find the educational program inherently worthwhile, whereas others are interested mainly in impressing the staff or avoiding more disagreeable tasks. Those who attend classes outside the institution may exploit the opportunity in the same manner that fellow inmates misuse work-release—committing crimes outside prison walls and importing contraband upon their return. A high school diploma or other educational achievement does not alter a person's criminal life style. He simply becomes a more educated criminal who later may utilize his new knowledge to stake out new territory for crime.

Teaching inmates how to get along with other people has long been a rehabilitative objective. A Canadian report on prisons suggested, "Inmates should spend as much time as possible outside their cells and in general have conditions of socialization as much like those of the outside community as possible."[10] To that end, attempts are made to teach social skills and interpersonal awareness. These programs are intended both to help the inmate adjust to confinement and to develop skills he can use outside. Courses such as nutrition and money management are designed primarily to prepare him to reenter the community. In 1979, California's Atascadero State Hospital for mentally ill offenders offered to its approximately 1,000 patients instruction in self-government, assertiveness training, interpersonal communications, community planning, and ethnic projects.[11] Counterparts to these programs exist in prisons around the country, although it is perhaps unusual for one institution to offer so many. Because inmates are isolated from the community, the community comes to the inmates. More than a quarter-million volunteers throughout the nation are demonstrating that they care about prisoners.[12] They establish relationships through tutoring, counseling, coaching sports, coordinating social events, and providing cultural enrichment. To inspire civil concern and leadership, community organizations such as the Jaycees invite inmates to become members of prison chapters.

Those who would help the criminal become a social being assume that although his needs are the same as those of most people, he does not know how to fulfill them in a socially acceptable manner. Programs are designed to teach offenders "the importance of interpersonal relationships as a source of happiness, enrichment, and satisfaction."[13] Although this is a worthy objective, it is totally misdirected when geared to the criminal, who has a very different set of needs. "Happiness" is the charge he gets from knocking off a bank, the kick out of cracking a safe, the thrill of incinerating a building. The "enrichment" he seeks from relationships is profit through a con game. "Satisfaction," if it is ever experienced, is the short-lived flush of triumph felt after a "big score." Criminals may find human relations classes an agreeable way to pass the time, but to teach a criminal social skills without addressing lifelong thinking patterns is as useless as pouring a delectable sauce over a slice of burnt, rancid meat.

Whenever parents, teachers, and others who have close contact with a criminal discover that he has a special talent, they seize upon it and hope that its cultivation will be the key to the criminal's reforming. In school, an art teacher may believe that if a talented delinquent pupil expresses himself through painting he will no longer resort to crime. A shop teacher who recognizes a criminal's knack for high-quality woodworking may encourage him to make it his life's calling. In confinement, the same thing often happens.

The prisons are bulging with talent. Millions of dollars are spent on programs designed to discover and nurture the inmate's creative potential. It is reasoned that he will think more highly of himself and, in the process, discover a constructive and rewarding hobby, perhaps even a full-time occupation.[14] The "Theater Without Bars" in Trenton, New Jersey, purported to provide inmates "redirection to their lives" by uncovering and changing their attitudes through a program of acting workshops.[15]

The short-term outcome of such endeavors may be positive. Programs that occupy inmates constructively reduce tension and contribute to a better institutional climate. But neither artistic accomplishment nor a green thumb significantly alter a criminal's outlook on life. In the unlikely event that he channels his talents into a full-time occupation, he remains without integrity and thus a crooked artist or gardener.[16]

That criminals pervert the use of their talents and skills is graphically illustrated in the story of flourishing capitalism at the Maine State Prison. In that relatively small maximum security institution (about 370 inmates), the fashioning of handicrafts and novelty items was big business, with sales in 1979 exceeding a half-million dollars. But an outside team evaluating the prison found that the institution's social structure was dominated by this business and that the prisoners controlled the institution. According to the evaluators, a few powerful inmates exploited the labor of others and the strong intimidated the weak. The enterprise has been drastically curtailed.[17]

Because criminality has been seen as symptomatic of an

underlying psychological disturbance, psychotherapy has been utilized as another rehabilitative tool in institutions. (The techniques are virtually identical to those used in treating responsible people who have a wide range of emotional disorders.) Treatment is expensive, and there appears to be greater reliance on it with juveniles than with adults. According to government figures, an institutional psychotherapy program for juveniles costs $28,000 per year per youngster.[18] In institutions, group therapy is offered more extensively than individual therapy because of the prospect of harnessing peer pressure as a positive force for change.

Because intensive individual psychiatric treatment is time-consuming and very expensive, it has never been widely available to offenders, even to those who have been patients in psychiatric hospitals. The "rational" therapies developed in the 1960s have been more practical and efficient and require far less staff training than does psychodynamic psychotherapy.

In 1965, the book *Reality Therapy: A New Approach to Psychiatry* was published. Its author, Dr. William Glasser, introduced a radical departure from the then still prevalent psychoanalytically oriented psychotherapy. Teaching responsibility was the objective, and Glasser considered it unproductive to dig into the past for causes. Mental illness was discarded as a concept, and Glasser emphasized "the morality of behavior." Since Glasser, other "rational" therapies have been developed, including "rational-emotive therapy" by Albert Ellis, "rational-behavioral therapy" by Maxie Maultsby, and cognitive therapies by A. T. Beck and D. H. Meichenbaum. All of these have provided a welcome alternative to the time-consuming, costly, and often unproductive procedures of psychoanalysis. These approaches have been utilized with a wide variety of patients, including criminals. The originators of these new therapies seemed to fail to recognize that the criminal is almost like a different breed of person. Glasser said, for example, "Children want to become responsible," and in most instances he is right. The criminal is an exception. So there is an erroneous premise from the outset. Glasser further stated that people learn responsibility "through involvements with responsible fellow human beings, preferably loving parents."[19] But criminals who had loving parents nevertheless rejected both the parents and their teachings and chose to live irresponsibly.

The new therapies are an improvement on past practices in that criminals are not given the convenient "out" of delving into the past to dig up excuses for current behavior. But they do not get down to basics and succeed in helping the criminal alter his view of himself and change his life objectives. In fact, he is able to pervert the treatment and become a more accomplished criminal.

The National Academy of Science panel that I referred to earlier in this chapter stated what has not been recognized until very recently: "The Panel believes that the magnitude of the task of reforming criminal offenders has been consistently underestimated. It is clear that far more intensive and extensive interventions will be required if rehabilitation is to be possible."[20] The rational therapies are not powerful enough tools.

In all correctional facilities, the staff rewards desirable behavior and ignores or punishes that which is undesirable. When the approach is dressed up in the psychological language of "behavior modification," it is still centuries-old reward and punishment but with an attempt to be consistent. The inmate earns points for cleaning his living area, completing other chores, going to his job assignment or school, and participating in activities. Points are converted into privileges, which permit the inmate increased amounts of freedom. The criminal finds this one of the easiest systems to exploit because he does not have to guess what the staff or therapist wants. Because behavior modification programs spell out expectations, compliance is easy, provided he does not balk at doing things on others' terms. At best, behavior modification results in token temporary changes by the criminal. The staff has less trouble with him, and he earns his privileges. Still, he remains a criminal.

Perhaps the most candid type of statement about the effectiveness of current psychological methods was made by Dr. William Dobbs, a former director of the criminal psychiatry division at Saint Elizabeths Hospital, the federal institution in Washington, D.C. "I'm not convinced," said Dr. Dobbs, "for whatever it's worth that any approach we have—that we really do that much to change people, that we have the tools we need."[21]

"Jailing is costly. Its benefits are few," states a 1977 report issued by the National Institute of Law Enforcement and Criminal Justice.[22] Community corrections is regarded as not only less expensive but more humane because, instead of being caged with others like himself, the criminal can be "reintegrated" into the mainstream of society.

The desire to find alternatives to full-time incarceration has given rise to a proliferation of community programs. Halfway houses have been established for offenders as a transition between prison and freedom. Community facilities offer offenders adult education, vocational training, and psychotherapy and counseling. The 1970s saw the innovation of releasing the offender on condition that he make restitution directly to the victim or perform services for the community, such as driving for the handicapped, painting a housing project, or helping run a youth club.

Actually, the concept of community corrections is not new. Since the late nineteenth century, offenders have been placed on probation and allowed to live in society provided that they report at regular intervals to a probation officer.[23] As of June 30, 1980, there were 64,450 offenders on probation in the federal system alone.[24] Community correctional programs are available to the serious offender after he has served a portion of his sentence and is released from prison on parole. Probation and parole are designed to keep track of offenders and in some cases to counsel them. But in many communities probation and parole have no teeth; they are hardly an inconvenience to the offender, much less a sanction. A half-hour appointment every other week (or even less often) hardly provides enough time for an overburdened probation or parole officer to complete paperwork, much less hold a meaningful discussion. Some probation officers with active caseloads of 200 or more have so little contact with their clients that they would not recognize many of them if they saw them on the street.

Repaying the victim or public service work may be court-ordered as a condition of probation and an alternative to serving a sentence. Restitution programs may have deterrent value for some offenders who have to labor many weeks to compensate their victims. But how does a criminal who is a rapist, bank robber, or arsonist who sets a multimillion-dollar fire make restitution? For the repeat offender, it is possible that making restitution will have an effect opposite to what is intended. The criminal does not regard the victim as a victim at all. *He,* himself, is the victim for having been caught. Compensating a person whom society claims is a victim may bolster his already elevated view of himself as a decent person and thereby give him even greater license for crime.

Restitution may leave the victim better off. Thus the fact that the chronic offender is unlikely to be deterred or rehabilitated is by no means reason to discard restitution altogether. However, it argues for selectivity in its application. The shortcomings lie not with restitution or for that matter with any other program but rather with its sponsors' unrealistic expectations of its power to change criminals. Like the institutional programs described above, many community correctional programs help criminals acquire skills or pay a debt to society, but they have very little effect on how they live their lives.

Eighteen-year-old Frank was on probation for unauthorized use of a motor vehicle. He had not been caught for a string of other car thefts, shoplifting, and drug use. Even he admitted that he had a "rotten temper" that had resulted in vicious assaults, especially when he was drinking. Having just graduated from high school, Frank wanted his own apartment because he was fed up with his parents telling him what to do. He was eager to work because "I like to spend money." After being fired from three jobs, he was unemployed for several weeks, maintaining that he could not find a job "where I'd feel right." Frank had turned down waiter, fast-food cook, and other positions that didn't "feel right" because he considered them beneath him.

Frank decided that a job training program was the path to high earnings and persuaded a high school counselor to refer him to the Department of Vocational Rehabilitation. The state was willing to foot the bill for the training if a case could be made that Frank had a "diagnosable emotional disability." Frank was referred to me for an assessment. In my report, I concluded, "The Division of Vocational Rehabilitation would be wasting its time and resources by offering Frank opportunities that others would better utilize." I then predicted, "Frank might begin job training with enthusiasm, but become bored and disenchanted. Competing desires for excitement might result in his quitting. This is not a young man with serious ambitions to launch a career and lead a responsible life. There is no diagnosable emotional disturbance." Because one of the people at DVR who knew Frank insisted that he deserved a chance, he was accepted.

Sure enough, after initial enthusiasm, Frank lost interest, became irregular in his attendance, and finally dropped out. Meanwhile, he was continuing to use drugs and was arrested for possession of a substantial quantity of marijuana. His probation period was extended for that offense. He knew he had to work and couldn't afford to be too choosy as to where. Immediately he got a job at a restaurant, where things went well until he was accused of stealing from the cash register and was fired. Frank's probation officer never knew of this because management did not press charges. Not wanting to endanger his probation, Frank quickly landed a job as a stockboy in a supermarket. As soon as he set aside several hundred dollars, Frank purchased a car but eventually defaulted on the payments. As long as he was working and avoided arrest, he remained in good standing with the probation officer, whom he saw once a month for 30 minutes. However, his drug use and drinking continued, and he was still stealing.

Because Frank hadn't raped or murdered anyone, he appeared to be a suitable candidate for community corrections. However, community programs do not help offenders like Frank make fundamental and lasting changes. But neither does prison.

Writing in *Corrections Magazine,* John Blackmore said that community corrections had consisted of a "shotgun approach" of establishing projects here and there. He called for new, carefully planned and coordinated programs.[25] Community corrections has a major challenge. Rather than continue to offer palliative and superficial measures, community corrections must offer well-thought-out programs that will equip criminals with a new set of concepts that correct lifelong patterns of thought and action. In the long run, this will be less costly than building more prisons.

Unless criminals are serving terms of life without parole, which very few do, they will be free eventually to prey upon us all. There is still a job for corrections to do in the institution and the community—that is to correct. But rehabilitation as it has been practiced cannot possibly be effective because it is based on a total misconception. To rehabilitate is to restore to a former constructive capacity or condition. *There is nothing to which to rehabilitate a criminal.* There is no earlier condition of being responsible to which to restore him. He never learned the ways of getting along in this world that most of us learned as children. Just as rehabilitation is a misconception, so too is the notion of "reintegrating the criminal into the community." It is absurd to speak of reintegrating him when he was never integrated in the first place. The criminal has long stood apart from the community, contemptuous of people who lived responsibly.

That one can engage in "career planning" with an unchanged criminal is still another misconception and results in an enormous waste of time and resources. A counselor discusses career alternatives in terms of skills, aptitudes, and interests that develop over a lifetime, whereas the criminal is thinking quite differently. Behind a criminal's seemingly sensible discussion of his career plans lie unrealistic expectations and colossal pretensions. Before he attends his first job training class, he envisions himself the top man in the program and later on the job. He is already spending his earnings before he acquires any proficiency. Career planning is futile until the criminal sees himself more realistically and develops a set of attitudes basic to getting along with people in any kind of work. Of what use to an employer is a skilled employee who flares up at the slightest criticism, refuses to take orders, and is erratic in attendance? (I wish I could say you can identify that rare prisoner who can go "legitimate" with proper career training, but I can't—because I haven't met one yet.)

Some people in the criminal justice system and in the community at large think that to help a criminal change means to induce him to give up crime. The 1973 National Advisory Commission on Criminal Justice Standards and Goals articulates the major objective as "motivating [the criminal] to refrain from breaking the law."[26] But to conceive of the task in this limited way is like calling a patient healthy when two cancerous kidneys are removed, and he is offered no transplant. If a criminal gives up crime, what will replace it?

Change demands more than keeping his hands off others' property or his fly zipped. It requires giving up a whole way of life. Rehabilitation specialists recognize that the criminal must be offered an alternative. They endeavor to provide him with opportunities for "success experiences," which they think he has been denied in the past.[27] This too is a misconception. The criminal doesn't think he's a failure except when he gets caught for a crime. If he failed at school, work, and elsewhere, it is because of choices that he made. It is not his self-esteem that needs building. He is not a shy, neurotic individual who feels he can't do anything right. Rather, he thinks of himself as an exceptional person who is superior to others. If people want to pat him on the back as he learns new skills and does what he is supposed to, that is fine with him. While receiving praise for success in their programs, he is scheming his next holdup or thinking about where to find the best heroin.

The criminal may convince others that he has one special problem with which he needs help. One mother said of her son, "Paul has no larceny in his heart. He just has a drug problem." She had no idea that Paul had been breaking and entering long before he ever touched drugs and that drugs gave him courage to commit armed robberies. Sometimes a criminal convinces himself that he'd straighten out if he could resolve one problem. He may genuinely desire to cut back on his drinking, stop using hard drugs, or control his temper better. "My drinking governs my whole attitude toward life, myself, and the world," declared one gunman. If a counselor concentrates on a single problem such as alcohol consumption, he is only beginning to deal with a criminal's irresponsibility. In fact, if a counselor can get the criminal to stay off the bottle, he may inadvertently help him become more adept in crime, for if the criminal stops drinking, his judgment and coordination are better. Similarly, if a criminal is detoxified and stays off narcotics, he doesn't run the risks in the drug world of dealing with shady characters, buying contaminated drugs, or worrying about dosage and physical side effects.

Many states have sexual psychopath statutes and conse-quently make special provision for psychological treatment of sex offenders. Counseling or therapy frequently focuses on sex-related problems, a practice comparable to spraying one leaf of a philodendron to cure a totally bug-infested plant. A rape or child molestation is a dot on the landscape of the criminal's irresponsibility. Psychologists have developed methods of conditioning sexual responses of offenders. While the offender views slides of deviant sex acts, his erec-tion is registered by a gauge attached to his penis. As he gets aroused by the slides, an aversive stimulus is introduced, such as a shock, loud noise, or foul odor.[28] Consequently, just the thought of the deviant act becomes an adverse stimu-lus. Even if one conditioned a criminal so that deviant sex behavior no longer appealed to him, that would not stop him from injuring people in other ways. Sex is only one outlet for the excitement that he seeks at the expense of other people. Issues even more basic than sexual orientation or specific sexual practices must be addressed.

Not only is there a conventional wisdom about causation of crime and treatment of criminals, but there is also a con-ventional wisdom about how to tell whether a program is successful. Assessment of change is sometimes based on ob-servations of the criminal's adjustment to institutional life. An environment may be offered in which criminals find it worthwhile to abide by the rules and participate coopera-tively, even enthusiastically, in programs and activities. If you were an observer in such a situation, you might be so impressed by the normalcy of the residents' behavior that you would wonder why they are confined at all.

On one offender treatment unit, I saw residents who were well-groomed, neatly dressed, polite, highly involved in treatment, and productively occupied throughout the entire day. They also seemed to discuss problems with considerable frankness during their therapy groups. In reality, the residents had adapted to their environment, but their outlook on life was little different from what it had been on the street. In fact, I heard one patient proclaim that his life prior to confinement was "exciting and exhilarating." He said that in this program he would "take my classes, become more sociable, and increase my awareness in some areas." Finally, he declared, "My intention is to be a higher plane criminal, more of a white collar type." Upon hearing this, another fellow confessed, "There isn't a day that goes by that I don't think to myself, 'I'm here picking up things to tighten my game up.' It's what I did in the last place. I just try to keep things positive as much as I can." These revelations, unusual only because they were so explicit, underscore the peril of equating compliance with inner change. When a criminal voices intentions to change but simply adapts to confinement, a corrosion in his attitude and behavior will occur once he is released if not before. Furthermore, successful adaptation to a highly regimented environment does not necessarily prepare a person to cope responsibly with the pressures and temptations of the real world.

Recidivism is the major measure of change.[29] Although the term generally means "the repetition of criminal behavior," [30] it most frequently refers to rearrest. Reliance on arrest statistics is heavy because these are not subjective appraisals and can be readily obtained from official sources. Statistics, however, do not show how the criminal is living his life. They reveal nothing of his honesty, his dependability, his decision making, or his concern for other people. Throughout his life, the criminal has always gotten away with far more than has been discovered. After a taste of prison, he may become shrewder and more cautious, but he continues his exploitative way of life and commits crimes. Recidivism statistics indicate only whether he has been careless enough to be caught.

Combating crime is a multibillion-dollar undertaking. According to a 1980 survey, there were 829 federal justice agencies and 55,279 state and local criminal justice agencies. The total expenditure for the entire criminal justice system—federal, state, and local—in fiscal 1979 was close to $25.8 billion.[31] Yet, despite this massive outlay of funds, nothing so far seems to be effective in helping criminals change.

The dismal failure of one program after another has left the public in a quandary. Citizens clamor, "lock 'em up and throw away the key." Yet they deplore the criminal emerging from custody totally unchanged, ready to resume his preying upon society. Is it fair to conclude that criminals, by nature, are unchangeable just because efforts to help them change have so far been unsuccessful? This, too, would be a misconception.

The criminal has periods when he becomes fed up with himself and wants to straighten out and start a new life. He is sick of running, looking over his shoulder, and disappointing and injuring those who care for him. He has neglected and exploited his family as well as many others.

Lloyd, 22, had committed many crimes but never served a day in jail. Still, as he perceived his life going to pieces, he was becoming increasingly apprehensive. He had lost job after job, his girlfriend was on the verge of leaving, friends had deserted him, and his family was ready to disown him. Lloyd wrote a letter to me in which he said, "I am completely estranged from my family and girlfriend. I realize that I don't have friends because I treat them irresponsibly. I stopped collecting unemployment, determined to change, and am now nonarrestable. My working hours have increased, and I am a full-time student. But I cannot continue these activities knowing what I know about myself." Going on, he wrote somewhat despairingly, "I have no real conception of what is expected of me now, and I keep going back to my original tendencies to make myself feel better. I have been in many kinds of therapy. It didn't work—none of it. Internally I am frightened and I realize I am not functioning as a human being. Fortunately, I have never been caught for a serious crime, although I have committed them. If it weren't for various members of my family bailing me out, I would have been incarcerated by now.''

A criminal is most likely to have doubts about his way of life after he has been apprehended for a crime and is facing unknown consequences. The door of a detention center locking behind him may render an adult or juvenile especially vulnerable to thinking about change, especially if it is his first lockup.

I interviewed Dick, age 21, shortly after he was locked up and experiencing his first taste of confinement. He said that he started ''going wild'' at 15, when he hung out with the wrong crowd, became a tough guy, and was ''screwing around with dope.'' Since then, he had used practically every kind of drug floating around the streets, going on long binges of amphetamine and barbiturate use. Finally he was arrested and charged with two counts of armed robbery, two counts of larceny, and carrying a pistol without a license. He told me that the first five days in jail he was so scared that he vomited every time he ate solid food. So terrified was he that he hardly slept a night during the first two weeks. He was not so much afraid of other inmates as he was about his future. Night after night, he lay awake thinking and reading. He called himself a ''social retard'' and cried because his way of life was emotionally ''killing'' his father. He was also depressed because his girlfriend had written him a ''Dear John'' letter. ''I want to change,'' Dick said with considerable fervor. ''I just can't do it myself, and I have nobody to help me. But my desperate desire to change is what I feel is most important.''

Does a criminal like Dick say he wants to change just as one more con? Does he say it because he is momentarily afraid and seeks reassurance about his future? At any particular time, it is impossible to be certain how genuine such a state of mind is. The important point is that there are times when a criminal is vulnerable, when his life is not working out as he hopes, and he casts about for an alternative. Vulnerability is highest when the criminal is faced with losing something he values, usually his freedom, possibly also a girlfriend or his family. He may also be vulnerable after he has lost his freedom and he has had time to think and become despondent about the course of his life. At such times, straightening out has its strongest appeal. The best time to reach a criminal then is when he is vulnerable, for otherwise his sincerity about change will slip away, and he will continue the only life he has ever known. Thus, the work of habilitation can begin in prison or in the community. The critical factor is not where it takes place but the state of mind of the criminal.

Reflecting on his wasted life, a middle-aged inmate of a state penitentiary posed to me what really is a challenge to society. First, he said that people like himself are rarely reached by current methods. Then he despaired as to whether it was possible to change at all. "In my opinion," he said, "the human mind is ever reduplicating itself, acquiring more finesse, sophistication, technique, subtlety, and science. I am sure that a controlled setting that is humane in its approach, that is moral, principled, and courageous, can inspire the most lowly to become a working and functional part of this country." Said another criminal, "I know it is not easy to change someone's whole concept and evil ways, but I am aware of this. For me to become a law-abiding citizen would be my greatest triumph."

The question is, can society effectively utilize its resources to help criminals become responsible instead of throwing billions of dollars into human warehouses or down the drain into well-intentioned, but misguided, partial solutions that turn out not to be solutions at all?

Chapter Thirteen
To Change a Criminal

A TALL, GAUNT, white-haired, elderly psychiatrist was doing most of the talking as he leaned back in the chair across from Leroy, a bearded black housebreaker and armed robber, who appeared cowed into silence. In a direct, yet polite manner, Dr. Samuel Yochelson was telling Leroy that he was a menace to society.

Yochelson had dealt with criminals this way many times before, but he was a different man in his approach to them than he had been ten years earlier in 1961, when he arrived at Saint Elizabeths Hospital in Washington, D.C., to begin a second career. One of Buffalo's most eminent psychiatrists, he was known not only as a successful practitioner but also for his contribution to the public's knowledge of psychiatry through his regular appearances on a local television series. As he approached his mid-50s, the time had come when he aspired to make a contribution to this field that would be both scholarly and practical. From being a public figure in Buffalo, he chose the obscurity of a new environment where he would not be heard from for 15 years. Yochelson undertook the research–treatment program in criminal behavior at a hospital rather than a prison because he thought that a treatment environment would be more conducive to a clinical study, and in addition, he could draw upon the expertise of the huge hospital's medical and social work departments.

When he began the research, Yochelson didn't consider his patients "criminals." Rather, he regarded them as disturbed people who were products of adverse family situations and oppressive social conditions. He spent hundreds of hours taking detailed histories and hundreds more treating them in individual and group psychotherapy using traditional techniques with which he had been successful in Buffalo. Yochelson believed that if he could help the Saint Elizabeths patients gain insight into their past behavior, they could resolve their conflicts and would no longer commit crimes. After several years of probing into their early experiences and psychosocial development, he observed something quite sobering. Despite all their insight, these men still were committing crimes right on the hospital grounds and, when caught, used their newfound insight as justification.

Undaunted, Yochelson realized that he would have to take a new tack. Having discovered that the search for causes was futile and contributed only to rationalization, he stopped swallowing his patients' self-serving stories and concentrated on their current thinking. As he did this, he saw that they were rational, not crazy at all. He concluded that the insanity defense through which they escaped imprisonment had been a farce. In fact, they were no different from criminals whom he studied who never were hospitalized for a psychiatric condition.

Increasingly, Yochelson became a hard-liner, not in the sense of wanting to punish criminals but in insisting that they be treated as responsible for their behavior and held accountable. Only by seeing them as the victimizers they were, not as the victims they claimed to be, could he surmount the barriers that they set up to confuse and distract not only him but everyone else they encountered.

The work with these men whom he now called criminals was arduous and unrewarding for a long time. But Yochelson persisted, meticulously recording on thousands of pages all of his observations, even those he couldn't immediately make sense of. Eventually, he realized that significant and lasting change in the behavior of criminals could occur only with a 180-degree alteration in their thinking. He developed a technique to teach criminals to report their thinking so that it could be monitored and errors pointed out and corrected.

In its format, Yochelson's new program resembled a classroom more than a therapy group. The procedures that he developed are time-consuming to apply, but they offer promise of revolutionizing practices in many parts of the criminal justice system and in the mental health field.

Leroy did not walk into the doctor's office from the streets begging for help. Yochelson had encountered a few criminals who did this. Some wanted to kick a drug habit or lay off booze. Others were momentarily depressed or anxious and wanted him to get a wife or parent off their backs. But they were not interested in making profound changes in themselves. Leroy declared that he had nothing to show for his 30 years. He had abandoned his wife and children for sex, heroin, alcohol, guns, and other excitement in the streets of Washington, D.C. After beating a charge for bank robbery by faking insanity, Leroy was committed to Saint Elizabeths Hospital, where he met Yochelson. Now he wanted two things—to get out of the hospital and to make changes in his life. What changes he wasn't sure, but he was certain that he wanted things to be different.

Yochelson began by stating that he knew Leroy sized up everyone whom he met. Since the purpose of the first meeting was primarily to let Leroy know whom he was dealing with, the psychiatrist did not worry about establishing rapport. Instead, he assumed control of the interview by presenting his own view of what Leroy was like. Yochelson was not searching for explanations, which Leroy would readily feed him in the form of self-serving stories and excuses. He declared that he would not fall prey to Leroy's diversions, excuses, and other attempts to mislead and confuse him. Leroy would be offered no chance to ramble on about his mother, his father, his "bad breaks" in life, or even his crimes. Yochelson knew practically nothing about Leroy's background, nor was he interested. He didn't even know the charge on which Leroy had been declared not guilty by reason of insanity. But having studied many criminals in depth and having found identical elements in many of their thought patterns, the doctor knew a great deal about the workings of Leroy's mind.

Yochelson asked Leroy to listen to his statements and then tell him whether he agreed. He asserted that very early in life Leroy had carved out a path different from most of those around him, that he had lived a secret life and gloried in being slick enough to fool others. Yochelson pointed out that Leroy's early and frequent violations grew out of a demand that the world suit Leroy rather than that Leroy suit the world. He cited Leroy's insistence that others respect him while he respected no one. Whereas Leroy paid lip service to responsibility, he actually had scorned all but extremely successful people, whom he thought he could surpass in brilliance and accomplishment. He stated that Leroy had a "glass jaw." He could dish out abuse but couldn't take even the slightest criticism. He told Leroy that although he might brag about his friends, he didn't know what friendship was. He contended that by a twist of mind, Leroy considered himself decent despite having committed crime after crime and having neglected and then abandoned his wife and children, whom he still professed to love. After each statement, Yochelson would pause, gaze intently at Leroy and ask him, "Am I right?" Sometimes, Leroy nodded solemnly. At other times, he would shrug his shoulders and remark, "You could say that." Yochelson would pounce on that statement and point out that it showed Leroy to be a coward who presented a tough exterior to the world but who didn't have the guts to face up to who he is. When Leroy replied, "I don't know," Yochelson said that "I don't know" is typical of a criminal who fears tarnishing his image by being truthful. Yochelson demonstrated how everything that Leroy said was revealing of his personality.

Like a bloodhound, Yochelson pressed on for close to three hours, unmasking Leroy. Leroy didn't like what he was hearing, but he found it hard to deny. He quibbled with a word or phrase here or there but found his resistance crumbling. Later Leroy admitted that early in the interview, he had sensed that this wasn't another "shrink" whom he could lead by the nose, that it was going to be a lot tougher than he had expected to take on Yochelson. Leroy began to wonder if the doctor was reading his thoughts. Fleetingly he thought that because Yochelson knew so much about criminals, he might be one himself. What amazed him most was that he was sitting there and taking it while this elderly man painted a dismal picture of him as a human being. Although he was being exposed, he did not feel attacked. Yochelson had remained calm and polite, even when he expressed his total opposition to Leroy's way of life. He did not ridicule Leroy, browbeat him, berate him, or treat him with anything less than respect. So Leroy continued to sit there and take it, almost mesmerized while Yochelson picked him apart and presented him with a mirror image of himself.

This was only the beginning. The doctor invited him to return for more of the same. Leroy had heard about Yochelson's program, but in the interview not a word about it had been mentioned. The doctor stated that until he completed laying out Leroy's personality there would be no discussion of a program.

Leroy did return for further interviews. No aspect of his life was sacred, not even Leroy's new girlfriend, whom he regarded as responsible because she had gone to college. Yochelson's probing questions revealed that she was not the Madonna-like figure he portrayed. She smoked marijuana, was an "easy lay," and offered to be an accessory to his crimes by concealing his guns in her home. After several meetings, it became apparent that Yochelson did not detect any redeeming feature in Leroy. Even his musical talents had been misused as he played in dives where criminals hung out. Bluntly, Yochelson told him that he was a thoroughbred criminal and that three options were possible: Leroy could continue in crime and experience the consequences; he could commit suicide, in which case society would be better off; or he could learn to live like a civilized human being and become a responsible person. Leroy had ruled out the first two. That left only change, which he thought would be a snap.

Behavior follows in the wake of thought. To eliminate criminal behavior, it is essential first to change the way a man like Leroy thinks. This is by no means a fast or easy process. The task requires demolishing old thinking patterns, laying a new foundation by teaching new concepts, and building a new structure wherein the criminal puts into action what he is taught. All his life, Leroy had heard the word "responsibility" bandied about, a word used so promiscuously that it means everything and nothing. Leroy was used to parroting the word even though he knew nothing about being responsible. To him, to be responsible meant to erect a facade and *appear* respectable. He commented, "Once a person is responsible, he can get away with a hell of a lot.'' Responsibility also meant to be a big wheel, to acquire fame and fortune overnight by any means that he could think of. But in the program that Leroy was about to enter, responsibility embraced all it takes to be an effective, constructive person with total integrity. It meant learning and putting into practice specific patterns of thinking that are second nature to most people but brand new to the criminal.

Leroy was told that none of his hard luck stories were relevant. The circumstances of his life were of no concern. He was not a victim. At the heart of this program is the premise that man can choose between good and evil. Rather than relieve Leroy's fears and guilt, Yochelson would try to intensify them. Having had some psychotherapy, Leroy was used to expressing feelings, ventilating anger. He was surprised that Yochelson, a psychiatrist, had no interest in his feelings. There would be nothing in this program to make Leroy ''feel better'' about himself or accept himself. Rather, in order to change he would have to grow intensely fed up with himself. Leroy was intrigued, but, more important, he saw no choice but to trust this man and see what the program was all about. He told Yochelson he would make an ''honest effort.'' Refusing to let that phrase slip by, Yochelson pointed out that there could be no effort that wasn't honest. He asserted that Leroy seemed to be placing the program on trial. If things did not go the way he wanted, Leroy would then do what he pleased, secure in the belief that he had tried. Yochelson continued to unmask Leroy by dissecting his every statement or question.

Leroy then was permitted to join a group of five men who already were at different points in the change process. Groups were organized in this manner so that a new man could see how others were functioning and the current members could see themselves all over again as they heard the questions, arguments, and excuses of a totally unchanged criminal. Leroy had been accustomed to therapy groups where patients decided what to discuss and where the doctor said little. Yochelson's group did not begin to resemble those freewheeling discussions. In this situation the doctor, not the criminals, was running the meeting. From a sheaf of notes made during the past 24 hours, each criminal reported what he had been thinking—thoughts about other patients on the ward, thoughts about the nursing staff, thoughts about family, thoughts about a violent movie on television, thoughts about the group, thoughts about Yochelson, thoughts during masturbation. The others listened in silence until Yochelson broke in to comment on a particular thought or sequence of thoughts. That became the focus of discussion, with Yochelson applying corrective concepts to everyone in the group, not just the man who was giving the report.

When Leroy entered the program, he had been given a preview of the life he would lead. Yochelson warned that it would seem like the cloistered existence of a monk. He would have to sever ties with other criminals. There would be no drugs, not even a beer; no sex until he learned how to have a responsible sexual relationship. Every day, he would have to attend group meetings. Even after he left the hospital, participation would still be required. His existence would seem regimented and frustrating as Leroy encountered problems that he never knew existed. Leroy heard these words and pondered them. The program sounded extreme to him, but what other choice did he have? His disgust for the past and fear about the future were strong enough for him to make a beginning.

Neither Leroy nor any other criminal can be passionately committed to change from the outset. It is impossible for a person to embrace immediately a way of life that he has previously scorned and about which he knows nothing. Commitment grows with experience. It's like learning to play tennis. This analogy made sense to Leroy, who had learned tennis while in the hospital. At first, tennis seemed glamorous, and he was eager to try it. After chasing the ball around on one of Washington's miserably humid August days and fighting off the gnats, Leroy was anything but committed to tennis. However, with lessons and practice, he improved. The harder he tried, the more skillful he became and the greater his eagerness to play and improve. Unfortunately, he had not made the generalization from tennis to life. Yochelson did, however, and told Leroy that with more experience and knowledge, commitment to change would develop just as had commitment to tennis.

Yochelson had no way of knowing why Leroy had agreed to be in the program. Was it to impress the hospital authorities so they'd let him out earlier? In his years of experience with criminals, Yochelson had learned to be neither gullible nor cynical. He knew if he believed everything that Leroy said, Leroy would manipulate him and lose respect for him. But Yochelson also knew that if he constantly disbelieved Leroy, there could be no dialogue between them. He made no immediate judgments, preferring to take the position, "time will tell." As he saw it, Leroy's life was at stake. The burden was on him to be truthful and then to put what he was learning into practice. Otherwise, the failure would be Leroy's, not Yochelson's.

Having heard that Yochelson's group met all morning every day, Leroy wondered what in the world consumed so much time. He quickly found out. Discussion was not limited to events or problems. Events may be few and unremarkable, especially during a routine prison or hospital day. A criminal considers himself having a "problem" only when he gets into a jam by doing what he isn't supposed to. So there was little point in limiting discussion to that. The heart of the meeting was the daily report of thinking. Then even the person who languished in bed all day with the flu would have plenty to report. First, Leroy had to be taught to stop and recollect what he had thought, then to make notes on paper. He was instructed to think of this exercise as though a tape recording of his thinking were being played back. The reason for the emphasis on thinking was that to-day's thoughts contain the seed of tomorrow's crime. Leroy began to understand this very quickly.

One morning, he reported being furious when he was called into an office and accused by a nursing assistant of being high on marijuana. He was especially outraged because he had used no drugs for a week, now that he was in the program. The thought flashed through his mind, "I'll bust the SOB's head wide open." In the group meeting, Leroy's thought of assaulting the attendant was treated as seriously as if he had actually done it. Yochelson knew that unless such thinking was controlled, it would be only a matter of time before Leroy became violent. But it was not only thoughts about committing crimes that were considered important. No element of Leroy's thinking was to remain obscured. As an unchanged criminal, he was in no position to determine what was important. What seemed trivial to him could provide the substance for a morning-long discussion. As reports were made, Yochelson listened carefully and, from the hodgepodge of thoughts, selected a focus. One criminal living in the community happened to mention that en route to the meeting, he thought of cutting off a driver who abruptly had pulled out in front of him. This thinking flashed by, consuming seconds out of a 24-hour day. Though most people would forget it instantly, this man had been trained to turn a magnifying glass on his thinking. Reporting this seemingly insignificant incident provided substance for a discussion that could have been approached on the basis of several themes—the criminal's expectation of other people, his attempt to control others, his fears, and his anger.

Leroy found that the morning meetings were like a classroom in that they were structured and orderly. But they were not in any sense dry or academic because the teaching was directly related to group members' immediate experiences. Leroy initially wanted to impress others by showing how perceptive he was. During the first meeting, one criminal was heatedly arguing with Yochelson. In a self-righteous tone, Leroy lambasted the other man for arguing at the expense of learning something. He advised the criminal, "Doc knows what he's talking about. You better listen!" Leroy expected praise but was taken aback by Yochelson's informing him that the purpose of the meeting was not to criticize one another but to *learn* from others' mistakes and experiences. Yochelson observed that all his life Leroy was quick to pick others apart but rarely applied his criticisms to himself. The doctor's most frequent question to each criminal in the group was, "What did you learn?" Early in the program, Leroy persisted in pointing out flaws in the group members or in Yochelson but shrank from looking at himself. He had never believed that he was a criminal and fought that notion with all his being.

One afternoon, an attendant offered him a ride from the tennis court to his living quarters. Leroy accepted only to find that the attendant went by way of the grocery store and purchased beer. Leroy took a few gulps and returned to the ward. No one had missed him, and no one knew about the beer except for the attendant, who wouldn't tell. When Leroy reported the incident to the group meeting, Yochelson reacted to it as though he had murdered someone. Leroy saw no big deal because "everyone" wandered off the grounds. For an experienced criminal, it was easy to get past the guards. Beer didn't hurt anyone. No one was the wiser. Wasn't he entitled to a slip? He wasn't perfect. In this single incident lay many errors in thinking. First, he had committed two violations of hospital regulations as well as a violation of the program by leaving the grounds without permission and drinking. Then there was Leroy's insistence that he could make exceptions for himself. It was the old story of making what was wrong right because he considered it right for him at the time. It wasn't the danger of a few gulps of beer that was at issue but Leroy's lifelong practice of making exceptions, with one offense leading to another. Furthermore, Leroy rarely stopped at one beer. Rather, beer was the first link in a chain of Scotch, heroin, women, crime. His claim that he had slipped and wasn't perfect only meant that he had not exercised the necessary restraints to eliminate old patterns. Whether everyone went off the grounds and drank was irrelevant, a lame excuse. Everyone was not in the program. Leroy was. The main question was whether a beer was worth the sacrifice of his opportunity to become a responsible member of society.

One of the obstacles that criminals pose to nearly every interviewer or change agent is the argument that "everyone does it," or "people are like that." Criminals point an accusing finger at society for being corrupt and claim that the only difference between them and others is that they have been caught. They'll point out how people in business and government get away with things, citing specific scandals. Leroy did his share of this. While acknowledging that many offenders avoid getting caught, or if caught don't get punished, Yochelson refused to be diverted from the task at hand—dealing with Leroy's irresponsibility.

The standards in Yochelson's program were stricter than almost any he would find in the straight world itself. Leroy found it difficult to accept the fact that to change he had to go from one extreme to another. He didn't view himself as an evil person to begin with. Coming to terms with the truth about himself was excruciatingly painful, the most difficult undertaking he had ever experienced. The criminal's reluctance to face the truth was verbalized by one group member who confessed, "The reason I don't examine this stuff is that when I really look at it, it's like touching a live wire." The most basic requirement of the program is that the criminal report his thinking without embellishing, editing, or omitting. Leroy deliberately concocted some lies because he didn't want to touch the "live wire." At other times, lies spilled out of his mouth automatically. He would deny something, admit to only a part of the truth, or shade his answer to make himself look good. As he pointed out, he had lied since he could talk, so lying was second nature.

Because of the criminal's habitual lying, it is important that in a program like this the agent of change maintain contact with a responsible person who knows the criminal well, such as a parent, wife, or employer. This must be done regularly with the criminal's knowledge and consent, especially once he is released. Yochelson was able to talk to the institutional staff who lived around the clock with Leroy and later to family members once Leroy was in the community. Access to an outside source is essential to evaluate the criminal's progress and also because another person may see a problem brewing that the criminal fails to recognize because of a lack of experience in the responsible world.

Leroy found the first month of the program new and exciting. He was sure that he could change faster and more completely than anyone else. He got a high out of small accomplishments. On a pass, he went to the cleaner's and asked to purchase some storage bags. The owner graciously gave them to him. He stopped by the grocery store to ask for cartons and was loaded up with more than he could carry. His asking was a real change. In the past, he'd just take whatever he wanted. Leroy proclaimed that he was getting high on responsibility. The trouble was that he still was in search of highs. It wasn't long before the novelty of the program wore off and Leroy grew bored. Whereas he had had tremendous stamina in his criminal life, he had little endurance for this. In the past, he always did things his way and found shortcuts, but in this program there were no shortcuts, only endless drudgery. Every time he opened his mouth, the doctor discovered something to criticize. There were no rewards for doing the expected. Yochelson would ask, "Do you want orchids for living like a civilized human being?" Observing that there seemed to be so much to learn at once, Leroy commented, "The more I do, the more there is to do." He found the whole program literally a pain in the neck and complained frequently of tension in his neck and a blistering headache. Although Leroy had been off drugs for months, he suffered other symptoms identical to those he had experienced during withdrawal from heroin. He knew that stomach aches, sweating, and other miseries would disappear if he cheated on the program. "Violation is the only comfort," he thought.

This man, who had always considered himself at the top of the heap, in control of all around him, suddenly seemed a helpless victim, if not of others, then of his own makeup. He acted as though his emotions arose from outside himself and he had nothing to do with them. Leroy claimed that because he couldn't control his anger, he slapped his girlfriend during an argument when she came to visit. He said he resorted to smoking reefer because he was so bored and depressed. He skipped a ward meeting because he was so anxious he couldn't sit still. It was up to Yochelson to alter his feelings and interest him in change.

Leroy's feelings had governed his interests and so he'd repeatedly balk at other's requests, saying, "I don't feel like it," or "I'm not interested." In fact, Leroy thought it was the duty of others to give him reasons why he should fulfill an obligation that he didn't recognize as an obligation at all. The hospital eventually permitted Leroy to work in the community, returning to the institution just for sleeping. He also was allowed passes on weekends. Yochelson had stressed repeatedly the importance of programming time, especially on weekends. On one of his first Saturdays out, feelings prevailed. Leroy didn't feel like doing much at all and made no plans. After visiting his mother, he went to the heart of the drug and crime area at 14th and U streets. Despite ideal spring weather, he didn't give tennis a thought. He had no interest in visiting friends of the family. He wandered by the bars and roamed through pool halls, feeling as if he wanted to get drunk more than anything else. He paused in front of one of his old haunts, told himself no, and returned to his mother's. On Sunday, he had a couple of beers, returned to the hospital grounds, and began flirting with a female patient. As the sexual repartee grew increasingly animated, Leroy grinned and patted her buttocks. The woman was ready for anything, but Leroy stopped, asked himself what he was doing, and returned to his ward. Monday morning, he complained that he just couldn't get interested in the program. He was angry at Yochelson for trying to make him a lackey and rob him of his manhood. He exclaimed that he wasn't going to be like "no white man." Throughout the program, every time Leroy injected the racial issue he was angry and seeking an excuse for irresponsibility. Then Yochelson was a "no good honky."

Leroy discovered that Yochelson was on a crusade against anger—quite the opposite of Leroy's earlier psychiatric treatment in which doctors encouraged him to express his anger. Yochelson asserted that the angry criminal does far too much damage "ventilating" his fury. Whenever the world does not suit him, whenever he fails to control a situation, the criminal flies off the handle. Anger is his habitual response whenever he thinks he's being threatened, and this happens many times every day of his life. When a responsible person is angry, he may offend others, think less clearly, and be less efficient at whatever he is doing at the time. But the anger usually stops there. For the criminal, anger is a malignancy that must be removed before it spreads and results in a crime. Leroy was shocked when Yochelson told him to swallow his anger rather than unleash it. Yochelson advised Leroy that for the present, it was better to risk an ulcer than for someone to suffer a cracked skull.

But neither ventilation nor suppression is an adequate solution. What must be done with a criminal like Leroy is to help him gain a realistic view of himself and of the world so that fewer things bother him and so he reacts constructively when things go wrong. The thin-skinned criminal has to learn to benefit from criticism, cope with rejection, and roll with life's punches. Columnist Ben Stein put it succinctly when he wrote that life requires "taking the lumps and calling them sugar."[1]

But the criminal must do even more than that. He must learn to anticipate situations in which he might be angry and think them through in advance. For example, if he leaves his car at a repair shop, he already knows from experience that mishaps are likely. The car won't be ready on time, the car will not be fixed, the bill will be higher than expected, the wrong thing will be fixed, or, worst of all, the service manager won't be able to find the car anywhere on the lot. A customer can be realistic in his expectations and thereby avoid anger. He can phone before leaving to check if the car is ready. He can request an estimate before a repair is made. He can instruct the shop to notify him before making any additional repairs. En route to pick up his car he can remind himself that even though he has taken precautions, something still may go wrong. This does not mean that he will be a doormat for others to step on. But by anticipating problems, he can preempt anger. If the need arises, he can be firm without being angry. Psychologist Paul Hauck makes the point that it is possible to live without anger: "It is perfectly possible to raise children who will not get angry over most normally provoking situations." He asserts, "One can be as solid as the Rock of Gibraltar and as peaceful as a sunny day, both at the same time."[2]

The responsible person may not take such steps to avoid anger. But the consequences of his anger usually are far less devastating than what ensues when the criminal becomes enraged. Criminals like Leroy establish their place in the world through anger, often at enormous cost to others. Who is Leroy if he can't control people? What is life if others don't jump to his command and anticipate his every wish? From a report of a single episode of anger, the role of anger in his life is examined.

To Change a Criminal

One Saturday, Leroy dropped by his girlfriend Jackie's apartment. When her phone rang, he grabbed it and heard a man ask to speak to Jackie. He handed the receiver to her and stood next to her straining to hear both ends of the conversation. She tried to get rid of the caller by pretending that he had reached the wrong party. Leroy accused her of lying about not knowing the caller since he had asked for her by name. Jackie denied it, and Leroy had sense enough to drop it. That evening, they went to a nightclub. While Jackie was in the ladies' room, a stylishly dressed buxom girl asked Leroy to dance. Jackie returned and, seeing the couple cheek to cheek on the dance floor, she created a commotion that wound up with Leroy's proclaiming that no "bitch" was going to tell him what to do, particularly after being called by every guy in the city. As Jackie rose from her chair to leave, he wheeled around and slapped her across the face. This was how Leroy handled life.

Leroy had not yet relinquished his view of himself as divine monarch, nor was he putting himself in the place of other people. He expected to be Jackie's "man," her one and only, no matter how many women he had or how he mistreated her. When others did not fulfill Leroy's expectations, he was outraged. And so he lived in a perpetual state of anger. To help him become more realistic, Yochelson introduced Leroy to "Murphy's Law," which says that if anything can go wrong, it will. Leroy heard a group member quip that he had discovered a corollary to Murphy's Law; things that he was absolutely positive couldn't go wrong also went wrong. For the rest of his life, Leroy could expect to be plagued by Murphy. Murphy's Law was only one tool. Basic questions to be addressed throughout the program were, Who are you, Leroy? How do you affect people? What do you want to become? What do you expect of others?

Despite doubts about the program and whether the whole thing was worth it, Leroy saw little choice other than to stick with it. Leroy's state of mind was captured by thoughts he jotted down late one Friday afternoon.

"Near the first gate where I spend some afternoons, I saw a guy who I talk with often," Leroy reported. "I don't know his name and doubt seriously if he knows mine. We talked, and it's very obvious he had been drinking and was feeling no pain. I thought to myself that everybody I came in contact with was high on something and enjoying themselves. Then I wondered is the square life worth it, with all its loneliness and no fun. As the pretty cars left the grounds through the gates, I thought the cars were only just a small portion of what square people have along with homes, children, sweet, beautiful wives who love them, relatives and friends who respect them, and many other small, but wonderful things. Then I felt my struggle and fight would bring to me those wonderful things, or I could get hip again and go no place, but the hell with it all, it's agony." His report ended with his writing, "I don't know why, but right now I feel like crying. So I'll stop and continue tomorrow. I hate this feeling, so help me God."

The worst problem Leroy faced in the early period was that as an unchanged criminal, criminal thoughts flooded his mind every day. The only barrier between himself and his life on the streets was a fear of getting caught and a threadbare conscience. These had not been very potent before, and he knew he could not rely on them in the future. Yochelson began to teach him ways to deter criminal thinking. The first method was to consider the many consequences of acting on a thought. At his job as a clerk, Leroy was positive that the boss was prejudiced against blacks and was afraid that he would be passed over for promotions. Each day he took a dimmer view of his boss, who appeared indifferent, if not antagonistic, to him while being cordial to the other personnel, all of whom were white. One day Leroy was reprimanded for coming in late. He had never seen anyone else spoken to so sharply. He held himself in check but stalked into the group meeting vowing that he wasn't going to take "shit from that mother fucker" any longer. The next time he was going to let him have it. Patiently, Yochelson pointed out that this declaration told the story of Leroy's life. If something didn't go as he wanted, he'd teach the other person a lesson. If a situation was bad, he'd make it worse. He had always demanded fair play but had treated others shabbily.

Yochelson pointed out that in typical fashion, Leroy was jumping to conclusions after only a few months on the job. He warned Leroy that he would encounter situations far more trying than this. In fact, Yochelson advised criminals to be grateful for things going wrong so that they could learn to cope with adversity and be better equipped for it in the future. If Leroy told off the boss, he'd not only enrage him, but if the boss were racially prejudiced, Leroy's behavior would reinforce that prejudice as well. Furthermore, Leroy would make other enemies in the office and find it more difficult to get work done. He might be fired and lose a job reference. Most important, his anger would unleash a chain of events that would be apt to culminate in his committing a crime, for this had been his pattern. Thinking of the consequences in advance was one form of deterrence. Later, Leroy would learn new concepts that would offer greater insurance against repeating old response patterns. He would understand the need for long-range thinking, the necessity of teamwork, and the importance of putting himself in the place of others. But until then, it was critical to equip him with deterrents for immediate use. Just as the criminal learns to abort anger, he also learns to nip criminal thinking in the bud before it flowers into criminal activity. He does this by preparing himself for any adversity.

Mark, one of the men most advanced in change in the group, reported that he and his wife Liz were driving to the mountains for a holiday weekend. In the past, the two of them had had arguments, long, cold silences, tears, and bitter recriminations whenever they were together, but especially on vacation. Weekends and trips had totally fallen apart over the most inconsequential incidents because Mark had always insisted on having his way. He tried to control Liz, even to the point of deciding what she should order from the menu for dinner. This time Mark was trying to anticipate everything that could possibly go wrong—getting lost, car trouble, illness, dirty accommodations, cold weather, rain, weak coffee, inconsiderate people, crowds at recreational facilities, a wife wanting to do something he didn't have any interest in, her moving at a slower pace, her having her period and refusing sex.

This was all new to Leroy, who had planned little in his life other than a bank robbery. In this program, he was taught to think not only about future *events* but also about what his *thinking* might be. Yochelson stressed the importance of *thinking about thinking*.

Summer was approaching, and the days were hot and sultry. Pete, another member of the group, reported being "dizzy with desire" as he gazed at young women in shorts, halters, and bikinis. He contrasted the "lush female animal" on the third-floor balcony across the way with his "old hag" wife, who actually was neither old nor a hag. He caught himself thinking this way and reported to Yochelson that he had put a stop to it. If he had allowed it to proceed, he would have mentally stripped her nude and imagined "balling her like she had never been balled before." From past experience, he knew that then he would go beyond fantasy, prowling the corridor, seeking an opportunity to accost her and drag her into an area where he would tear her clothes off and gratify his desires.

Leroy was impressed with how quickly Pete had put the brakes on thinking. But Leroy pointed out that there were occasions when he didn't have time to ponder the consequences. Furthermore, he couldn't anticipate everything he'd think about, much less do. There had to be a more efficient way to deal with his immediate desires. How could he quickly squelch thinking about the pleasures of snorting coke when the thoughts seemed to hit him out of the blue? Yochelson suggested that perhaps the best way to deal with thoughts about drugs or other violations was simply to ask himself if they were worth throwing away his life and returning to the gutter. If Leroy answered no, he could direct his thinking elsewhere. This Leroy tried.

At the office, Leroy saw a young woman removing a splinter from her foot with a needle from a syringe. Immediately, he thought about drugs. He dealt with this thinking by reminding himself, "drugs are death," then thinking about something else.

Pete reported spotting a pair of rubber gloves lying on a shelf in a physician's examining room. He thought about putting them on, grabbing the nurse, and raping her. Immediately, Pete stopped this stream of thought and began to think about problems at work. Another man reported going out to buy a quart of milk and passing a liquor store. He instructed himself, "Keep your mind on the milk." The thought that the responsible person can allow himself to think and perhaps savor is dynamite to the criminal, who will elaborate on it and translate it into action.

Finally, a deterrent process that Yochelson emphasized repeatedly was teaching each of the men to take stock of himself. Yochelson had been holding a mirror up to Leroy, rubbing his nose in the slime of the past. Now it was time that Leroy held it up to himself. Alcoholics Anonymous requires its members to conduct a "searching moral inventory." In the same way, if a criminal does not make a habit of reflecting on his life, he will not progress because there is little incentive to change.

Inculcating fear and guilt are essential to change inasmuch as they prompt consideration of other people and the making of responsible decisions. Leroy knew well the spine-tingling fear and knot in his stomach that came whenever he was approaching the scene of the crime and leaving it to make his getaway. The only conscience he knew was that of momentary remorse when he realized he had hurt or disappointed someone. Leroy could shut anything out of his mind long enough to do whatever he wanted. The criminal must learn that fear is built into life. Some people diet out of fear. They exercise because of fear and drive safely because they are afraid. Fear is an incentive to do better. Out of fear of hurting others, people take precautions before they act. Fearing for the future, a person does what he must for his family and himself. He purchases life insurance, saves money, schedules health checkups, services the car. Leroy was told that if he were to hurt someone or be thoughtless, he should experience pangs of guilt. Without fear and guilt, he could never live responsibly. Leroy's fear and guilt would grow only by subjecting his irresponsible thinking to scrutiny, then by struggling to grasp corrective concepts, and finally by putting them into practice.

Leroy believed that once he learned to be responsible, he would have no worries, but Yochelson warned him that he'd be tension-free only if he were dead. Through new experiences, Leroy was learning what the doctor meant. He began to worry about work because he had processed fewer requisitions in November than in October. It wasn't just that or the boss hassling him. There were constant interruptions, incompetent co-workers asking asinine questions, unreasonable deadlines, being placed interminably on hold while people in other agencies looked up information that turned out to be inaccurate so that eventually he had to redo work. Leroy complained that all this was meaningless. There'd be a ray of sunshine as one problem was solved and then clouds seemed to descend—another day, another set of problems. Leroy wanted to say, "The hell with it." Why should *he* bother? Why should *he* worry? If this was life, it was not what he bargained for. Patiently, Yochelson did what he had done so many times before. He asked Leroy what alternative he had. Every job had its difficulties.

Yochelson was having his own with Saint Elizabeths. Life was full of problems. It was only reasonable to expect that before one was solved, another would crop up. Did Leroy want to return to hustling, holdups, and heroin? Did he want to kill himself? If not, the only other course was to press on and do what had to be done.

The program requires massive amounts of endurance because life itself demands that. This is a quality that Leroy was short on. He was forever expecting to reach the summit of achievement without taking the beginning steps and was angry when it didn't happen. His had been a life of emergencies, all of his own making. There were no goals, only an interminable series of conquests to shore up an inflated but precarious self-image. Leroy could not see any light at the end of the tunnel. He couldn't understand why anyone would work and work and work without a guarantee that it would all pay off. He demanded insurance against failure, and by failure he meant being anything less than tops at whatever he did. He said, "For some reason or other, I'm unable to go into a situation where there's a chance of failure." Since a guarantee of success was not forthcoming, Leroy began to doubt everything. "What's the purpose of it all?" he asked. "Every day is like you have to put on your armor to fight a battle. It's too much."

While Leroy was entertaining doubts, the hospital thought he was doing superbly and discharged him on a conditional release. By this time, he was immersed enough in Yochelson's program to keep attending the group meetings each day. Although there was a momentary flurry of elation at being released, Leroy still found himself in a prison, the prison of a program that demanded making what he considered extreme sacrifices. All he could see was deprivation, not opportunity to start life anew. He had rejoined the wife and children whom he had abandoned years before. But still, what was life? Day after day, it was work, home, and the program.

Leroy lamented that all he had gotten out of the program was an aching head, upset stomach, and constant fatigue. He had reached the point of saying what he had said all his life when he tired of something: "Fuck it." At this point, he had ruled out crime, but not other things. After working overtime one Saturday, Leroy came home late in the afternoon and found his wife Mary not yet back from shopping. He strolled down to the corner and started chatting with some of the winos hanging around. As he was talking, friends of Mary's called to him and offered him a ride home, chiding him about his poor choice of companions. Leroy replied that he was lonely. Seeing that Mary was still not home, he knocked on the landlady's door, and she invited him in to a party. Leroy had a drink or two and eyed a young lady who seemed to be about 20. She was aware that he was watching her and soon came over to him. They bantered flirtatiously. He nuzzled her cheek, then planted a kiss on her lips, and finally drew her into the bedroom shutting the door behind them. After embracing and kissing, they undressed, and the girl began lionizing Leroy, telling him what a great build he had and admiring and fondling his penis. In a frenzied manner, they had intercourse and dressed. In the nick of time, Leroy returned to the party to find his wife just bursting in the door, looking for him. Mary accused him of nothing, but he was angry because "she shouldn't have been checking up on me." Leroy saw no harm whatsoever in this rendezvous. He claimed he was entitled to a "release." Yochelson viewed it differently, asking Leroy if a quick tumble with a tramp was worth risking the loss of his wife and children and the stability of the life that he was trying to build. He was not sexually deprived. He had sex with his wife almost every night. Finally, Yochelson reminded Leroy that once he made an exception for himself, it would be only the beginning. Whenever he said "fuck it" because of a momentary dissatisfaction, he came perilously close to abandoning the entire effort to become responsible. It was a question of his choice and will. Leroy became contrite, admitted he had erred, and moaned that he was a hopeless case. Yochelson was unrelenting. He reminded Leroy that he said "I can't" only when he didn't want to do something. "Are you a man or a mouse?" queried the doctor. Then he asked Leroy if he'd take criticism like a man and improve or give up and blame others.

In Yochelson's program, the theme of the criminal's injury to others always hung heavily in the air. Leroy knew what injury was when his own home was burglarized. He knew what injury was when his son was threatened by a boy with a knife. But he never thought of himself as injuring others. He equated injury with drawing blood, something he rarely did. But he was completely oblivious to others' rights and feelings. A fellow in the group reflected, "I do have feelings for other people. If I saw people trapped in a burning house, I'd experience a certain horror." The man continued, "And yet I really don't have any feeling for those I hurt. Were I to rape a woman, I wouldn't feel one second of her pain or anguish. I can't explain the contradiction between my pain for those in the burning building and my complete lack of feelings for my victims. I think it's because, where my own interests and pleasures are concerned, my feelings for others are automatically so totally suppressed and discarded as to be totally absent. I don't know. I only know that if I could appreciate the sufferings of my victims, they wouldn't be my victims."

Learning what constitutes injury is critical to learning about oneself. Throughout the program, Leroy experienced new waves of awareness and then disgust as to the scope of the damage that he had inflicted in almost three decades as a criminal. Beyond physical suffering and financial loss, injury extends to the emotional damage, to the climate of fear engendered in the aftermath of a crime, and to the disruption of lives. A small violation has a far-reaching effect. If a man pays for a meal with a bad check, the business suffers a direct loss. But the customers are hurt too, because if enough of these losses occur, management will refuse to take checks and customers will have to pay by cash or credit card. Furthermore, because the cost of losses is passed on to customers, the offender's own mother will have to pay more in that very restaurant. One of the men in Yochelson's group had committed burglaries and had been in a few fights. But he hadn't fought or broken into anyplace lately. He asserted that he wasn't much of a criminal because "I only dealt drugs." Yochelson pointed out that there was no telling how much injury this man contributed to through his drug sales. The criminal did remember that one of his buyers, after purchasing some heroin, held up a store, terrorized the customers, and shot the lady behind the cash register. But never before had he thought about these or other injuries resulting from his drug trafficking.

The criminal's habit of blaming others is a persistent obstacle to the process of change. Yochelson told Leroy that what others do makes no difference in this program. Only what he does matters. Does he create a bad situation? Does he make an already bad situation worse by anger or poor judgment? He must evaluate himself before criticizing others. If his wife is unreasonable, the important issue is how *he* reacts. If he fails to meet a deadline at work because of someone else's incompetence, what matters is not the shortcomings of the other person, but how *he* deals with the situation. Even were he to be attacked totally without provocation, the focus in the group meeting would be his thinking about his assailant and what *he* actually did. Leroy and the others were totally accountable for changing their own lives. Blaming circumstances was futile and only gave vent to anger. One of the fellows reflected, "When you look over your whole life and you see the total harm, it is up to you to create a new life for yourself. Nobody else does it for you."

As Leroy learned new ways to think and behave, he gradually emerged from his own private universe into a world of sharing, teamwork, loyalty, and trust. His attitude shifted from "screw everybody else but me" to "I have to learn how to share. I don't even know what it means." He slowly relinquished his perch of solitary grandeur to discover the give-and-take of relationships. In the group meeting, he found out what a discussion is, witnessing that it is possible to disagree with a person without insulting him. He learned to listen. In the past, Leroy didn't think anyone could teach him anything because he knew it all to begin with. First in the group and then at work and with his family, he began to learn and practice the rudiments of civilized behavior. He became a team member instead of demanding to be the captain. As Leroy traveled along this new road in life, unremarkable everyday events called up memories of his sordid past.

Leroy and Mary were discussing their priorities in fixing up the apartment. Because both were working, they had been able to set aside more than $500 for the project. But they needed so much, it was hard to decide whether to purchase a couch, chairs and a lamp, or some drapes and a coffee table. They listed each item they hoped to buy and what it was likely to cost. The next morning, as he rode the bus to work, Leroy was absorbed in thinking about their discussion. He winced to himself as he thought about the way he used to "borrow" Mary's hard-earned wages on false pretenses and spend it on drugs and other women. He gasped as he realized what they could have owned by now had he been a responsible person.

Two other fellows who had been in the program longer reported sobering reflections arising from their current progress. Pete had done well in sales and had received a promotion. Now he was authorized by management to attend an out-of-town convention. Pete picked up the phone book to look up the airlines number to make reservations. As he ran his finger down the page, he thought of the obscene phone calls he had made to clerks at nearly all the airlines, as he

tried to find a female agent who would engage in sexual repartee while he clung to the other end of the line masturba-
ting and fantasizing. As these recollections flashed through
Pete's mind, he was revolted to the point of feeling physically
nauseated.

Tony talked about his experience reading a psychology
book in the library now that he was out of prison and in
school part time. He reported with satisfaction that by con-
centrating for two full hours, he had absorbed a tremendous
amount. His head was swimming with ideas, and he was
bubbling over with enthusiasm. However, he remembered
that before prison, his library habits were very different. He
rarely could sit still for two hours, and when he did, only 15
minutes were spent in study. The rest of the time his mind
was in the streets or he was staring at girls' legs or breasts.
He also reflected how during that period of his life he wasted
thousands of the dollars that his parents had saved over the
years for his college education.

Several years before meeting Yochelson, Leroy had been a
patient in psychotherapy in which the therapist probed his
unconscious mind and searched for hidden complexes. He
also had participated in programs where he was rewarded or
punished for his behavior. Yochelson's program was neither
as complicated as the psychodynamic approach nor as simplistic as behavior modification. He found its concepts made
sense, and he could glimpse progress when he allowed himself to be guided by them. The more he learned, the more
starkly the present contrasted with the past, and the more he
saw there was to learn. Leroy was surprised to learn that he
knew virtually nothing about making decisions responsibly.
He had been one of those people who didn't like to ask a
question because to do so was a humiliating admission of ignorance. He had no need to plan ahead except in scheming a
crime. He recalled, "I thought about tomorrow, tomorrow." Now he was beginning to realize that to admit ignorance is wiser than pretending to know it all. Leroy began to

weigh alternative courses of action and consider both short- and long-range consequences.

There are other programs that teach criminals how to make decisions as well as acquire many other skills. However, they focus upon situational problem solving and feelings, not upon thinking patterns that are all-pervasive. Yochelson's program aimed to help a criminal change 180 degrees by learning an entirely new way of thinking and acting that would permeate his entire life. Leroy continued to be amazed at the tremendous attention to tiny details. For example, he reported that from time to time, he put a quarter in a pay phone rather than 20 cents because he didn't want to take time to get the proper change. Yochelson developed this pattern into a major theme for discussion—the criminal's view of money. Leroy had never valued money. A nickel, a quarter, a thousand dollars meant little. More money had passed through his hands in a few weeks than most people earn in years. To manage money, Leroy first would have to keep track of it. Again, it was the matter of going from one extreme to the other, from squandering thousands of dollars to counting every penny. Establishing the discipline of saving was what mattered, not whether Ma Bell gained 5 extra cents on the pay phone. In this program, the smallest breach of integrity became a major issue, even when no one was hurt by it. One of the men in the group ate ham at Thanksgiving rather than turkey. When asked by a friend whether he enjoyed his turkey, he responded that he had. This was a lie, a trivial one to be sure, but one that not only was unnecessary but that a criminal can ill afford. Leroy and the others in the group had lied all their lives, even when there seemed to be no advantage to it. One lie had led to another. To destroy this pattern, a criminal must maintain total integrity. Leroy's friend in the group could have replied, "This year it was ham." The discipline in being totally truthful is important in the same way as the discipline in accounting for every cent.

* * *

Leroy had ups and downs in change as did all the men. As Leroy achieved more and more in the responsible world, it became increasingly hard to think of turning back. He viewed the old life as a living death. It was true that meeting deadlines at work, worrying about bills, balancing his checkbook, enduring the stresses of children, and working out differences with his wife were not the highs he was accustomed to. There were periods of self-pity and departures from the program—a nip of sherry, followed by a tumbler of Scotch, staying home from work on a day when he just didn't feel like going, slapping Mary in a pique of anger because now *she* was spending too much money. But from each such departure, Leroy learned. The most important reinforcer of change was that by adhering to the program, he was accomplishing new goals *he* had set. Leroy and Mary bought a small house in which Leroy took great pride. After coping with delays in securing financing and the drudgery of moving, he plunged into fixing up the place, spending practically every spare moment plastering, painting, cleaning, and working on the yard. Tending a vegetable garden became almost an obsession. After months of physical labor, he was finally able to say, "As soon as you hit the corner, my house stands out." But many more projects remained—repairing the fence, enlarging the garden, sodding the front lawn, and painting the bedrooms.

Leroy's family life meant more and more. His boys, approaching adolescence, looked to him for approval and guidance. He fought back tears of joy as Tommy powered his school football team to victory with the encouraging cheers of the fans. Leroy had always believed he had to have more than one woman or else he was not a man. But he was starting to change his mind about this.

One day in the group, Leroy reported that a "sexy looking thing" was waiting at the bus stop. Catching himself thinking, "She'd be a nice piece to have," he shifted his gaze, then boarded the bus and buried himself in the newspaper. She made her way down the aisle, plopped down beside him, and brushed her thigh against his. Leroy shifted his leg and responded politely to the conversation. Deciding to keep things light, he discussed the weather and bus breakdowns. When he got off, he thought he was a "damn idiot" for not taking her phone number. But as he walked to his office building, he had an image of Mary, who had suffered so much in the past because of him. Now she was beginning to trust him, to plan a life with him as her husband and father of their two boys. He felt ashamed of his thoughts about the girl on the bus and dug into the work piled up on his desk.

As things continued to go relatively smoothly at home, Leroy found he was thinking less about other women and looking less too. "I look once and don't allow myself to look again," he reported. "I am never going to let myself go. It makes me feel good to be in control of myself."

Leroy believed that he had gone through too much in the past and was working too hard now to soil a clean record. Hard work was yielding results—a promotion at work, an attractively decorated and immaculately clean home, two sons who loved him, a wife who depended on him, neighbors who respected him. Leroy had altered his spending habits. He and his wife had a savings certificate in a bank and had far fewer debts. Leroy said, "I value money. Excitement is when I have it stashed away." Leroy saw similar changes occurring in some of the other men in the group. One who had been insensitive and angry was referred to at his job as "the Easter bunny" because he was so affable. Another rose from busboy to manager of a large restaurant. Perhaps what Leroy and the others prized most was not so much the tangible accomplishments but rather the feeling of being clean. One man asserted, "I so prize the cleanliness that everything could go, including my health, but I'd still prize the cleanliness." What had been temptation was no longer tempting. Leroy severed his connections with other criminals, prostitutes, the drug world. No more looking over his shoulder for the police. He said with pride and some amazement, "That world is like a dream."

Leroy did not become complacent. The criminal life may have seemed like a dream, but Leroy knew it could quickly become real if he failed to be self-critical or ceased to struggle to improve himself. Although he was no longer legally accountable to the hospital, he put himself on a parole, so to speak. Voluntarily, he continued to seek Yochelson's counsel long after the intensive phase of daily sessions was over. Meeting with Yochelson once a week, he spontaneously brought out his thinking. Rather than fearing the doctor's picking him apart as he used to, Leroy welcomed it. He was afraid of getting too cocky from compliments that were being showered upon him at work, at home, and by his friends. Leroy agreed with Pete, who drew an analogy between his current status and rowing a boat away from the brink of Niagara Falls. Pete contended that unless he kept straining at the oars, he'd drop over the edge of the falls. Another man put it this way, "My wife, our little apartment, the car, the stereo. It's like it's all sitting on sand that could be blown away with one little slip."

In November 1976, tragedy struck Leroy, something he never envisioned, although Yochelson had warned him it might occur. On Yochelson's first trip away from Washington to speak about his work, the 70-year-old psychiatrist collapsed in the St. Louis airport and died a few days later. Leroy was stunned, but he knew what he had to do: "Damn what I feel, do I must. I have got to be stronger than ever." More than a year later, he was still watchful of his own thoughts, had received another promotion at work, and, above all, had continued to make the program his life.

As Yochelson had instructed him, Leroy continued engaging in a daily moral inventory. He knew that he would never reach a point at which he would "have it made." Rather, he was positive that the effort had to be constant and that he had to bear in mind what his life had been. This program seemed less and less burdensome because Leroy no longer harbored his former grandiose view of himself. The more he reaped rewards of this new life, the more crime repulsed him. He lived a quiet life, one that he could never have imagined before, dividing his time among family, work, and a few friends. Leroy budgeted his money and his time, the latter being too short for all that he wanted to accomplish. He knew what had to be done to progress. He had the tools—the new patterns of thought that Yochelson had taught him. Leroy reflected, "It's easy to figure out things when my mind isn't bollixed up." Going back to crime was unthinkable. Declared Leroy, "There are too many things I want. I don't want anything interfering with my goals."

Chapter Fourteen

Corrections That Correct

SHOULD WE lock up criminals and throw the key away, or should a nation that prides itself on being compassionate and valuing human life embark on a program of corrections that is truly corrective? Criminals experience brief periods of dissatisfaction with their lives during which they sincerely want to change. Those in corrections must learn how to take advantage of these periods by helping the criminal to see himself as the rotten person he is and then teaching him new ways of thinking.

"Corrections is 150 years of undocumented fads," remarked Professor George Beto, former commissioner of corrections in Texas and an internationally known figure in the field.[1] It is time to change that. Instead of climbing on bandwagons to embrace fads or traveling in comfortable, well-worn ruts that lead to dead ends, it is time to become knowledgeable and then more effective. Only when the public and professionals know what criminals are really like can they make reasonable decisions as to what should be done with them.

The criminal justice system stands accused of protecting criminals who are victimizers more than it protects potential victims. As crime flourishes, citizens suffer. Their homes and places of business are being converted into maximum security fortresses with locks, alarm systems, TV surveillance, guards. They are reluctant to leave their homes unattended and fear for their safety on the streets. Almost every adult American or someone close to him has been a victim of crime. People clamor for greater protection. But because prisons are considered nothing more than expensive, overcrowded warehouses, thousands of criminals are committed to community programs rather than institutions. Americans have doubts as to how satisfactory this alternative is and fear even more that their government cannot protect them. In addition to the despair of millions of Americans, there is the desperation of parents and spouses of criminals and also the despair of criminals themselves, who know from personal experience that the conventional wisdom is bankrupt. It is instructive to listen to what these people say.

Writes one distraught mother of a 17-year-old boy who is in jail for the second time in a year, "Eddie has been in and out of schools for emotionally disturbed children, social workers' and child psychiatrists' offices, and reform schools since he was 12. He's a bright handsome kid, and we're desperate to help him save his future." Eddie's mother pleaded, "Can you help? This whole area is sadly lacking in the rehabilitation of criminals. Eddie will be 18 soon, and then he'll be playing in the big leagues, and there are so many like him."

Another mother wrote me describing an ordeal with her child that had dragged on for years. "We are in the process of fighting for the sanity of a 13-year-old child," she said.

"He has had a very normal upbringing. Yet this child at 4 years old started to steal. Since then, he has continually stolen money at every opportunity. He lies about it, and as he gets older he denies it more." She said that she and her husband had had no success in getting him help. "All we can see now for this child is a future in prison, and yet our hands are tied, not knowing what to do or where to run. Our hearts are breaking for this child."

The wife of a criminal who had spent his life in and out of institutions made a heartrending statement. "He feels life is over for him, it's too late, he wasted too much of it in prison. I try to tell him he's not too old to start over. You see, if he had cancer or some other disease, I would do everything in my power to find a cure. I don't give up that easy, he's a human being, even if at times he doesn't act like one." Then she begged, "Please help me help him. I know he doesn't know what real love means, but I do know he tried to love me with the only love he had to give."

Finally, a criminal in prison for the third time in less than a decade was certain his parole board considered him "unrehabilitatable," but still he hadn't given up on himself. "Frankly," he said, "I am tired of 'doing time' and getting absolutely nothing out of it. I am willing to try anything to find an end to this type of existence. I am desperate in trying to find anything to help me stay out of this type of situation again—I don't want my life to become a waste."

The system grinds on, guided by theories and practices that have neither made the public safer nor achieved lasting change in criminals. How to deal with criminals is a highly charged issue, guided less by sound information than by emotion-laden attitudes and rhetoric.

Crime soars, citizens remain afraid, and criminals navigate the criminal justice maze only to emerge substantially the same as when they entered. Judges make decisions based, in part, on presentence reports, which are often misleading because they contain irrelevant or biased information self-servingly supplied by the criminal and his family. Psychiatric evaluations are a charade in which the criminal, maneuvering to beat a charge, practically selects his own diagnosis. Punishment has not altered the criminal's personality; nor has the grab bag of remedies that are considered "rehabilitative." Prisons restrain criminals, but only temporarily. Except for the tiny number of criminals serving life sentences without parole, all the rest will return to the community to prey upon society.

Effective policies, decisions, and programs cannot be formulated by those who do not know how criminals think. The belief persists that the criminal is basically like the responsible person except that he's turned to crime because he has been neglected, deprived, abused, or excluded by society.

Federal, state, and local training programs in corrections strongly emphasize regulations and procedures but neglect educating personnel as to the true nature of the criminal. The curriculum of the Kentucky Division of Corrections Training, for example, offers a variety of courses, but not one deals specifically with the personality of the criminal.[2] In graduate school programs, scant attention is paid to working with criminals. The general consensus there seems to be that because criminals are untreatable, few psychiatrists, psychologists, or social workers will bother with them. Some universities now are offering training in forensic psychiatry and psychology, but the curriculum is grounded in conventional theories that have prevailed for decades. When a person first begins working with criminals, he is likely to be in the position of a man who is expected to perform a cardiac bypass operation but has a degree in theology, not medicine. The criminal is quick to make mincemeat of such a well-intentioned but ill-equipped person.

The greatest occupational hazard to people working with criminals is not physical attack. More serious is a rapid burnout of enthusiasm, commitment, and interest. Mention the word "burnout" to people in corrections, and they will solemnly nod. Increasing numbers of idealistic, genuinely concerned young Americans are entering corrections, eager to do a good job. Almost immediately, they confront a huge array of obstacles for which they are poorly prepared. Despite the fact that their clients are among the most difficult anywhere, they think they are expected to accomplish what parents, teachers, employers, clergymen, and others failed at for years. In addition, their caseloads are overwhelming. Time with clients is cut short by stacks of paperwork and lengthy meetings. The new employee encounters apathy, cynicism, and occasionally hostility from senior workers, who are battle weary from struggles with criminals and the bureaucracy. A worker in juvenile corrections expressed some of his frustration in a piece that he titled "Psalm."

> *Minimum Standards is my Bible,*
> *I may not meet them;*
> *It makes me labor over Treatment Plans;*
> *It leads me to send off Birth Verification Forms;*
> *It keeps me at my desk;*
> *It causes me to do weekly Detention Reviews*
> *   for Certification's sake.*
> *Yea, though I may go to work in the morning*
> *   with the hope of helping out a young person,*
> *I never get the chance, for It consumes my time.*
> *Coming up with "specific behavioral outcomes that*
> *   are measurable" puzzles me;*
> *It presents me with two hours of paperwork*
> *   for every hour I spend counseling with a family;*
> *It tires my brain;*
> *My stack of overdue case record reviews overflows;*
> *Surely the Court Specialist will never tell me*
> *How to get "client participation in the development*
> *   of a treatment plan" (only that I haven't done it),*
> *And I will stay Uncertified forever.*

Anonymous[3]

Disillusionment leads to burnout. The new employee eagerly tries to strike up a relationship with a criminal. Just as he thinks he is making headway, he discovers he's been "had." The criminal does what he's done time and again—providing one impression while concealing his true intentions and illicit activities. Just as the new worker starts to believe that his efforts are bearing fruit, he is jolted into a new awareness. For instance, he learns during a shakedown of cells that the criminal whom he has been counseling has for weeks been stashing away contraband, including several homemade knives. At first, the new employee attributes his lack of success to his own inexperience. After repeated failures, his morale drops, and he wonders if he was really cut out for such a job. Resentment mounts toward clients who defy all his efforts. Some workers develop the attitude that their clients are "no good SOBs" and hopeless cases. Of course, some are, but it is a poor attitude to bring to one's work before the evidence on any particular case is in. One senior corrections official described the cycle from enthusiasm to burnout. "The first year," he said, "the new guy can't do enough *for* the criminal. The second year, he can't do enough *to* the criminal. The third year, he doesn't give a damn." The human element vanishes when workers become cynical or indifferent. Some quit their jobs. Some endure, grateful simply to survive each day. A minority plug along, still hoping to accomplish something.

In the early years of his work, Dr. Yochelson was unsuccessful in helping criminals change. This was because he was utilizing traditional concepts and techniques rooted in theories about causes. As he used to say, the result of his efforts was that he had "criminals with psychiatry, rather than criminals without psychiatry." Despite all their insight, they still committed crimes. By 1970, he had piloted an entirely new approach based on years of studying how criminals think. Statistics can be presented about nearly anything in different ways. The only meaningful statistics with respect to Yochelson's work occur during the years 1970 to 1976 (the year of his death). For during that period, he was utilizing the habilitative procedures (described in Chapter Thirteen) with 30 hard-core criminals. As of May 1976, 13 out of 30 were living responsible lives. This was ascertained by regular followup in the community and verification by contacting families and employers.

Yochelson's criteria of habilitation went beyond remaining arrest-free. These men not only were arrest-free, but they reported having very few desires to commit a crime. They were accountable for how they spent their money and time. Not only did they hold jobs, but they had developed stable work patterns and were advancing. Those who had families were described as accommodating and dependable. One could contend that because the numbers are small, it is hard to generalize beyond them. On the other hand, 13 out of 30 represents better than a 33 percent success rate with men whom others had given up on. Each of the habilitated criminals had been a one-man crime wave. Yochelson's work was a start. It clearly showed that a demanding program that corrects the thinking patterns of the criminal and holds him accountable for implementation of corrective patterns is effective. In my outpatient clinical practice, I have found the approach powerful in helping criminals make far-reaching changes in their lives.

Changing a person's thinking may suggest brainwashing or conjure up ominous images of prisoner of war practices, drug-induced treatment, psychosurgery, and other insidious or coercive methods. Procedures described in Chapter Thirteen and advocated here do not remotely resemble any of these. Change is possible only when a criminal makes a *choice* to participate in a program like Yochelson's, when he is fed up with himself and consents to expose his thinking to criticism and correction. In this program, decisions are not made for the criminal. The *process* of decision making is the focus, but the specific decision is up to the individual. A criminal maintains his own political and religious views, his aesthetic tastes and interests. Eventually, he chooses his life's work and advances as far as his talents and efforts allow. This program does not manufacture robots. Within the limits of responsibility lie countless opportunities and tremendous variations in life style. Nothing in this program imposes a life style or values of a particular social class. (Responsibility and decency are not limited to any particular social class.) In short, the change process calls for criminals to acquire moral values that have enabled civilizations to survive. The objective is to teach them to live without injuring others.

As he begins, no criminal can be aware of all that it will take to change. Some criminals will not be interested in finding out and, from the beginning, will reject any opportunity to reform. Some will make a stab at changing on their own but in time give it up. Criminals who refuse to change remain a danger, and society must be protected from them. In such cases, only two alternatives exist—lengthy confinement in humane institutions or release under a kind of close supervision that does not now exist. Supervision would require as a minimum that the offender meet weekly with an officer of the court and that the officer make home visits and maintain regular contact with someone reliable who knows the offender well, such as a spouse, parent, or employer. Those criminals who are amenable should be offered the opportunity to participate in an intensive program like Dr. Yochelson's—a program designed to help them make fundamental changes in their thinking and behavior.

This is a tough approach to crime, tough because some criminals will have to be locked up for a long time. It is tough because it stipulates that far more is necessary to effect *significant* and *lasting* change than current theories or practices suggest. Some criminals who want to change still must be confined in institutions for a while because no court will allow them to remain in the community after they've committed a heinous act. The most important part of the change process must be conducted in the community. It is a pipe dream to release a criminal from an institution and expect him to function responsibly without guidance in a world for which he is not equipped. It would be like insisting that a two year old solve a quadratic equation. For those who are not confined at all, there must be a period of "trial probation." That is, the criminal could be placed on probation with the understanding that he elect the intensive program for change. If he decided to abandon the program, the court would rule whether probation should be continued under different conditions or revoked. Whether in the institution or the community, the person who will guide the criminal in this enterprise will show compassion not by shedding tears for him but rather by devoting considerable time and effort to a gigantic undertaking that has life and death importance to both society and the criminal.

How long does the process of change take? Clearly, the task with the career criminal is the greatest. In piloting the first "habilitation" program, Yochelson found there was wide variation, depending upon how quickly a criminal got down to business. If a criminal residing in the community on probation or parole regards the opportunity to change as his "life line," he can complete the intensive phase of the program in one year of daily meetings with regular followup meetings thereafter.

In describing the change process, Yochelson spoke of "the criminal" with few distinctions as to degree of severity. Obviously, not every person who commits a crime is a hardcore criminal. But still, crimes result from the way a person thinks. The program described in the previous chapter can be modified to help both youthful and adult offenders who are not career criminals become more responsible and function more effectively. However, the complete, intensive process is mandatory for career criminals.

There are two requirements to launch this kind of program—training personnel and developing community resources that will enhance the effectiveness of such a program. Were this program to be conducted in the community, participants would live at home and attend daily meetings at a facility provided for this purpose. To be effective, the program must have the backing of the court, which would play an active role throughout the participation of each criminal. The offender would agree to participate in the program as an alternative to incarceration. Should he fail to fulfill the requirements of the program, the court would reconsider his sentence. The criminal would not only attend meetings but would work full time with any hours remaining in the day carefully programmed. Each participant's accounting of himself would be verified by outside sources such as relatives, employers, or friends. This verification would act as a safeguard for society against the possible harm it could suffer at the hands of a criminal who, pretending to change, is really not changing.

This program could be initiated in an institution where staff would be trained and criminals would be evaluated daily. Once a criminal was released, however, the work would have to be continued in the community on an intensive basis.

The people operating the program would be trained in the thinking and behavior patterns of offenders. The first phase of training would be didactic and would concentrate on motivational issues and on patterns of thought that are integral components of the criminal's self-image and world view. Then the trainer would discuss and demonstrate the approach to be used in the change process. The final stage would be to supervise trainees as they applied this knowledge.

A cadre of psychiatrists or psychologists is not required to help criminals change. Rather, the concepts and methods are straightforward and can be transmitted to people who do not hold advanced degrees but who do have the dedication and stamina for this arduous work. It is essential that the men and women who operate such programs be responsible themselves, for there is little more futile than having one ir- responsible person try to teach another irresponsible person how to become responsible. In other words, the personal qualities of those who are to help criminals change are im- portant. To undertake this task, a person must have a blend of firmness, compassion, and considerable patience, because quick results are unlikely.

Criminals can participate in this process either individu- ally or in groups. Each offender should be informed at the time of screening for the program and then again at sentencing that his failure to cooperate in the program will result in a reconsideration of his sentence by the court. Criminals cannot be forced to change. They must reach a point in their lives when they are becoming fed up with themselves and desire to change. There are only three paths—crime, change, or suicide. Many offenders have be- lieved that there is a fourth—that is, to *appear* responsible but get away with violations on the side. Partial participation in this program is analogous to being a little bit pregnant. It is not a viable option. A person either shuts the door com- pletely on crime or he does not. No middle ground exists. There is a parallel to Alcoholics Anonymous in that AA calls for total abstinence. A sip of alcohol becomes a glass, then a bottle, and in time the alcoholic is back to where he started. So it is for the criminal. If he begins to lie, eventually lying becomes pervasive. If he takes home a few supplies from work, it is not long until he is cheating or stealing from his employer in other ways and then committing more crimes.

This program differs radically from previous efforts at "rehabilitation" by psychiatrists and psychologists. As I have said throughout this book, mental health professionals have not understood who the criminal is. Because of this, they have applied concepts and procedures that are not suit- able for this population. What I am proposing here is a pro- gram soundly based on a detailed understanding of how criminals think. It places total responsibility upon each criminal, who has the capacity to make a new series of choices. The program does not require new types of facilities or tremendous manpower.

How expensive is such programming? Very, but it promises to cost less than most of what is now being done. It has been estimated that it costs $18,000 a year to confine one youngster in a California Youth Authority facility and $15,000 to confine an adult for one year in a California prison. The cost soars to many times that when these figures are multiplied by the number of years a person is incarcerated and to that is added the toll of future crimes by released unchanged criminals. (Of course, the costs of crime are not really calculable because it is not possible to place a price tag on emotional distress, psychological damage, physical injury, or loss of life.)

Educators, mental health professionals, social workers, and counselors who have heard me speak have seen potential in this approach for intervening before youngsters are entrenched in a criminal life style. They have regarded the concepts of responsibility as being simple enough to transmit, in the proper form, to students in the elementary grades. Whether this will prevent antisocial behavior remains to be seen. The youngster who will be tomorrow's career criminal is unlikely to be affected by such intervention for he has been impervious to nearly everything else. But there are other youngsters who might be deterred by early systematic exposure to concepts that will help them think and behave responsibly.

I have presented many of the ideas included here at professional meetings and workshops throughout the United States, Canada, and in England. My presentation often strikes an especially responsive chord in priests, ministers, and rabbis who have an interest in the philosophy and practices of the criminal justice system. One minister said to me with some excitement, "This is so old, it's new. It's all in the

Bible.'' What he meant was that the issues I've addressed here are as old as man himself—man's power to choose, free will, good versus evil, man's response to temptation, his courage or cowardice in the face of adversity. The Ten Commandments enjoin man from certain crimes, and the Golden Rule of ''Love thy neighbor as thyself'' offers a guide for living. The Holy Scriptures are filled with admonitions against deceit, anger, pride, and guilt. In addition, the Old Testament says, ''As a man thinketh in his heart, so *is* he'' (Proverbs 23:7).

We are as we think. It is impossible to help a person give up crime and live responsibly without helping him to change what is most basic—his thinking. Criminals have been rewarded, punished, manipulated, probed for unconscious dynamics, and taught to read, work, and socialize, but they have not been helped to learn brand-new thinking patterns in order to change their way of life.

It is critical that all of us know who the criminal is, that we realize that he thinks and acts differently from the rest of us. Only then will realistic and compassionate decisions, effective programs, rational policies, and sound legislation be forthcoming. As a result, we will be a lot safer in our businesses, neighborhoods, and homes.

Notes

Chapter Two

1. Alfred Adler, "Individual Psychology and Crime," *Police Journal* 17 (1930), reprinted in *Quarterly Journal of Corrections* (1977), 7-13.

Chapter Three

1. S. A. Szurek's paper was reprinted in a 1970 collection of papers on antisocial children. See "Childhood Origins of Psychopathic Personality Trends," in S. A. Szurek and I. N. Berlin, *The Antisocial Child: His Family and His Community* (Palo Alto: Science and Behavior Books, 1970), pp. 2-12.

2. Norman Cameron, *Personality Development and Psychopathology: A Dynamic Approach* (Boston: Houghton-Mifflin, 1963), p. 656.

3. Joseph W. Rogers, *Why Are You Not a Criminal?* (Englewood Cliffs, N.J.: Prentice-Hall, 1977).

4. Robert Wallace, "Parents Smoke Pot; He Doesn't," *Tele-gram-Tribune* (San Luis Obispo, Cal.), November 8, 1979.

5. Psychiatrist David Abrahamsen said, "Parents too often say to a child, 'If you don't like it here, you can leave.' " Abrahamsen observed that such an attitude instills in the youngster "a feeling of complete rejection" (*The Psychology of Crime* [New York: Columbia University Press, 1960], p. 306). The question is what came first, the mother rejecting the child or the child rejecting the mother? Rather than reject the youngster who is having problems, many a mother keeps showering him with more attention and affection.

6. L. Joseph Stone and Joseph Church, *Childhood and Adolescence* (New York: Random House, 1968), p. 544.

Chapter Four

1. E. H. Sutherland, *Principles of Criminology* (New York: Lippincott, 1939).

2. Martin Gold, *Status Forces in Delinquent Boys* (Ann Arbor, Mich.: Institute for Social Research, 1963).

3. National Institute on Drug Abuse, "Growing Pains—Transitions to Maturity," *Prevention Resources* 3 (Spring–Summer 1979), 9.

4. Francis W. King, "Marijuana and LSD Usage Among Male College Students: Prevalence Rate, Frequency, and Self-estimates of Future Use," *Psychiatry* 32 (August 1969).

5. "Most U.S. Young People Conservative on Drugs," *Michigan Alumnus* (June 1980), 30.

6. "Suburbanites Shop in District for Hard Drugs," *The Washington Post,* July 26, 1981, A-1.

7. Elizabeth Douvan and Joseph Adelson, *The Adolescent Experience* (New York: Wiley, 1966), p. 198.

Chapter Five

1. Kenneth Polk and Walter Schafter, *Schools and Delinquency* (Englewood Cliffs, N.J.: Prentice-Hall, 1972), pp. 17, 18, 163.

2. Edgar Z. Friedenberg, *The Vanishing Adolescent* (New York: Dell, 1962), p. 122.

3. Robert J. Rubel, Testimony Before the President's Task Force on Victims of Crime, Houston, October 19, 1982.

4. From the Asklepieion Society Northwest, Minnesota Correctional Facility, Stillwater, Minn.

5. National Institute of Education, *Violent Schools—Safe Schools,* Vol. 1 (Washington, D.C.: Government Printing Office, 1978), p. iii.

6. The provisions on "assault leave" are contained in article 20 of the teachers' contract of the Dayton, Ohio, Public Schools.

7. Winston Churchill High School, "Discipline Code," Montgomery County, Md.

8. Rubel, "Testimony."

9. The Wechsler Intelligence Scale for Children.

10. Charles A. Murray, *The Link Between Learning Disabilities and Juvenile Delinquency* (Washington, D.C.: Department of Justice, 1976), p. 2.

Chapter Six

1. National Advisory Committee on Criminal Justice Standards and Goals, *Juvenile Justice and Delinquency Prevention: Report of the Task Force on Juvenile Justice and Delinquency Prevention* (Washington, D.C.: Department of Justice, 1976), p. 127.

2. Robert J. Samuelson, "A Weak Link Between Crime and Joblessness," *The Washington Post,* May 10, 1983, D-1.

3. Frederick Spencer, "The Effects of an Experimental Vocational Intervention Model Upon Hard-Core Unemployed Ex-offenders," *Journal of Offender Counseling, Services and Rehabilitation* 4 (Summer 1980), 346.

4. "An Inside Job," *The Wall Street Journal,* February 5, 1970, 1.

5. Mark Peterson and Harriet B. Braiker, *Doing Crime: A Survey of California Prison Inmates* (Santa Monica, Cal.: Rand, 1980), p. 132.

Chapter Seven

1. Ann W. Burgess, Testimony Before the President's Task Force on Victims of Crime, Washington, D.C., September 15, 1982.

2. "Rape: An Analysis," *The Evening Star* (Washington, D.C.), November 12, 1971, A-1.

3. Robert White, *The Abnormal Personality* (New York: Ronald Press, 1956), p. 397.

4. Joan Petersilia, Peter W. Greenwood and Marvin Lavin, *Criminal Careers of Habitual Felons* (Santa Monica, Cal.: Rand, 1977), p. 21.

5. "The Menace of Any Shadow," *Time* (December 22, 1980). This article on violent crime briefly recounts the slaying of Dr. Michael Halberstam.

6. J. L. Barkas provides an eye-opening discussion of how even responsible people tend to blame the victim rather than the offender in *Victims* (New York: Scribners, 1978).

7. U.S. Department of Justice, *Sourcebook of Criminal Justice Statistics, 1981* (Washington, D.C.: Department of Justice) p. 233.

8. The Task Force issued a final report in 1982: "President's

Task Force on Victims of Crime. Final Report.'' (Washington, D.C.: Department of Justice, December 1982).

9. U.S. Department of Justice, *Crime in the United States, 1981* (Washington, D.C.: Department of Justice) p. 152.

Chapter Eight

1. *Dorland's Illustrated Medical Dictionary,* 24th ed. (Philadelphia: Saunders, 1965), p. 782.

2. American Psychiatric Association, *Diagnostic and Statistical Manual of Mental Disorders,* 3rd ed. (Washington, D.C.: American Psychiatric Association, 1981), p. 295.

3. James T. Reese, ''Obsessive Compulsive Behavior: The Nuisance Offender,'' *FBI Law Enforcement Bulletin* (August 1979).

4. American Psychiatric Association, *Manual,* pp. 164, 291.

5. S. Freud, ''Some Character-Types Met Within Psycho-analytic Work,'' in *Collected Papers,* Vol. 4 (London: Hogarth, 1946), pp. 318–344.

6. S. Freud, ''The Ego and the Id,'' in *The Complete Psychological Works of Sigmund Freud,* Vol. 19 (London: Hogarth, 1961), pp. 12–68.

7. ''Sam Told Me to Do It . . . Sam Is the Devil,'' *Time* (August 22, 1977), 21.

8. '' 'Son of Sam' Killer Berkowitz Says 'Urge to Kill,' not Demons, Drove Him,'' *The Washington Post,* February 23, 1979.

9. ''Poison in Drugs,'' *Rocky Mountain News* (Denver), October 6, 1982, 58.

10. A letter to *The Los Angeles Times* described a tragic case when an attempt to feign mental illness failed. At the Juvenile Hall, a 15-year-old boy was told by other kids that if he faked psychosis he could be sent to a hospital, where he could suddenly regain his sanity and be released. That scheme worked. Later,

the youth was arrested and confined in a county jail, where he planned once again to convince the authorities that he was mentally disturbed. He knew when the guard would bring lunch and so he planned to hang himself just at that time so he could be cut down. He would have succeeded had not a telephone rung and diverted the guard's attention. The 15-year-old boy died of strangulation while the guard was on the phone ("A Cry for Help, but No One Listened," *The Los Angeles Times,* January 14, 1978, II-5).

11. See, for example, the fourth annual report of Chicago's Isaac Ray Center, "The Isaac Ray Center: Programs in Psychiatry and the Law," Dept. of Psychiatry, Rush–Presbyterian–St. Luke's Medical Center (Chicago, Illinois, 1982).

Chapter Nine

1. Department of Justice, "Prisoners at Midyear 1982," *Bureau of Justice Statistics Bulletin* (October–November, 1982), 1.

2. Smith Hempstone, "One Picture, One Crime, Two Tearful Mothers," *The Washington Star,* October 21, 1972.

3. In the federal system, the end of the road used to be Alcatraz. That prison was closed, and now the inmates needing tightest security are housed at the facility at Marion, Ill.

4. Stephen Gettinger, "Informer," *Corrections Magazine* (April 1980), 17–19.

5. "Rape Is the Way Some Master the Violent Art of Jail Survival," *The Washington Post,* September 28, 1982, A-8.

6. Joan Petersilia, Peter W. Greenwood and Marvin Lavin, *Criminal Careers of Habitual Felons* (Santa Monica, Cal.: Rand, 1977), p. 13.

7. Richard A. Schwartz, "Psychiatry and Crime Control," *Diseases of the Nervous System,* 36 (February 1975), 58.

Chapter Ten

1. Joseph W. Rogers, *Why Are You not a Criminal?* (Englewood Cliffs, N.J.: Prentice-Hall, 1977), p. 4.

2. Willard Gaylin, "On Feeling Guilty," *The Atlantic* (January 1979), 78–82.

3. H. J. Eysenck, *Crime and Personality* (London: Routledge & Kegan Paul, 1979), p. 13.

4. "Woman Raped in Georgetown," *Washington Daily News,* August 11, 1965, 5.

5. "The Mafia: Big, Bad and Booming," *Time* (May 16, 1977), 32ff.

Chapter Eleven

1. Marshall B. Clinard, *Sociology of Deviant Behavior* (New York: Holt, Rinehart & Winston, 1963), p. 55.

2. Frederic Wertham, *Seduction of the Innocent* (New York: Rinehart, 1953), p. 164.

3. David Loth, *Crime in the Suburbs* (New York: Morrow, 1967), p. 47.

4. Ira Goldenberg, "An Alternative Definition and Conception of Juvenile Delinquency: Implications for Planning," *Professional Psychology* 4 (November 1973), 455.

5. U.S. Department of Justice, "Prisons and Prisoners," *Bulletin of Justice Statistics* (January 1982), 2.

6. U.S. Department of Justice, *Sourcebook of Criminal Justice Statistics, 1981* (Washington, D.C.: Department of Justice), p. 477.

7. "Justice Aid Says Poor Hurt by Counsel System," *The Salt Lake City Tribune,* June 20, 1977, B-1.

8. Louise I. Shelley, *Crime and Modernization* (Carbondale: Southern Illinois University Press, 1981), p. 137.

9. Commission on Law Enforcement and Administration of Justice, *The Challenge of Crime in a Free Society* (Washington, D.C.: Government Printing Office, 1967), pp. 5, 6.

10. Larry Cole, "Juvenile Crime in the Suburbs: Cruising the 'Privileged Precincts' with the LAPD," *Los Angeles* (November 1977), 148ff.

11. William Healy and Augusta F. Bronner, *New Light on Delinquency and Its Treatment* (New Haven: Yale University Press, 1936), p. 201.

12. Karl Menninger, *The Crime of Punishment* (New York: Viking, 1968).

13. Anneliese F. Korner, "Mother–Child Interaction: One- or Two-Way Street?" *Social Work,* 10 (July 1965), 47–50.

14. In 1937, Samuel Beck stated that psychopathy is a vague category and called it "the wastebasket of psychiatric classification." See Samuel Beck, *Introduction to the Rorschach Method,* American Orthopsychiatric Association Research Monograph, no. 1 (Menasha, Wisc.: George Banta, 1937), p. 4.

15. H. J. Eysenck, *Crime and Personality* (London: Routledge & Kegan Paul, 1979).

16. "Genetic Link Seen in Chronic Criminality," *The Washington Post,* January 8, 1982, A-24.

17. Joan Beck, "Are There Born Criminals?" *Philadelphia Inquirer,* January 13, 1982.

18. C. Robert Cloninger et al., "Predisposition to Petty Criminality in Swedish Adoptees," *Archives of General Psychiatry,* 39, November 1982, p. 1242.

19. Professor K. E. Moyer has written two books in which he re-

views studies of the physiological aspects of aggression. See K. E. Moyer, *The Psychobiology of Aggression* (New York: Harper & Row, 1976), and K. E. Moyer, *The Physiology of Hostility* (Chicago: Markham Press, 1971).

20. Robert D. Hare and Janice Frazelle, "Psychobiological Correlates of Criminal Psychopathy," paper presented at a symposium on the Biosocial Correlates of Crime and Delinquency, annual meeting of the American Society of Criminology, Washington, D.C., November 1981.

21. Stanton E. Samenow, "Cryptorchism and Character: A Case Study," *Medical Arts and Sciences* 25 (1971), 9–22.

Chapter Twelve

1. Ramsey Clark, *Crime in America* (New York: Pocket Books, 1971), p. 200.

2. Max Rafferty, "There *Is* Such a Thing as a Bad Boy," *Globe-Democrat* (St. Louis), September 22, 1977.

3. Robert Martinson, "What Works? Questions and Answers About Prison Reform," *The Public Interest* (Spring 1974), 22–54.

4. National Academy of Sciences, *The Rehabilitation of Criminal Offenders: Problems and Prospects* (Washington, D.C.: National Academy of Sciences, 1974), pp. 11, 34.

5. National Advisory Commission on Criminal Justice Standards and Goals (NACCJSG), *Corrections* (Washington, D.C.: Government Printing Office, 1973), p. 43.

6. Raymond H. C. Teske and Nancy L. Powell, "Texas Crime Poll" (Huntsville, Tex.: Sam Houston State University Criminal Justice Center, 1978), p. 10.

7. "A Talk with Ed Meese," *The Washington Post,* July 7, 1981, A-15.

8. The National Advisory Commission recommended, "Each institution should have prevocational and vocational training programs to enhance the offender's marketable skills" (NACCJSG, *Corrections,* p. 368).

9. Confined juvenile offenders participating in a federally funded program are reported to have increased their reading ability by one grade level in one-third the time it would have taken them normally ("Why Johnny Reads: Ask Detention Man," *The Evening Star* [Washington, D.C.], March 27, 1977, A-6).

10. Sub-Committee on the Penitentiary System in Canada, *Report to Parliament* (Ottawa: Supply and Services Canada, 1977).

11. "Mentally Ill Offender . . . Atascadero State Hospital," fact sheet (Atascadero, Cal., Atascadero State Hospital, November 1977).

12. Jack B. Parker and John A. LaCour, writing on volunteerism, have said, "To the person who has been locked away from society the mere presence of a concerned volunteer is therapeutic in itself" (Jack B. Parker and John A. LaCour, "Common Sense in Correctional Volunteerism in the Institution," *Federal Probation,* 42 [June 1978], 47).

According to M-2 Sponsors of California, perhaps the single largest volunteer effort in corrections, the overall objective of such programs is "to enlist community participation in our correctional institutions with the prime concern being the prisoners—to alleviate their feelings of alienation and rejection" (*Successful Habilitation of Ex-Offenders* [Hayward, Cal.: M-2 Sponsors, 1978], p.3).

13. "Mentally Ill Offender."

14. The Law Enforcement Assistance Administration funded project CULTURE ("Creative Use of Leisure Time Under Restrictive Environments") to the tune of $1 million the first year and $800,000 the second year ("Culture from Inside," *American Journal of Correction* 40 [November–December 1978], 10).

15. "Theater Without Bars," descriptive material, 831 Parkway Ave., B15, Trenton, N.J. 08618.

16. Nancy Flinn, "Garden Yield: Prisoners' 'Good Time' plus Six Tons of Vegetables," *Gardens for All News* (Autumn 1979), 28ff.

17. Edgar May, "Maine: Was Inmate Capitalism out of Control?" *Corrections Magazine* (February 1981), 17–23.

18. National Institute for Juvenile Justice and Delinquency Prevention (NIJJDP), *Intervening with Convicted Serious Juvenile Offenders* (Washington, D.C.: Government Printing Office, 1976), p. 25.

19. William Glasser, *Reality Therapy: A New Approach to Psychiatry* (New York: Harper & Row, 1965), 19.

20. National Academy of Sciences, *Rehabilitation,* p. 34.

21. "60 Minutes," CBS News, February 20, 1977.

22. National Institute of Law Enforcement and Criminal Justice, *Instead of Jail? Issues and Programs in Brief,* Vol. 1 (Washington, D.C.: Government Printing Office, 1977), p. 1.

23. Probation was regulated by statute for the first time in the United States in 1878, when Massachusetts provided for a probation officer's being appointed to serve Boston courts that had jurisdiction in criminal matters (David Dressler, *Practice and Theory of Probation and Parole* [New York: Columbia University Press, 1959], p. 18).

24. U.S. Department of Justice, *Sourcebook of Criminal Justice Statistics, 1981* (Washington, D.C.: Government Printing Office, 1981), p. 451.

25. John Blackmore, "Community Corrections," *Corrections Magazine* (October 1980), 4–14.

26. NACCJSG, *Corrections,* p. 606.

27. The National Institute for Juvenile Justice and Delinquency Prevention observed, "Most of the exemplary practitioners we contacted agreed that persistent failure was a hallmark of the background of delinquent youths. Thus, it was important to give them reasons to believe in themselves and in their own efficacy. Tasks structured to be eminently 'doable' contributed to that" (NIJJDP, *Intervening*, p. 78).

28. Aversive conditioning is one of many conditioning approaches that has been utilized in training sex offenders. Dr. R. L. Laws of the Sexual Behavior Laboratory at Atascadero State Hospital in Atascadero, California, has worked extensively in this area. See, for instance, D. R. Laws and A. V. Pawlowski, "An Automated Fading Procedure to Alter Sexual Responsiveness in Pedophiles," *Journal of Homosexuality* 1 (1974), 149–163, and D. R. Laws, J. Meyer and M. L. Holmen, "Reduction of Sadistic Arousal by Olfactory Aversion: A Case Study," *Behavior Research and Therapy* 16 (1978), 281–285.

29. Task Force on Criminal Justice Research and Development, *Criminal Justice Research and Development* (Washington, D.C.: Government Printing Office, 1978), p. 1200.

30. National Criminal Justice Information and Statistics Service, *Dictionary of Criminal Justice Data Terminology* (Washington, D.C.: Government Printing Office, 1976), p. 78.

31. U.S. Department of Justice, *Sourcebook of Criminal Justice Statistics, 1981* (Washington, D.C.: Government Printing Office), pp. 2–4.

Chapter Thirteen

1. Ben Stein, "Taking the Lumps, Calling Them Sugar," *Los Angeles Herald-Examiner*, July 27, 1978.

2. Paul Hauck, *The Rational Management of Children* (New York: Libra, 1967), pp. 100, 101.

Chapter Fourteen

1. George Beto, Remarks before a criminality colloquium sponsored by the Indiana Lawyers Commission, Indianapolis, September 23, 1978.

2. Kentucky Department of Justice, Division of Corrections Training, *1980 Schedule of Classes* (Richmond: Bureau of Training, Kentucky Department of Justice, 1980).

3. From *The Advocate,* a publication of the Virginia Juvenile Officers Association (Spring 1978).

Index

273

Index

Index